The Travel Writings of Marguerite Blessington

ANTHEM STUDIES IN TRAVEL

Anthem Studies in Travel publishes new and pioneering work in the burgeoning field of travel studies. Titles in this series engage with questions of travel, travel writing, literature and history, and encompass some of the most exciting current scholarship in a variety of disciplines. Proposals for monographs and collections of essays may focus on research representing a broad range of geographical zones and historical contexts. All critical approaches are welcome, although a key feature of books published in the series will be their potential interest to a wide readership, as well as their originality and potential to break new ground in research.

Series Editor

Charles Forsdick – University of Liverpool, UK

Editorial Board

Mary Baine Campbell – Brandeis University, USA
Steve Clark – University of Tokyo, Japan
Claire Lindsay – University College London, UK
Loredana Polezzi – University of Warwick, UK
Paul Smethurst – University of Hong Kong, China

The Travel Writings of Marguerite Blessington

The Most Gorgeous Lady on the Tour

Aneta Lipska

ANTHEM PRESS

Anthem Press
An imprint of Wimbledon Publishing Company
www.anthempress.com

This edition first published in UK and USA 2020
by ANTHEM PRESS
75–76 Blackfriars Road, London SE1 8HA, UK
or PO Box 9779, London SW19 7ZG, UK
and
244 Madison Ave #116, New York, NY 10016, USA

First published in the UK and USA by Anthem Press 2017

© Aneta Lipska 2020

The moral right of the authors has been asserted.

All rights reserved. Without limiting the rights under copyright reserved above,
no part of this publication may be reproduced, stored or introduced into
a retrieval system, or transmitted, in any form or by any means
(electronic, mechanical, photocopying, recording or otherwise),
without the prior written permission of both the copyright
owner and the above publisher of this book.

British Library Cataloguing-in-Publication Data
A catalogue record for this book is available from the British Library.

Library of Congress Cataloging-in-Publication Data
Library of Congress Control Number: 2019953391

ISBN-13: 978-1-78527-252-3 (Pbk)
ISBN-10: 1-78527-252-7 (Pbk)

This title is also available as an e-book.

CONTENTS

List of Illustrations	vii
List of Abbreviations	ix
Acknowledgements	xi
Preface	xiii
Introduction	1

Part I. TEXTS

1. Paratexts	23
2. From Life to Text	35
3. Fictional Strategies	43

Part II. IMAGES

4. Natural Sceneries	55
5. Ruins and Edifices	67
6. Sacred Art and Religious Practices	77

Part III. SPACES

7. Genoa: Byron's Companion	91
8. Naples: Lady of the House	99
9. Rome and Venice: Romantic Traveller	109
10. Paris: Writer of Fashion and Revolution	117
Conclusion	127
Notes	133
Bibliography	143
Index	153

ILLUSTRATIONS

P.1 James Godsell Middleton (fl. 1826–1872), *Margaret Power, Countess of Blessington (1789–1849)* (after Sir Thomas Lawrence)   xv

1.1 *Advertisement of works by Lady Blessington published by Mr. Colburn.* Back matter of the second edition of *The Idler in France* (1842, vol. 2)   33

4.1 Samuel Bradshaw (fl. 1832–1880), *The Undercliff, Isle of Wight, as seen after passing the church of St. Lawrence, on the way to Black Gang* (after William Leighton Leitch)   61

8.1 Italian (Neapolitan) School, circa 1800. *Palazzo Belvedere, Naples.* Watercolour and black wash on paper   100

ABBREVIATIONS

CLB Marguerite Blessington. *Conversations of Lord Byron*
IiI   Marguerite Blessington. *The Idler in Italy*
IiF Marguerite Blessington. *The Idler in France*
IoW Marguerite Blessington. *A Tour in the Isle of Wight, in the Autumn of 1820*
NtP Marguerite Blessington. *Journal of a Tour through the Netherlands to Paris, in 1821*

See the bibliography for full references.

ACKNOWLEDGEMENTS

This book would not have been written without the help and encouragement of several people. I am particularly grateful to Professor Zbigniew Białas for being an enthusiastic reader of my work, for his expert advice on travel writing and his continued support over the years of my research. I also want to thank Dr Ewa Wełnic, who introduced me to the field of literary studies and has always shown genuine interest in my work.

My thanks go to Professor Ann R. Hawkins and Professor Susanne Schmid for sharing with me their expertise in the life and work of Marguerite Blessington and for reaffirming my conviction that she is worth devoting years of scholarly pursuit to her. I am indebted to the readers of the manuscript, Professor Magdalena Ożarska, Professor Grzegorz Moroz and the three anonymous reviewers for Anthem, who offered insightful comments and valuable suggestions, as well as my proofreader, Dr Stuart McWilliams, for his accuracy and meticulousness.

My gratitude is also due to the editorial board of the Anthem Studies in Travel series for accepting my book proposal, and to the Anthem team for a fruitful and professional cooperation.

Finally, I want to thank my son, Tadeusz, for being my ever-present joy and motivation to do my best, and my husband, Jakub, who has been my severest critic, erudite guide and constant companion throughout this long journey. I dedicate this book to them.

PREFACE

This book is about a largely overlooked woman travel writer, an author whose texts merit scholarly attention yet tend not to receive it, even in the most appropriate contexts. To give but two examples, in the recently published *Idleness, Indolence and Leisure in English Literature* (Fludernik and Nandi, 2014), there is a chapter on Victorian travel writing, and in another work devoted to similar issues – *Leisure and the Irish in the Nineteenth Century* (Lane and Murphy, 2016) – there are essays on 'Leisure in Literature', 'Leisure, Tourism and Travel' and 'Leisure and Female Élites'. None of these mentions Marguerite Blessington's two travel accounts, *The Idler in Italy* (1839–40) and *The Idler in France* (1841). Blessington's works are relevant examples in every way, yet they are not familiar enough today to be included, even though they were popular among readers in her time,[1] and the author's life and activities have been of interest to today's scholars. The idea that lies behind this book is thus to propose a critical reading of Marguerite Blessington's four travel narratives, and to broadly contextualize them within social, cultural and literary phenomena of the first half of the nineteenth century.

Marguerite Blessington's first recorded journey, to the Isle of Wight, took place in 1820. In 1822 she anonymously published a journal from the tour – *A Tour in the Isle of Wight in the Autumn of 1820*. In 1821 Blessington made a relatively short tour of the Continent, the anonymous account of which, *Journal of a Tour through the Netherlands to Paris, in 1821*, also appeared in print in 1822. In the same year Blessington commenced her proper Continental tour, which continued until 1830. This long-lasting journey resulted in the publication of two travel accounts – the three-volume *Idler in Italy* in 1839 and 1840, and the two-volume *Idler in France* in 1841.[2] There was a gap of almost 20 years between Blessington's early and later texts. What is more, her Continental tour lasted nearly a decade, and the account of it was published 10 years after its completion. That interval of 20 years was not only an eventful period in Blessington's life but also in the history of British tourism.

The period was framed by two significant events. In 1820 the first regular cross-Channel streamer service started, and in 1845 Thomas Cook organized his first commercial tour. Within that period, it was fashionable among British travellers to explore their own country (Hooper 2002, 174; Buzard 2002, 38), yet after the end of the Napoleonic Wars in 1815, a great number of them also headed to the Continent (Buzard 1993, 19). With the advance of travel infrastructure, travelling became more accessible and affordable for anyone who wished to travel, irrespective of their social and financial status. Little by little, the traditional Grand Tour was superseded by mass tourism (Buzard 2002, 47–48).

These events greatly influenced the contemporary understanding of travel. After the opening of the Continent in 1815, British travellers would gradually depart from the established itineraries of the Grand Tour, searching for individual and authentic contact with the foreign (Cardinal 2002, 137). Yet, as the number of people travelling with this very purpose significantly increased, destinations favouring personal experience would become consumer products (ibid., 154). Travel writing of the period was a barometer of these evolving attitudes – anchored in tradition, saturated with Romanticism yet heralding the coming of a new Victorian reality – which manifested itself in the evolution from standardized handbooks to private records of personal experience and then to texts geared towards mass consumption.

The two-decade period was also diverse in literary terms. Richard Cronin designates the writers of the years between 1824 and 1840 as 'Romantic Victorians', since they were suspended between the two literary epochs. Their texts drew on their predecessors, yet they already bore the hallmarks of the coming literary trends (Cronin 2002, 2–3). Blessington is present in Cronin's study as Byron's biographer, but she also fits well in this circle as a travel writer.

In what follows I demonstrate how the tendencies in tourism and literature as well as the changing aesthetic and social trends in the period in question favoured Blessington's predilection for self-fashioning. Depending on the circumstances, she constructed a number of identities for herself in such a manner as to enhance her status as a celebrity back home. In recent years she has been rediscovered, mostly as a representative of the celebrity culture of the time (Ives 2012, 5). Her great personal asset was her physical appeal, which was recognized by, among others, Sir Thomas Lawrence, who painted a highly acclaimed portrait of her (Figure P.1). As a result, Hawkins observes, 'What was believed about Blessington was shaped largely by her lovely image' (Hawkins 2012, 54). This book argues that Blessington's late travel texts had the same function as the image – that of an index of her socio-cultural status. The subtitle of the book – *The Most Gorgeous Lady on the Tour* – is indicative of the relation between Blessington's celebrity and her travels. It refers to Dr Samuel Parr's designation of her as 'the most gorgeous Lady Blessington', which circulated among her contemporaries (Molloy 1896, 1: vii).

Figure P.1 James Godsell Middleton (fl. 1826–1872), *Margaret Power, Countess of Blessington (1789–1849)* (after Sir Thomas Lawrence). Oil painting on canvas. © National Trust Images.

Survey of Literature on Marguerite Blessington

The majority of the publications on Marguerite Blessington in the nineteenth century were of a biographical character and concerned her eventful life, her beauty and personality as well as her skills as a salonnière. The first biographical information on Blessington appears to have been issued in 1838 as a short chapter in Henry Chorley's *Authors of England* (1838). A medallion showing the countess's portrait is followed by a three-page notice that summarizes her life to date and also offers appraising comments on her. In terms of her social and writing activities, Chorley ranks Blessington alongside such women as Mary Wortley Montagu, Elizabeth Montague, Hester Piozzi and Frances Burney (Chorley 1838, 34–36). The tone of the comments vacillates between moderate and favourable and considerably differs from that prevailing in Blessington's biographies after her death.[3]

Following her death in 1849, there soon appeared three biographical works on Lady Blessington. The first was *Memoir of Lady Blessington*, which was authored by Blessington's niece Margaret Power and prefaced Blessington's posthumously published novel *Country Quarters* in 1850. It seems to have been a response to accusations against the countess concerning her immoral conduct, which had appeared in the press. In Power's *Memoir*, Blessington is idealized, some facts from her life are passed over and some of her actions are justified. Blessington's second biography, *The Literary Life and Correspondence of the Countess of Blessington*, was written by a friend of hers, Richard Robert Madden, and published in 1855. Madden aspired to introduce Blessington to his readership as a literary figure by means of an edited collection of not only his own and Miss Power's recollections, but also the countess's handwritten genealogical sketch, transcripts of letters by and to her friends and family members, and other papers. Although he thus achieves a wide scope, Madden nevertheless admits that he strived not to 'hurt the feelings, or to injure the character of individuals' (Madden 1855, 1: 4). After Madden's death, the family letters and documents that were in his possession were published separately by Alfred Morrison as *The Blessington Papers* (1895) and were used by the next biographer – J. Fitzgerald Molloy – for composing *The Most Gorgeous Lady Blessington* (1896). Molloy recorded Blessington's life and career in the form of a narrative in which he wove quotations from those who befriended her. Nevertheless, since the commentaries are mostly by men and to a great extent concern the countess's female charm, this biography has been criticized as obviously gendered (Hawkins and Kraver 2005, xiii–xiv).

The same rhetoric dominated the next account of Blessington's life, which was published in the twentieth century. Michael Sadleir, a biographer and a novelist, authored *Blessington–D'Orsay: A Masquerade* (1933), the American edition of which was entitled *The Strange Life of Lady Blessington* (1947). The writer's flair for storytelling, character creation and intrigue is evident here, and is indicated by the titles themselves. Yet, to maintain the appearance of objectivity, in a manner similar to his predecessors, Sadleir also cited the commentaries by the countess's contemporaries. Another romanticized version of Blessington's life was *Notorious Lady: The Life and Times of the Countess of Blessington*, a biographical novel written by Doris Leslie (1976). In 1969, Ernest James Lovell edited Blessington's *Conversations of Lord Byron* and prefaced it with an extended biographical note, which presents her life as simultaneous and, at one point, identical with Lord Byron's. Thus Lovell invested the countess's life with a new meaning.[4]

The year 2016 saw a new, scholarly biography of Marguerite Blessington, written by Susan Matoff and published by the University Press of Delaware. The title of the book, *Marguerite, Countess of Blessington: The Turbulent Life of a Salonnière and Author*, alludes to the forerunners' narratives of Blessington's changing fortunes, yet it also draws attention to her life accomplishments. This stance is confirmed in the introduction, in which Matoff sets herself the goal of 'plac[ing] her [Blessington] where she belongs in history – as an important and influential salonnière, a writer of many books, some of which deserve serious attention, an editor of two of the most popular annuals of the day, and a valued friend and confidante' (Matoff 2016, vx). Matoff proposes a novel approach to the figure of Blessington by acknowledging her as having a great impact on 'the great men of her time', in particular Edward Bulwer-Lytton and Benjamin Disraeli (ibid., xv). Matoff also rightly distances herself from the dominant story of Blessington's relationship with Alfred, Count d'Orsay, lest it should overshadow her achievements and delineate her as unworthy of scholarly attention (ibid., xv–xvi).

In recent years, Blessington has been rediscovered by both Irish studies and genre studies. She is discussed in such publications as *Hibernia's Muses: The Daughters of Thalia and Melpomene. Portrait Sketches of Irish Women Writers* (2005) by S. W. Jackman and *Wild Irish Women: Extraordinary Lives from History* (2012) by Marian Broderick. In literary terms Blessington has been acknowledged mostly as Byron's biographer and as a novelist. Riana O'Dwyer's essay in the collection *New Contexts: Re-Framing Nineteenth-Century Irish Women's Prose* (2008) expands on Blessington's literary career and provides close readings of her first novel, *Grace Cassidy; or, the Repealers*, and of *Conversations of Lord Byron* (ibid., 35–54).[5] This biographical work is the subject of analysis in Julian North's study 'Self-possession and Gender in Romantic Literary Biography' (2002, 109–38). Blessington is also frequently referred to in publications concerning the genre of silver fork novels, in which she specialized. Edward Copeland considers her 'a talented observer of fashionable life' (2012, 177) and provides comments on her several texts in *The Silver Fork Novel: Fashionable Fiction in the Age of Reform* (2012, 11–13, 176–80). Her novels also serve as exemplars of the genre in Sheryl A. Wilson's book *Fashioning the Silver Fork Novel* (2012, 31, 86–119, 147–48).[6] Her poetry, in turn, has been commented on by Paula R. Feldman in *British Women Poets of the Romantic Era* (2000, 147–53).

As a result of the growing interest in book history, Blessington has been a subject of study for scholars concerned with the influence of aristocratic women on the literary marketplace of Victorian England. Muireann O'Cinneide, in *Aristocratic Women and the Literary Nation*, designates Blessington as 'probably the most famous aristocratic writer' of the period (O'Cinneide 2008, 8) and expands on her 'essentially socialized mode of writing and publishing' (ibid., 4). From this perspective, she analyzes *Conversations of Lord Byron*[7] and Blessington's silver fork novels.[8] In a similar vein, Terence Hoagwood and Kathryn Ledbetter, in *"Colour'd Shadows": Contexts in Publishing, Printing, and Reading Nineteenth-Century British Women Writers*, demonstrate how Blessington took advantage of her social status, feminine charm and the scandalous aura surrounding her life to succeed as an editor (Hoagwood and Ledbetter 2005, 54–56, 79–85). Susanne Schmid claims that Blessington appealed to her contemporary female readership for the same reasons (2008, 88–92). In *British Literary Salons of the Late Eighteenth and Early Nineteenth Centuries* (2013), in turn, Schmid investigates the phenomenon of Blessington's success as a salonnière, ranking her alongside Mary Berry and Lady Holland. The book is a major contribution to the acknowledgement of Lady Blessington's significance to the culture of literary salons in England.[9]

A thorough work on Blessington's writing and editorial activity and its significance to the mid-nineteenth-century women's book market has been done by Ann R. Hawkins. Her introduction to the 2005 edition of Blessington's *Victims of Society* (written with Jeraldine Kraver) offers a detailed survey of literature on and by Blessington (2005, vii–xxvi). In a number of articles[10] and in her chapter in the book *Women Writers and the Artifacts of Celebrity in the Long Nineteenth Century* (Hawkins 2012, 49–78), Hawkins investigates the reception of Lady Blessington during her lifetime and attributes the phenomenon of her celebrity to the ability to 'trade on her beauty', manage her public reputations and fashion her selves in her poems, fiction and editorial publications (Hawkins 2012, 77; Hawkins 2003a, 1–2).

Notwithstanding the growing interest in the figure of Marguerite Blessington and her other fields of activity, her travel texts have not yet been comprehensively studied, even though she has been mentioned in studies of women's travel writing. Jane Robinson claims in her *Wayward Women: A Guide to Women Travellers* that Blessington's travel writing 'did much to popularize the Grand Tour amongst "women of quality"' (1990, 83), and Maria H. Frawley, in *A Wider Range: Travel Writing by Women in Victorian England*, more specifically ascribes to her the popularization of an 'idle' type of traveller (1994, 49, 52).

Blessington's *The Idler in Italy* has been acknowledged in several works concerning the reception of Italy by English travellers. Manfred Pfister, in *The Fatal Gift of Beauty: The Italies of British Travellers. An Annotated Anthology*, cites three passages from this text as well as providing a short referential note mainly concerning Blessington's Italian journey and the *Idlers* (Pfister 1996, 471–72). The value he finds in the *Idlers* consists in the 'glimpses they allow into the fashionable society of international tourists' (ibid., 472). Devon Fisher, in turn, analyzes several passages from the book to exemplify the attitude of early Victorian writers towards Roman Catholicism, in the book *Roman Catholic Saints and Early Victorian Literature* ... (Fisher 2012, 29, 35, 42). Finally, Sharon Ouditt, in *Impressions of Southern Italy. British Travel Writing from Henry Swinburne to Norman Douglas* (2014), looks into Blessington's reflections of Naples, Neapolitan people and customs, comparing them to those by John Chetwode Eustace, Hester Thrale Piozzi and Charles Dickens (Ouditt 2014, 14, 25–26, 34–36).[11]

The significance of the Italian period for Blessington's lifetime achievement has been mostly appreciated by Susanne Schmid. In the aforementioned monograph, she observes that in *The Idler in Italy* Blessington focuses not only on the value of sightseeing but also on 'the quality of interaction, the combination of playfulness, learning, and the ability to perform oneself' (Schmid 2013, 149). Having analyzed these aspects mainly in the accounts of Genoa and Naples, Schmid concludes that it was through her 'early immersion into the conversational culture of the continent', that Blessington would become one of the leading London salonnières (ibid., 173–74).

The Idler in France, in turn, has only served Barbara Pauk as material for discussing the French salon culture in one of the chapters of her PhD dissertation,[12] whereas Blessington's early travel journals – *A Tour in the Isle of Wight in the Autumn of 1820* and *Journal of a Tour through the Netherlands to Paris, in 1821* – so far have not received any attention whatsoever.

Contents and Methodologies

The three analytical parts making up this book are preceded by the introduction, which is divided into two sections. In the first section, I aim at situating Marguerite Blessington's travels and travel writing in the contexts of British women travel writers of the first half of the nineteenth century. The second section of the introduction presents the life and career of Blessington, with emphasis on the stretches of time she spent travelling or sojourning in Continental cities.

In Part I of the book, I approach Blessington's writings from textual and generic perspectives with the aim of displaying her evolving identity as a travel writer. I juxtapose the early and late travel accounts here in order to demonstrate how the writer manoeuvred within the genre of travel writing so as to create a particular vision of herself. Drawing on Gerard Genette, Chapter 1 discusses the paratext of Blessington's four books, thus situating them in the context of book marketing and also of celebrity culture of the time. Chapter 2 concentrates on those features of the texts proper that allow their categorization as nonfictional travel writing. In Chapter 3, in turn, I adopt narratological and cultural perspectives in order to analyze the affinities of the *Idlers* with the genre of the fashionable novel. Part I does not attempt to label Blessington as a woman travel writer in a strictly feminist vein, but it rather relies on textual and extra-textual evidence to form some ideas of the way she might have wished to be viewed.

Part II argues that, notwithstanding the illustrated fictional techniques, the literary quality of Blessington's both early and late travel accounts is best revealed in her sketches of landscapes (Chapter 4) and architecture (Chapter 5) as well as her visualizations of religious art and practices (Chapter 6). As she travelled to countries offering but little novelty to readers, Blessington would attempt to distinguish her travel writings from others. One way of doing so was by adopting elements of the genres popular among readers; another was by depicting the visual in such a manner as to highlight the texts' artistic merit. My purpose in these text-oriented chapters is both a close reading of Blessington's word paintings and their contextualization in the light of the aesthetics and visual culture of the late eighteenth and early nineteenth centuries. I focus in particular on the aesthetic categories of the picturesque, the beautiful, the sublime as well as the Gothic, and on the guidelines developed by Edmund Burke and the practical instructions provided by William Gilpin. I argue that Blessington's incorporation and at times reinterpretation of aesthetic conventions express her attempt to be considered a refined and artistically literate English lady.

Part III of this book offers cultural readings of those chapters of the *Idlers* in which Blessington recounts her sojourns in five continental cities of distinct character.[13] It aims at establishing possible links between the representation of space and Blessington's perception of her self. Each of the chapters in Part III is a separate study of place, examining Blessington's techniques of appropriating its historically or culturally determined meaning in such a manner as to impart a specific characteristic to herself as a traveller and travel writer. My selection of the cities is motivated by their distinctive cultural identity, understood as the established outcome of representational practices throughout history; a 'legible form', as Balshaw and Kennedy put it, constituted by 'signifying practices, discourses and images' (Balshaw and Kennedy 2000, 4). Nevertheless, since in most cases Blessington followed the conventional Grand Tour itinerary and there were some cities she visited more than once, I make no attempt here to discern a linear evolution of the writer's identity. The scope of this part is broader than the previous ones, as it draws on the history of tourism, social and national studies, as well as broadly understood intertextuality.

The goal in each of the chapters is to propose a critical reading of Marguerite Blessington's somehow neglected travel accounts from a particular perspective, situating them in the varying historical, social, cultural and literary contexts. This book thus relies on several methodological approaches, which are determined by the stated objectives and also by the studied texts themselves. My conviction throughout is that it is appropriate not only to closely read the text itself, but also to confront it with its extratextual reality. In the three parts making up the book, the idea prevails that writing literature in general, and recording travel experiences and composing travel texts in particular, may become a way to fashion the author's identity in accordance with the dominant norms and values; a form of self-fashioning, defined by Stephen Greenblatt as 'a manipulable [and] artful process' (Greenblatt 1980, 2).

INTRODUCTION

British Women Travellers and Travel Writers, 1820s–1840s

Although women had travelled long before the nineteenth century, it was then that travelling became fashionable among them (Korte 2000, 111).[1] With the improvement of travelling conditions, it was no longer considered too inconvenient and dangerous for them, and so they could well accompany men on their tours, as Mary Shelley, Lady Morgan, Frances Jane Carey and many others did. Sometimes they would travel as caretakers to their relatives, like Mariana Starke, or as governesses, as in the case of Anna Jameson. Nevertheless, over time, an increasing number of women travelled solely for their own sake. Just as men did, they would travel for many reasons, including self-development.

A great number of British women going to the Continent considered their journey to be an educational one, their Grand Tour.[2] They followed the traditional itinerary, on their way devouring travel books by their predecessors, as, for instance, Mary Shelley did.[3] Drawn by their classical and artistic interests, they would visit the cities where they could best refine their tastes, just like Charlotte Eaton, who went to Florence and then to Rome and described its 'creations of gifted genius' in her book *Rome in the Nineteenth Century* (1820, 1: 148). Others aspired to broaden their knowledge of European manners and culture by staying for a longer time in European capitals and surrounding themselves with members of Continental elites. Frances Trollope sojourned in Paris, where she was admitted into the salons of the cosmopolitan aristocracy, as recorded in her *Paris and the Parisians* (1836).[4] Finally, for some women travel was a chance to deepen their professional knowledge (Frawley 1994, 22). Louisa Stuart Costello, for instance, specialized during her travels as a historian studying medieval France.[5]

Notwithstanding their educational goals, women also participated in the increasingly popular leisure travel. The idle traveller, commented upon in a rather critical manner by Laurence Sterne in *A Sentimental Journey Though France and Italy* from 1768 (Sterne 2002, 14–15), began to take on positive connotations from the turn of the eighteenth century. Idleness was embraced by those who recorded their travels to define their state of mind while on tour. One reason behind that was Romantic ideology, which considered idle repose and contemplation as potentially creative and morally enriching activities. When recording her travel experiences in *Letters Written During a Short Residence in Sweden, Norway, and Denmark* (1796), Mary Wollstonecraft, for instance, tends to withdraw from the outside world, and particularly its cruelties, into aesthetic contemplation of Scandinavian landscapes, which provoke a rush of personal thoughts and emotions (Adelman 2011, 89–90).

An aesthetic appreciation of the countries visited was part and parcel of leisure travel. Travel accounts of the period reveal that, prior to their journeys, their authors were often well read and had familiarized themselves with the aesthetics of the picturesque and the sublime. There were those who documented the picture-like beauty of their own country,[6] as did Dorothy Wordsworth in her *Recollections of a Tour Made in Scotland, A. D. 1803* (published posthumously in 1874) or, four decades later, Louisa Stuart Costello in *The Falls, Lakes and Mountains of North Wales* (1845). Nevertheless, after 1815 a great number of scenic tourists were particularly attracted to Italian landscapes (Brand 1957, 167–68; Walchester 2007, 18). One of them was Anna Jameson, who admitted to 'hav[ing] understood the word *picturesque*' only when arriving in Italy, since there not only natural scenery but 'the commonest object of every-day life' becomes such (Jameson 1826, 357).[7] Women travellers also sought the sublime scenes they had known from Gothic stories. Adopting the same techniques, they would build the tension and create imaginative descriptions in their travel writings; this is what Costello did in her accounts of France (see Saunders 2015, 142–44).

As the process of journeying gradually accelerated and travel became common and standardized, idleness stood for a leisurely mode of movement and a personalized experience. Travellers would search for 'the fertility of unprogrammed, nonchalant itinerary [...] otherness without foreknowledge', as Cardinal puts it (2002, 147). Angela D. Jones observes that Romantic women travellers in particular searched for direct contact with the inhabitants of foreign lands and immersed themselves 'in the ordinary experiences' of their daily life (Jones 1997, 498). Among the women who valued authentic contact with the natives more than, for example, art was Mary Shelley (see Frawley 1994, 58–59). Frawley also recognizes this need to explore the unknown and the primitive among later women travellers, whom she designates as 'Victorian adventuresses' (1994, 105). They emphasized their relaxed, unscheduled and personalized manner of travelling in the titles of their travel accounts, using wording suggestive of idleness. Anna Jameson's *Winter Studies and Summer Rambles in Canada* (1838) and Mary Shelley's *Rambles in Germany and Italy* (1844) may serve as apt examples here.

Another popular form of reviving the travel experience in the period was literary tourism, that is, visiting those places that were associated with notable poets and writers, which often were depicted in their works. One of the literary figures that aroused the interest of those who travelled in Britain was Robert Burns (Hagglund 2010, 28–29). In her *Recollections of a Tour Made in Scotland A.D. 1803*, Dorothy Wordsworth melancholically recalls visiting the poet's grave and talking to his wife's servant maid in their home (1874, 5–7). Those who travelled to the Continent after 1820 would, in turn, make their travel experience 'live' by following in the footsteps of Lord Byron (Buzard 1993, 117). Anna Jameson was among many travellers to the places where the poet had actually stayed (e.g., Jameson 1826, 35; see also Buzard 1993, 118). As others did, she used Byron's *Childe Harold's Pilgrimage* as a guidebook and read the verses while admiring the views described therein (Jameson 1826, 195).

Roger Cardinal observes that the aspiration of the Romantics was 'travel with an aura of the challenging, the colourful, the exceptional' (2002, 137). For those travelling to the Continent in the years immediately after 1815, the Waterloo battlefield and other spots associated with Emperor Napoleon were an excellent opportunity to get the feeling of recent history. Charlotte Anne Eaton visited Waterloo only a month after the battle and recorded her impressions in *Narrative of a Residence in Belgium during the Campaign of 1815; and of a Visit to the Field of Waterloo, by an Englishwoman* (1817). Although these might have been very tangible experiences, over time participation in historical and literary tourism was identified with mass tourism.

Not only was travelling fashionable among women, but writing about travels also was. In the early nineteenth century, the mode of recording travel experiences by both men and women relied on eighteenth-century conventions of travel writing.[8] Nevertheless, rather than copying, writers would appropriate the traditional travel genres and use them to suit their purposes. Moreover, travel texts by women throughout the first half of the nineteenth century frequently incorporated a number of genres at the same time, thus defying any categorization.[9] As Mary Shelley pointed out in 'The English in Italy' (1990, 343), it is impossible for the 'multifarious material' accumulated during a long stay in a foreign country to be suited to a single form of travel writing. Another reason for adapting various genres was probably the feeling of '*belatedness*' that travellers to the Continent at the time were left with; that is, the awareness that everything they saw had already been not only discovered but also written about (Buzard 1993, 158).[10] What is more, travel writers struggled to differentiate their travel accounts from modern tourist guidebooks by Baedeker and Murray, which started to appear from the late 1830s onwards (Buzard 2002, 48–49). In effect, authors experimented with travel writing, diverging from its traditional forms.

Elizabeth Eastlake, in her 1845 essay 'Lady Travellers', takes a close look at travel writing by British women travellers to the Continent in the first half of the nineteenth century and observes three dominant trends. She notes that first, there are women who 'made their own personal movements the mere thread on which to hang the general history of the countries they are traversing, or the groundwork on which to introduce a narrative of fictitious interest'. There are also those who 'have remained long enough in one province or place [...] to obtain that living acquaintance with it which always commands interest'. And finally, there are women who, 'having launched out beyond the beaten track, are privileged to offer any description, however unpretending, on the score of novelty' (Eastlake 1845).

Women writers personalized their travel accounts in a number of ways. They frequently adopted the epistolary or diary form of recording their experiences in a foreign country, to keep up the appearance that their accounts were for private use. As the title indicates, such is the form of Mrs Ashton Yates's *Letters Written during a Journey to Switzerland in 1841* (1843); in the preface she specifies that the letters were addressed to her children, and that they were dictated by her 'gossiping inclination' (Yates 1843, v). The personal and unrestrained character of letters and journals enabled their writers to freely express their personal views, even those contrary to the standard ones. In this way the authors would associate their works with a particular group of readers, which could prove useful in the 1840s, when the travel book market had become quite saturated (Walchester 2007, 28).[11]

Women travellers would also foreground a particular image of themselves in their travel texts.[12] Though a married woman, Elizabeth Strutt wrote an account from the perspective of an unaccompanied lady traveller, which is emphasized by the title, *A Spinster's Tour in France, the States of Genoa, &C., during the year 1827* (1828). By such means, Strutt narrowed her account to feminine matters and thus indicated the implied reader. Notwithstanding marketing reasons, assuming a particular identity in travel writing could serve the purpose of self-expression (Bassnett 2002, 234, 239). In *The Diary of an Ennuyée* (1826) Anna Jameson, for example, portrayed the fictitious figure of a melancholic, broken-hearted young woman travelling to Italy.

Travellers who had spent a considerable period in a foreign country felt entitled to offer readers an authoritative guide. In the preface to *Paris and Parisians* (1836), Frances Trollope, though she too used the epistolary form, emphasizes that she does not present her personal impressions but, having gathered information from numerous sources, truthfully presents the foreigners (Trollope 1836, vi).[13] For the same reason Mariana Starke's guidebook-like accounts would become prototypes of Murray tourist books (Buzard 1993, 68–70). There were, however, travel narratives clearly geared towards attaining a particular goal. Having become attached to the Italian people, in her *Rambles*, Mary Shelley sets herself a task of 'say[ing] something that may incite others to regard them favourably; something explanatory of their real character' (1844, 1: viii–ix), and she makes it clear that she will mainly touch upon political matters (ibid., 1: ix–xvi).

Over time there were more texts manifesting women travellers' attempts not to follow typical routes and visit solely fashionable locations but, instead, to go off the beaten track. Even those travelling in countries already well trodden, such as Italy or France, were able to discover a niche. Thus, while Charlotte Ann Eaton aspired to give a 'complete account' of the whole city in *Rome in the Nineteenth Century* (1820), Maria Graham limited her scope to its neglected neighbourhood in *Three Months Passed in the Mountains East of Rome, during the Year 1819* (1820). Frances Trollope documented *Paris and the Parisians in 1835* (1836), but Elizabeth Strutt Byron left the capital and wrote *Six Weeks on the Loire* (1833). Many of these texts reflect the authors' refusal to participate in mass tourism.

The publication of women's travel writing was facilitated by the growing interest of the publishing industry in women's writing (Frawley 1994, 28). Editors of both periodicals and books followed up contemporary readership's predilection for vivid productions, such as travelogues, and hunted for those who could submit such texts (see Ericson 1996, 172; Frawley 1994, 28). Anna Jameson, whose *Diary of an Ennuyée* initiated her activity as a travel writer, is a case in point (Orr 1998).

There were also women who took advantage of their already-gained celebrity to promote their travel texts. When Mary Shelley published several articles on travel in the 1820s, she had already been acclaimed for her novel *Frankenstein*. More importantly, however, she was then the widow of Percy Bysshe Shelley, and years later she reinforced this celebrity status by publishing *Rambles in Germany and Italy in 1840, 1842, and 1843* (1844), which recorded her pilgrimage to the land where her husband and two children had died (Frawley 1994, 47). Sydney Owenson (Lady Morgan), too, prior to publishing *France* (1817) and *Italy* (1821), had gained recognition as the author of the novel *The Wild Irish Girl* (1805; Orr 1998). Moreover, her ladyship was a great asset to Henry Colburn, the publisher, who was particularly interested in texts by titled writers.[14] Lady Morgan was among many women whom publishers actually commissioned to write books on particular countries (Buzard 1993, 158), since, given the authors' recognizability and also their expertise, the books were bound to succeed. Another such author was Frances Trollope, whose *Paris and the Parisians* (1836) as well as *A Visit in Italy* (1842) were advertised as written by an already acclaimed travel writer.[15] As Elizabeth Eastlake put it, there were women who would even 'regularly make a tour in order to make a book, and have thus pretty well divided the tourable world between them' (1845).

Marguerite Blessington's Life, Travels and Literary Career

Who was 'the most gorgeous Lady Blessington'? Her biographers left detailed accounts of her life and career, and she herself recorded her travels. Yet nowadays she is mainly remembered for her extraordinary beauty, magnetic appeal, astonishing brilliance and eventful life. She has been even compared to contemporary popular movie stars, who have their life stories recounted in tabloids (Hawkins and Kraver 2005, viii). In the following account of Marguerite Blessington's life, I mostly concentrate on the periods of her tours and sojourns in foreign cities; the account is based on Blessington's own travel accounts and on the biographical texts mentioned in the preface.

Before the journeys

Margaret (not Marguerite) Power was born on 1 September 1788[16] in Knockbrit in County Tipperary, Ireland, the third child of Edmund and Ellen Power. Even though Margaret was not born a lady, ladyship, which came so naturally to her when she got married to the Count of Blessington, might in fact have run in her blood, since her mother boasted her descent from the Sheehys and the Desmonds, very old and revered Irish families. Her parents did not appreciate the 'great qualities' that Margaret possessed but that 'lay dormant' (Molloy 1896, 1: 4). Thus the girl had led the life of a recluse until a family friend, Anne Dwyer, took pity on her and resolved to take care of her education. Margaret developed an avid interest in studying and reading, which was to continue throughout her life. She also displayed a great talent for inventing imaginative tales with which she began to entertain her family members and visitors, thus finally winning her parents' approval.

When the eight-year-old Margaret had just began to flourish and appreciate her surrounding under Miss Dwyer's influence, her father's debts forced the family to move to Clonmel. The removal from Knockbrit was a great blow to her; to use Michael Sadleir's words, 'The first plate was forged in the armour of smiling self-sufficiency' which was to cover the future Lady Blessington (Sadleir 1947, 4). With time, however, she began to take advantage of the opportunities that the city offered, and attended the local dance evenings with her sisters. Thus she was admitted to the society of Tipperary, from whom she began to receive considerable attention, owing to 'the intelligence of her countenance, and the charm of her conversation' (Power 1850, 4).

When she was fifteen, her beauty also began to blossom, a fact that her father was to use to his advantage. Once in Clonmel, the family encountered new problems, since Edmund Power accepted the position of a magistrate. The role required him to prosecute Catholic Irishmen, and attempt to convert them to the Protestant religion, as a result of which he made numerous enemies. To ingratiate himself with the Clonmel officers, he invited them to dinner and expected his daughters to entertain the guests with conversation. Among them was Captain Maurice Farmer, who would become Margaret's husband. Lured by material benefits, Mr Power eagerly consented to the marriage, despite the fact that he had been informed of the suitor's insanity. In vain did Margaret implore her parents not to marry her off to 'a man who inspired her with nothing but feelings of terror and detestation' (Power 1850, 5).

Thus in 1804, when she was not yet sixteen, Margaret was sold into an unwanted marriage. Madden (1855, 1: 33) quotes Blessington's recollection of the time spent in her husband's house, according to which she was intimidated and maltreated. Such was her suffering that after three months, when her husband informed her of his being ordered to join his regiment, she stood up to him and refused to accompany him. Forced to obey the order, he finally allowed her to stay at her parents'. This, in fact, was the end of the relationship since, shortly after, due to one of his insane acts, Captain Farmer was expelled from the army and fled to India. Margaret lived for three years with her parents, but left Clonmel when she learned that her husband was returning from India.

Even though there are discrepancies in the accounts of the following years, it is believed that between 1809 and 1814 she resided in Hampshire, in the house of Captain Jenkins, whom she had met at her parents' house, and who offered her protection. Jenkins became Margaret's companion and patron, creating favourable conditions for her to enjoy tranquillity and continue her self-education, and kindling in her a particular interest in literature and art. He also provided her with the first chance ever to travel not only in country but also abroad to Paris.[17] As Sadleir claims, in these years she 'developed a brilliance and charm of conversation, a power of putting others at their ease and inviting their confidence, which remained her outstanding characteristics, and were the secrets of her success as hostess and as ruler of a *salon*' (Sadleir 1947, 11).

The year 1814 was a turning point in Margaret's life. In this year Jenkins was visited by his old army friend, Charles John Gardiner, second Viscount of Mountjoy, who was an affluent Irish nobleman, a widower in his early thirties with four children. Margaret had already met him once ten years earlier in Clonmel,[18] and this casual acquaintance was now renewed. In 1816 he became first Earl of Blessington and proposed marriage to Margaret, contingent on her getting a divorce. Margaret's response is not recorded, yet it is known that she soon moved to London and was established by Blessington in Manchester Square. She was now engaged to Lord Blessington and was seeking divorce, which status, as it turned out, did not last long. In October 1817

Margaret became a widow after her husband's sudden death. On 16 February 1818, when she was almost thirty, Margaret Farmer remarried and became Marguerite Gardiner, Countess of Blessington.

Early travels and the beginnings of a career

The first four years of their marriage, from 1818 to 1822, were an eventful period in Marguerite's life. The newlyweds spent their honeymoon in Dublin and at Mountjoy Forest in Tyrone, Ireland, as Lord Blessington wished to introduce his new wife to his children, family members and friends. There Marguerite learned about the extravagant and theatrical tastes of her husband, who put her on a pedestal and kept her in the lap of luxury. However, owing to her husband's prodigality, the resentment of his family, her unhappy memories of Ireland and her hope to begin anew in London, she soon began to put pressure on him to leave Ireland.

On their return to London the couple settled at a splendid town mansion at No. 11 St James's Square, which for the following three years would be 'the centre of attraction for the most remarkable men of the day' (Power 1850, 6). Initially, their dinners and soirées were attended mostly by politicians and statesmen, but also present were writers, poets and travellers, among whom were George Canning, Viscount Castlereagh, Thomas Moore, Samuel Rogers, John Galt and Samuel Parr. One of the frequent guests was also Sir Thomas Lawrence, the painter of Lady Blessington's portrait, which would bring her fame. In the same year the countess began her literary career, publishing four anonymous volumes: *The Magic Lantern; or, Sketches of Scenes in the Metropolis* (1822), *Sketches and Fragments* (1822), *A Tour of the Isle of Wight in the Autumn of 1820* (1822), *Journal of a Tour through the Netherlands to Paris in 1821* (1822).

Although male members of London society were enchanted by her, it is assumed that Marguerite Blessington was not on good terms with ladies of the high *ton*, who would not visit her at St James's Square or invite her to Almack's, ruled by Lady Jersey (Lovell 1969, *25*). In one of her debut sketches in *The Magic Lantern*, she writes: 'How often have I seen a lady-like, sensitive woman, shrinking beneath the fixed gaze of some dames of fashionable notoriety, on whom her apparent timidity has impressed the conviction of her being *nobody*' (Blessington 1822, 101). She might well have been thinking of herself, since in the years to come she would attempt to prove the contrary.

Two years earlier, in the autumn of 1820, the newly wed Lady and Lord Blessington had set off on a journey to the Isle of Wight, where they spent two weeks from 15 September to 2 October. The account of their stay on the Isle was her very first attempt at recording a journey. From the text we learn that she was unwilling to undertake the trip, as it meant abandoning her 'comfortable home for the noisy bustle of bad inns' (*IoW* 2). Yet with a heavy heart they settled on the plan for health reasons, as they had been advised to do so. The tour of the island turned out to be an occasion for her to indulge in 'the beauties of nature' (*IoW* 29), and this was probably where she developed her predilection for the picturesque. By steamboat they travelled from Southampton to Cowes, where they spent several days and went to explore the villages Wootton Bridge and Ryde. Then they rowed up the Medina River to Newport, where they stayed for the next few days. From there they made a number of trips to places of interest, such as the Appuldurcombe House, Shanklin Chine, Bonchurch Landslips, Carisbrooke Castle and Blackgang Chine. All in all, the trip to 'this lovely island' turned out a very enjoyable experience (*IoW* 75). Lady Blessington left it 'with reluctance'. Even twelve years later, she would still remember it fondly, which is evidenced in a letter to her friend Mrs Anne Mathews, wife to the actor Charles Mathews:

> I like the Isle of Wight – it is endeared to me by the recollection of having passed a delightful fortnight there, with my ever-to-be-lamented husband; the only *téte-à-téte* we ever enjoyed during our marriage, and which we both felt as children do their first vacation from school. How many souvenirs does each thought of it excite. (Madden 1855, 3: 369)

In the following year, 1821, the Blessingtons made a rather whirlwind foreign tour, as the countess noted, 'through the Netherlands and part of France'. The tour lasted one month and a half (from 10 September to 24 October), and the part of the Low Countries they saw included only a few Belgian cities. This was a shorter and cheaper alternative to the proper Grand Tour, also popular among the British. Like most tourists, they went to Dover in order to cross to Calais, and there they embarked on 'a regular sailing packet', as the steamboat was delayed. The crossing took three hours and is described as exceeding the 'horrors of crossing the Styx' due to a heavy swell, crowd pressures and seasick passengers (*NtP* 11).

From Calais they headed towards the Belgian border via Lille, where they devoted a considerable time to the Palace of Fine Arts, contemplating its pieces of art and its library collection. When in Belgium, they went to Tournay, which impressed the countess with its cathedral, and finally reached Brussels, where they stayed for several days. While there, Lady Blessington was impressed by the cathedral, the works of art in churches and the lace factory. Most of the time, however, she spent visiting the locations related to events from recent history, such as the Royal Palace of Laeken, where Emperor Napoleon I had resided, and the vicinity of Waterloo, where the great battle took place only six years earlier.

Then the couple returned to France and arrived in Paris on 26 September. Lady Blessington had already been to Paris. She had a clear idea about how she wished to spend the following few weeks in the city and its vicinity this time, but the plan would prove highly demanding. One of her goals was to cultivate her artistic tastes; therefore, her first destination was the Louvre, where she resolved to spend 'an hour or two' every day (*NtP* 93). Like most tourists, the countess also went sightseeing to the city's famous attractions, among which were places linked to Napoleon and Josephine, such as the Tuileries Palace, the Élysée Palace and the Château de Malmaison. Apart from contemplating art and sightseeing, Lady Blessington also had the chance to get the feel of the city when attending the opera and the theatre, loitering in the Palais Royal, visiting the Beaujon Gardens and taking tours through curiosity shops, for which she developed a real weakness. She was also privileged to make the acquaintance of such Parisian personalities as Francois Joseph Gall, a neuroanatomist, and Baron Dominique Vivant Denon, an archaeologist.

Three weeks later, on 17 October, the Blessingtons left Paris and headed for home. Passing through Amiens, where they saw the cathedral, they reached Calais. After a very rough crossing on board the *Rob Roy* steam packet, they saw the cliffs of Dover and finally returned home on 24 October. Ten months later the Blessingtons would cross the Channel again, but then they would stay abroad for much longer.

Setting out for the Continent

There are several plausible reasons for the Blessingtons' decision to set out for the Continent in the year 1822. Molloy relates that they both agreed on leaving London for the upcoming winter, but, although Lord Blessington wished to go to Mountjoy Forest, the countess, reluctant to return to Ireland, insisted on going to Italy (Molloy 1896, 1: 56, 60). Blessington might have wished to redirect her husband's expenditure on his estate to 'the delights of fashionable life [...] on the Continent' (Sadleir 1947, 25–26). Madden, on the other hand, claims that it was Lord Blessington's 'necessity for distraction, for novelty, and new effects' that occasioned his attempt to abandon their abode in St James's Square and to go abroad (Madden 1855, 1: 73). Such 'restlessness' and 'perpetual desire to be somewhere else' was supposedly typical of the British in the nineteenth century, as Pemble argues (1988, 96). Yet Sadleir also ventures to claim that this enthusiasm about the Continental travel was aroused by Alfred, Count D'Orsay, who on his way to France happened to visit the Blessingtons (Sadleir 1947, 37). Others point out that, as a result of their extravagant lifestyle, the Blessingtons had financial difficulties and therefore might have resolved to economize by moving to the Continent, which was a common practice at the time as well (Feldman 2000, 148). Whatever the reason, on 25 August 1822 Lord and Lady Blessington, along with the latter's youngest sister Mary Ann Power and their numerous entourage, left London for an 'indefinite period' (*IiI* 1: 1).

The Blessingtons went to Dover to cross the Channel, and just as before the crossing was far from a pleasurable experience:

> The packet was full, to overflowing; the cabins crowded, and the deck thronged. [...] Many of the ladies, and nearly all the males, declared that *they* never suffered from sea-sickness; but, before we had more than half crossed the channel, they had either disappeared, or were seen leaning over the ship's side, intently gazing on the sea. (*IiI* 1: 3)

The countess herself, however, on this occasion seemed prepared for such hardships. On their arrival she was also well acquainted with the common travelling routes. Instead of going through Abbeville, in her opinion 'the uninteresting, and often traversed route' to Paris (*IiI* 1: 7), the party decided to take that of Rouen and were repaid by viewing much prettier sites and encountering on their way the birthplace of Pierre Corneille. It had already become their practice during their first Continental tour to take such routes, so that they could visit the homes and haunts of renowned persons, and so it would remain for the next eight years.

Through Rouen they got to St Germain-en-Laye, the town where Lady Blessington would be buried twenty-seven years later. After two days they left the place, much to the countess's regret, and headed for Paris, which they reached on 31 August. This was the countess's third visit to Paris, and she spent the ten days meeting her acquaintances, such as Baron Denon and the poet Thomas Moore, walking in the city's gardens and seeking entertainment. She also visited the Louvre even though she had been there 'at least thirty times' during the two previous visits (*IiI* 1: 31). While the countess was enjoying herself, her husband was preoccupied with hiring servants, buying supplies and equipping their several carriages with furniture and luxurious appliances.

On their departure, the cavalcade made such an impression on passersby that one of them reportedly named it the 'Blessington Circus' (Sadleir 1947, 51). Lady Blessington was excited at the prospect of the journey into the unknown; however, to be on the safe side, she decided to 'go forth with no Smelfungus predisposition to be dissatisfied, nor yet with any very enthusiastic anticipations of being charmed' (*IiI* 1: 41).[19] Passing through Fontainebleau, where they visited the room in which Napoleon I had signed his abdication, the party made their way to Switzerland. On 15 September they arrived at the top of Mount Jura, from which the countess could delight in her first view of

Lake Geneva, where she would then go for a row. They spent almost a month travelling in Switzerland, where they visited the places linked to Voltaire, Rousseau, Gibbon, Gessner, Shelley and Byron.

Back in France, they stayed for a few days in Lyons and then for three weeks in Vienna, where the countess explored ancient ruins. There they also met the archeologist François Artaud, who provided them with 'letters of introduction to half of cognoscenti of the south of France and Italy' (*IiI* 1: 160). They moved on and arrived in Avignon on 20 November. During the three-month stay in the city, Lady Blessington developed a habit of making long excursions on horseback to all must-see sights, such as the Fontaine-de-Vaucluse, the tomb of Petrarch's Laura and the Pont du Gard and Villeneuve. She also evinced great interest in the local people's lives, visiting Avignon's lunatic asylum and the hospital. In the evenings, she was eager to attend the salons, where all the '*beau monde* of Avignon' assembled, and to invite newly acquainted friends to her place (*IiI* 1: 204). On 16 February, the 'Blessington Circus' left Avignon, its number increased by one – Count D'Orsay.[20] The party of now thirteen members stopped to see Aix-en-Provence and the coastal cities of Provence and after only two weeks decided to head for Italy.

Italy

The route to Italy taken by the party was the Grande Corniche, a tortuous road on a steep rocky coast leading from Nice to Genoa (Brockedon 1829, 1–2). Opened under Napoleon's reign, it was still under construction at the time of their visit. As it was not yet suitable for wheeled vehicles, the only possible means of transportation were a sedan chair or muleback. Nonetheless, the countess was satisfied that the road was 'boldly designed, and solidly executed, with a disregard of difficulties, or a complete triumph over them' (*IiI* 1: 359). Additionally, the travellers could ceaselessly delight in the views of the French and Italian Rivieras – the picturesque villages, luxuriant flora, mountains and the sea. After a six-day journey, they took leave of the mules, praising their sure-footed pace and agreeableness. Proceeding in 'coaches of the country', they headed towards Genoa.

On their arrival in Genoa on 31 March, the countess was impressed by the situation of the city, 'built on an amphitheatre, with the fine bay bathing its foundations' (*IiI* 1: 399). The prospect of visiting Genoa was all the more attractive because she knew Lord Byron resided there. The Blessingtons' daily activities mainly included meetings with the poet, but also visiting churches and palaces as well as attending the opera, having water parties and receiving visits from other English residents and naval men. Their stay there was interrupted by the sad news of the death of Lord Blessington's only legitimate son.

As a consequence of this tragedy, Lord Blessington decided to have a codicil made to his will. It was agreed that in the event of the Earl's death, Count D'Orsay, provided he would marry one of his daughters, was to inherit a great part of his estates, whereas the amount of one thousand pounds per annum was bequested to Lady Blessington.

Having left Genoa on 2 June 1823, the party travelled along the Tuscan coastland with the sparkling sea on the one side and a chain of woody hills on the other. When entering the city of Florence for the first time, the countess was equipped with 'a thousand of associations of the olden time', which she wished to confront with the city's present reality (*IiI* 2: 101). More than on other occasions she was now a typical tourist, wishing to make the most of her visit. In the mornings she was occupied by sauntering through galleries, mainly the Uffizi Gallery and the Palazzo. Afternoons were mostly spent on wandering about the city's streets and piazzas as well as visiting its innumerable palaces and churches. In the evenings, in turn, she would go on excursions to the city's environs. As the countess planned to return here on her way back home, however, the Blessingtons left the city after three weeks.

From Florence they travelled to Rome via the Chianti Hills, which, for rather practical reasons, did not appeal to the countess: 'The road is hilly, and the views it commands do not compensate for its tediousness' (*IiI* 2: 151). On 5 July Lady Blessington for the first time saw Rome, which at the time was not a welcoming place for tourists. The city was having a heat wave and there was a risk of contracting malaria. Moreover, on this occasion the countess was probably displeased with hotel conveniences; as Madden records, 'All the appliances to comfort, or rather to luxury, which had become necessary to Lady Blessington, had not been found in Rome' (Madden 1855, 1: 95). Thus, this was but a short visit to the city's highlights. After nine days, on 13 July, Lady Blessington left Rome, planning to return and stay there for several months on her way back home, so that she could pay to the city its due attention.

The Blessingtons set off towards Naples, taking the route along the Tyrrhenian coast. They reached their destination on 17 July 1823, and they planned a long sojourn there. Initially, they stayed in the Gran Bretagna, an excellent hotel with the view of Naples Bay, whose only disadvantage was the location in the Strada Chiaja, a touristic promenade. Its noise and dust, however, became unbearable for the countess, and she determined to find a more suitable abode. Finally, they moved in the Palazzo Belvedere, a beautifully situated residence at Vomero. In Naples, the countess's lifestyle became more regular – she allocated some time to everyday matters, reading and entertainment, as well as making excursions to places of interest in the city's environs. She would also regularly receive guests – Naples's esteemed residents and visitors.[21]

In February 1826, after two and a half years, Lady Blessington bid farewell to all her friends and left Naples. The party now headed for Florence, stopping on their way in Rome, where they spent about three weeks. There the countess met with her acquaintances and explored antiquities under the guidance of William Gell and Edward Dodwell. In March 1826 they reached Florence, and, unlike their first stay in the city, this sojourn was devoted mainly to social interactions, enjoyable parties and theatricals with which they were entertained by the Earl's friend, Constantine Henry Phipps, Marquess of Normanby. After nine months, the countess had become tired of the city's hustle and bustle, and therefore they resumed their journey and headed for Pisa. First, however, they diverted to Genoa, where they spent but a few weeks, missing the presence of Lord Byron, who was no longer alive.

Late in December 1826 they came to Pisa, where they spent six months. The countess liked the city's climate and its location close to the sea port of Livorno, thanks to which there was easy access to 'books and other comforts from England' (*IiI* 2: 485). This being their first stay in the city, the Blessingtons also went to see its monuments, among which were the Church of Santa Maria della Spina, as well as the Lanfranchi Palace, where Byron had stayed, and Tobias Smollett's grave in Livorno. Here they also met the Duc and Duchesse de Guiche, to whom they took an instant liking. The Duchesse de Guiche was D'Orsay's sister. The Guiches, the Prince and Princess Constantino Carragia and the poet Alphonse de Lamartine were among the acquaintances with whom the Blessingtons had spontaneous soirees in their Casa Chiesa and engaged in pleasant, casual conversations.

In June 1827 the Blessingtons were back in Florence, and on this occasion the countess was introduced to Walter Landor, who was to become her close friend, and out of regard for whom they probably decided to prolong their stay in the city. They thus settled in the Casa Pecori, on the banks of the Arno, where they were visited by Landor, Lamartine, Prince Borghese and other prominent guests. Just as during her first visit to the city, the mornings were devoted to visiting art galleries, whereas in the evening they went for drives in Tuscan environs. During their stay in Florence, the time came to execute Lord Blessington's will, made four years before, which offered Count D'Orsay the hand of one of his daughters. However, since the local minister refused to marry the Count to then fifteen-year-old Harriet, the party resolved to leave Florence immediately and head for Naples. They were on good terms with the British minister there and the wedding took place on 1 December 1827.

This journey to Naples is not recorded in *The Idler in Italy*, and thus the Blessingtons and the newlyweds are placed right in Rome somewhere at the end of 1827.[22] This time planning a longer sojourn in the city, the countess instantly went house hunting and hired the Palazzo Negroni. There, as usual, they started receiving numerous guests, among whom was her biographer R. R. Madden. Lady Blessington also made several notable acquaintances. One day the countess attended a masquerade where she was approached by a masked female who turned out to be Hortense Bonaparte, the stepdaughter of Napoleon I, and a masked man in a blue domino – in fact, Jerome Bonaparte, the emperor's brother.[23] The countess met them again on other occasions, once when she accepted the Duchess's invitation[24] and then when, walking in the gardens of the Villa Palatina, she encountered the Prince of Montfort with Madame Letitia Bonaparte, the mother of Napoleon I.[25]

On 9 May 1828 the Blessingtons and their companions left Rome and travelled northward through the eastern regions of the Apennine Peninsula. In Ravenna they stayed at the inn once occupied by Byron and visited the Palazzo Guiccioli and Dante's tomb. Traveling via Ferrara, where they visited Tasso's prison, they arrived in Padua, in which town they prolonged their stay to several weeks so as to visit its university and the local tourist attractions. From Padua the Blessingtons headed for Venice. They followed the route along the Riviera del Brenta, and in Mestre they got on a boat that took them to the Grand Canal. In Venice they spent another few weeks, which were devoted to intensive sightseeing.

Once the Blessingtons left the city, the pace of the journey increased. After six years spent in Italy, they finally commenced their journey back home. On their way they stopped again in Padua and explored Vicenza and Verona. Then they had a stopover in Desenzano, where the countess admired the view of Lake Garda and the Alps. They prolonged their stay in Milan to visit the Ambrosian Library and La Scala, and have a chance to see other Lombard towns. From Milan, they headed south to Genoa and then moved straight towards the French border, which they passed again through the Grand Corniche.

Paris

Once in France, the cavalcade went again along the Riviera to Marseilles. Blessington observed that the state of the villages had considerably improved over the six years and that the French hotels were superior to the Italian ones in terms of comfort and food, yet not 'in civility and attention' (*IiF* 1: 3). The travellers then settled on visiting several sites renowned for their well-preserved Roman ruins. They first made a detour to see Nîmes and its Maison Carrée, the Tour Magne and the Temple of Diana. Back in Provence, they stopped in Arles, where the countess was impressed not only by numerous Roman structures but also by the place's peculiarly primitive charm. The next stops were Beaucaire and Tarascon (with its famous medieval Church of St Martha) on the Rhône River. Finally, in Saint-Rémy-de-Provence they explored the archaeological site of Glanum, with its triumphal arch and mausoleum. Passing via Lyons, they finally arrived in Paris in June 1828.

Paris was the final destination on Lady Blessington's itinerary, where she would stay for almost two and a half years. On their arrival, the party first stayed at the hotel in the Rue de Rivoli, the noisiness of which, however, the countess strongly disliked and, as usual, she began house hunting. The Blessingtons rented the mansion in the Rue de Bourbon known as the Hôtel Maréchal Ney, whose apartments overlooked the Seine and the Tuileries Garden. Sadleir records that the residence 'seems to have marked the zenith even of Blessingtonian extravagance' (Sadleir 1947, 107). The plan of embellishing Lady Blessington's private suite was conceived by the Earl himself and was kept in secret from her until carried out. When they finally moved in, the countess's feelings were mixed, since, on the one hand, she felt excited and pampered, as she reflects, 'We feel like children with a new plaything, in our beautiful house.' Yet, on the other hand, she must have already feared the consequences of her husband's reckless expenditure; as she admits, 'the only complaint I ever have to make of his taste is its too great splendour' (*IiF* 1: 117). In their luxurious house, the Blessingtons would receive and entertain the prominent members of aristocratic, political and artistic elite, to which they had been introduced by Madame Craufurd, D'Orsay's grandmother.

Apart from socializing, Lady Blessington continued the same pursuits that she had followed during her previous stays in the city. Besides visiting the Louvre, she did some sightseeing, among other places to Rousseau's Hermitage in Montmorency and to the Pays Latin, the quarter inhabited by literary types. The countess would also take regular walks, attend the opera and theatres, as well as going on shopping sprees. She spent much time with the Duchess of Guiche, who was her guide to the Parisian world of fashion.

Unfortunately, the upcoming year in Paris was to be much less favourable. In April 1829, Lord Blessington received a letter urging him to return to London and appear in the House of Lords so as to vote on the Catholic Emancipation bill. Already in poor health, the journey there and back contributed to the deterioration in the Earl's condition. On 25 May 1829 Lord Blessington had a stroke of apoplexy and died suddenly. Once more Lady Blessington became a widow. She had to face the fact that, due to her husband's poor money management and a disadvantageous bequest he had made to her, her income would be reduced to merely 2,000 pounds a year. Another problem was that Lady Blessington became the subject of scandal, which now flared up in London and had emerged from the fact that after the Earl's passing she had continued to live with Count D'Orsay and his sixteen-year-old wife under the same roof.[26]

Lady Blessington stayed in Paris throughout the Revolution of 1830, but when it came to an end, the new political face of the city was no longer favourable to her friends and thus to her. Therefore, in November 1830, in very low spirits, the countess resolved to return to the even less welcoming London.[27]

After the journeys

Back in London, Lady Blessington did not return to the house in St James's Square, as it was to be reverted to her late husband's family on the expiration of the present lease. Instead she rented a house in Seamore Place, Park Lane, where she resumed the salon started prior to her Continental journeys. When residing in Avignon, Naples, Florence, Rome and Paris, Lady Blessington had mastered her skills as hostess; she learnt that the most desirable form of entertainment for 'men of talent and distinction' should combine 'luxury and mental stimulus' and allow them 'a pleasant freedom from the artificial constraints of polite society' (Sadleir 1947, 132, 125). By these means the countess might well compete with the three prominent London salonnières – Lady Holland, Lady Charleville and Lady Cork.

On her return from the Continent, the countess would also take advantage of the recognition she had gained prior to her journeys, the valuable contacts she had already made and her travel experiences in order to establish herself as a writer and editor. Her first publication now was *Conversations of Lord Byron*, based on her reminiscences of Lord Byron, which was initially published serially in the *New Monthly Magazine* in 1832 and then, in 1834, as a single volume. This publication made her famous as 'Byron's Boswell' (Hawkins and Kraver 2005, xvii) and opened the doors to her literary career. Unlike her early unsigned publications of 1822, from 1832 on her texts were printed with her name on the title page. She wrote more or less two works a year, for which she was handsomely paid.

Around this time Lady Blessington also committed herself to popular annual giftbooks. She not only contributed her own short stories and poems, but was also offered editorship of several annuals, which position she held till her death. Thus, she edited *The Book of Beauty* (1834–50), run by the well-known engraver Charles Heath, *The Keepsake* (1841–50) as well as *Flowers of Loveliness* (1835) and *Gems of Beauty* (1836–40). Her already established position as a salonnière would have been very helpful in attracting such distinguished contributors to her annuals as, among others, Benjamin Disraeli, Thomas Moore, Letitia Landor, Edward Bulwer-Lytton, William Thackeray and Walter Savage Landor.

At the same time Lady Blessington tried her hand at novel writing. Her first three-volume novel, entitled *Grace Cassidy; or, The Repealers,* concerned the Irish question and was published in 1833. As a *roman à clef*, the novel would enable her to criticize her enemies and to flatter her potential allies. Other novels followed, namely *The Two Friends* (1835), *The Confessions of an Elderly Gentleman* (1836), *The Victims of Society* (1837), *The Confessions of an Elderly Lady* (1838), *The Governess* (1839), *Meredith* (1843), *Strathern* (1845), *The Memoirs of a Femme de Chambre* (1846), *Marmeduke Herbert* (1847), *Country Quarters* (published posthumously in 1850). By 1849 the countess had authored eleven novels altogether, skilfully satisfying the demands of the readership. Lady Blessington also issued non-fiction works, among which were the travel accounts based on the journals she kept during her Continental tours.

In the meantime, in 1836 Lady Blessington moved to Gore House, Kensington, where she continued her salon for the next thirteen years. As she was now a professional writer and editor, her social meetings assumed a predominantly literary character, which was manifested by the practice of inviting guests to the library and not to the drawing room. She gathered together the most distinguished literary figures of the time, such as Edward Bulwer-Lytton, John Forster, Benjamin Disraeli, Charles Dickens, Henry Crabb Robinson, Thomas Moore, Albany Fonblanque, Joseph Jekyll, William Makepeace Thackeray, Walter Savage Landor and Samuel Rogers. Benjamin Haydon, also a friend of hers, once wrote in his diary:

> Went to Lady Blessington's in the evening, everybody goes to Lady Blessington. She has the first news of everything, and everybody seems delighted to tell her. She is the center of more talent and gaiety than any other woman of fashion in London. (quoted in Madden 1855, 1: 179)

Yet she was still shunned by ladies of London's high society, who not only resented her being held in such high esteem despite her dubious reputation,[28] but were also envious of her charm and competence as a salonnière. Among the few well-meaning women with whom she kept in touch were Letitia Landon, Countess Teresa Guiccioli and Anne Mathews, her only true female friend.

Among the reasons why Lady Blessington's soirées appealed to numerous writers was the possibility to benefit from the acquaintance of other writers, potential publishers and reviewers. From this the countess unintentionally profited herself, when her guest Nathaniel Parker Willis, an American journalist, praised the countess's salon in his *Pencillings by the Way* (1835), by which she won international acclaim. As a result, while she was rather shunned by London society, she would rise to a cultural icon in America. Her novels and keepsakes, considered as guides to English manners and style, became so popular among the American readership that they were reprinted there on a large scale.[29]

One of the motives behind Lady Blessington's becoming such a prolific writer was the need to supplement her finances. Her modest income would not have been enough to cover the expenses of her fashionable lifestyle and to support her family and Count D'Orsay, who moved to Gore House after his wife had left him in 1831. Nevertheless, this tremendous writing effort turned out to be insufficient when Lady Blessington was confronted with a series of financial crises. First, in 1833 her house in Seamore Place was broken into and her valuable jewellery was stolen. The next misfortune was the crash of the financial markets in the 1840s, which greatly reduced her writing income. Then came the failure of the crops in Ireland from 1845 to 1848, which diminished her profit, and the death of Charles Heath, who owed her a considerable sum of money. Finally, in the spring of 1849 the countess's biggest creditor, Howell & James department store, demanded that she settle her account. In this situation, and having refused all the offers of help from her friends, Lady Blessington made the decision to put up for auction all the contents of Gore House. Hoping for a cheaper, less arduous and more peaceful life as well as more friendly environment, she determined to return to the Continent, which was to be the final journey in her life.

In April 1849 Lady Blessington came to Paris with her niece, Miss Margaret Power, and found herself again among her old friends, but she did not long enjoy her retiring state there. Not even two months later, on 4 June 1849, having just settled in a cosy apartment, Lady Blessington woke up early in the morning with severe breathing difficulty and soon died of heart stoppage. She was not yet sixty-one. The countess was buried at Chambourcy, near St Germain-en-Laye, in a pyramid-shaped granite mausoleum designed by Count D'Orsay.[30]

Part I
TEXTS

Chapter 1

PARATEXTS

Before it is presented to the public, a text needs to be adorned by certain additions – 'the paratext' in Gerard Genette's terms (1997, 1) – which make it a proper book. These elements may be supplied by both the author and the publisher, and include the cover, front matter (including the title page and the contents), headings, footnotes and back matter. The paratext may have a profound influence on the reception and consumption of a book among readers, since this is what catches, or does not catch, their attention before they start reading the text proper. To use Genette's words, the paratext constitutes the book's 'threshold of interpretation' (ibid.), which may be a welcoming or an unwelcoming one. Philippe Lejeune, in turn, acknowledging their embellishing properties, characterizes these elements as 'a fringe of the printed text which in reality controls one's whole reading of the book' (quoted in Genette 1997, 2).

In this chapter I argue that Blessington's paratexts reveal much about travel writing conventions and commercial practices in the first half of the nineteenth century. When examining the title pages of Blessington's four accounts of her travels, one notices that there are striking similarities between *A Tour in the Isle of Wight, in the Autumn of 1820* (1822) and *Journal of a Tour through the Netherlands to Paris, in 1821* (1822), which distinguish them from *The Idler in Italy* (1839–40) and *The Idler in France* (1841–42). Therefore, I discuss the early and the mature texts separately throughout.

Neither of the two early journals identifies Marguerite Blessington as its author. The title page of *A Tour in the Isle of Wight, in the Autumn of 1820* includes the Latin phrase 'CURRENTE CALAMO', placed in the space commonly reserved for the name of the author. The phrase means 'written off at once, without premeditation', and it would have transmitted to the reader a twofold message. First, the identity of the author was not considered as vital as the fact that what followed was an immediate and thus authentic account of a journey. This would have been in accordance with the tendency in eighteenth-century travel writing to belittle the role of the writer and at the same time to attest to the text's veracity (Batten 1978, 39, 58). On the other hand, the use of the phrase is reminiscent of typical techniques women would adopt to 'break into' the genre of travel writing (McAllister 1988, v). At that time it was still easier for a woman to get published if she did not reveal herself to be a woman. Moreover, given the feminine tendency to assume self-protective strategies (ibid., 9), Blessington may have tried to avoid accusations of trying to gain recognition by means of these hastily written notes. In fact, it would have been impossible anyway, as not only was she a woman, but she also lacked both formal education and travel experience, and thus her journal would have been doomed to failure (ibid., 8).

Even though the journal is not signed, the identity of the author is hinted at in the prefatory note, at the end of which there is the information 'St. James's Square. July 6th, 1822' – this was Blessington's address (at no. 10) at that time. The Blessingtons' residence was an intellectual and artistic centre visited by a number of esteemed personages, and certainly those who attended their social meetings would connect the facts.[1]

In a manner similar to the previous book, *Journal of a Tour through the Netherlands to Paris, in 1821* was issued anonymously, but on the title page readers would find the information that would have helped them identify the author; it indicates that the text was written by the author of *Sketches and Fragments*. This was the second book published by Blessington, the title page of which, in turn, informed the reader that it was by the same author as *The Magic Lantern; or, Sketches of Scenes in the Metropolis*, her very first publication. The three volumes were published in 1822, which was a significant year in Blessington's career, as in May Sir Thomas Lawrence's famous portrait *Margaret, Countess of Blessington* was exhibited at the Royal Academy. The portrait received high critical acclaim, and as a result Blessington became a celebrity (Eckroth 2012, 5; Hawkins 2012, 66). This must have encouraged both the author and the publisher – Longman, Hurst, Rees, Orme, and Brown – to issue the three volumes. These circumstances indicate that not revealing the author's name on the title page was not intended to show Blessington's sincere embarrassment, but rather her adherence to the prevailing publishing practices at the time. Revealing their authorship in such a self-reflexive manner was a common strategy among writers. In any case, the identity of the author very soon came to light, as she was referred to by name by her reviewers in the *Monthly Magazine* and the *Literary Gazette,* and in the following years all the three texts appeared in popular magazines, along with Blessington's name (Hawkins 2012, 66)

Nonetheless, Blessington seemingly had not been confident as a travel writer in July 1822 when *A Tour in the Isle of Wight, in the Autumn of 1820* was issued. If she had been, she would have signed it as the author of *Magic Lantern*. This lack of confidence is clear from the short preface, written in a manner typical of eighteenth-century women travel writers. At that time women felt obliged to explain why they had travelled and written about their travels. Moreover, in order to 'create a place for their work', they needed to convince the reader of 'the significance of their contribution' to the field of travel writing (McAllister 1988, 9). Thus they applied a number of strategies aiming at their self-validation, which were of either a defensive or an offensive nature. Most of the women tried to combine apology with assertion, and some of them succeeded in turning excuses into subversively assertive statements (ibid.). In her very first travelogue, Blessington limits herself to defensive strategies.

In the preface to *A Tour in the Isle of Wight* entitled 'To the Reader', Blessington gives an explanation for publishing her journal, as if in anticipation of its critical reception. The reader is first informed that the tour described in the volume 'was written without any idea of its ever being perused, save by the partner of it' (*IoW*). However, she lent it to a friend who, partial to the author, 'induced' her to publish just a few copies only for distribution among acquaintances (ibid.). She adds that the aim of presenting them with the volume was solely to prove her regard for them. The excuse that the author had but few readers in mind was another typical eighteenth-century convention (McAllister 1988, 12–13). By assuming such an apologetic tone, the author presents herself as a modest novice, aware of the amateurish character of her work. What we learn from the preface is confirmed in the text proper, as at one point she tries to convince the reader that she did not want to travel, and that the decision was made only 'after serious consideration and mature deliberation'. In the end, the journey was undertaken with a heavy heart: 'It was therefore with a foreboding of evil that we commenced our journey; undertaken solely because we were told that change of air and exercise were absolutely necessary for our health' (*IoW* 3). The insistence that the author's reason for embarking on the tour was not her desire for enjoyment or literary fame but the pursuit of health was also typical in the period.

Similar rhetorical techniques are applied in *Journal of a Tour through the Netherlands to Paris, in 1821,* with the difference that defensive tactics are balanced by offensive ones. Already on the Continent, Blessington was not able to provide a preface to this account herself, and instead there is an advertisement by the editor who, well aware of the accepted travel writing conventions, may be assumed to be the writer's mouthpiece. Typically, the advertisement includes information that only several copies of the journal were intended for distribution among friends initially, but the friends persuaded the author that the text should go public (*NtP* vi–vii).[2] It also stresses that the writer has already 'been favoured with the approbation of the public' and is 'unwilling to lose any portion of fame' (ibid., v). In this way, through the editor, Blessington convinces her readers of her unassuming position, yet, already at this stage, she wishes them to consider her an author of some renown. Such apparent contradictions are the organizing principle of the introductory section of the journal.

In a manner typical of women's travel writing, it is also emphasized that the journal was written in haste and for private use: 'The Tourist wrote for amusement [only and] the observations and reflections were noted down at the moment [...] amid the confusion and bustle' of her arrivals and stays in numerous hotels (*NtP* v–vi). Then the reader is assured that on return home the author did not rewrite, polish or supplement her account with any additional materials (ibid.). Whether it was to express modesty on the part of the author or doubts on the part of the male editor, drawing the readers' and critics' attention to stylistic imperfections of the text may seem an ill-judged move. On the other hand, McAllister suggests that this was but another 'rhetorical stratagem', since the purpose of justifying the journal's possible flaws was in fact to fend off critics' attacks (1988, 16). This peculiar marketing strategy also aimed to win over the reader who valued matter-of-factness and authenticity in travel journals more than their refined form (Batten 1978, 44–45).

Not only the form but also the journal's content is belittled, as it states:

> The ground has been trod over and written over again and again [...] but different travelers observe different objects; and the reader will find that the book, like the journey, is short, and though it may afford but little amusement or instruction, it will, at all events, not occupy much of his time. (*NtP* vii–viii)

This passage, too, may be taken as an apology on the part of the writer, who expected accusations of inaccuracy, pointlessness and blandness of her account, because of its conciseness. Perversely, however, in providing such excuses, Blessington does not dismiss her work but recommends it to potential readers by pointing to the significance of its contribution to the well-trodden field of travel writing. Even if not very diverting in terms of content, it is not a lengthy and time-consuming book and hence will read well; thus, after all, the reader may expect to derive some kind of pleasure from it. Likewise, the journal is here claimed to offer little instruction, yet two pages earlier it is believed to make use of 'observations and reflections' (*NtP* vi), and the purpose of the two descriptive techniques is precisely to instruct readers – the former to 'teach facts' and the latter, 'the significance of the facts' (see Batten 1978, 82).[3] The two terms, taken word for word from the title of Hester Piozzi's *Observations and Reflections Made in the Course of a Journey through France, Italy, and Germany* (1789), situate Blessington's journal in the canon of travel writing.

The advertisement proves both the editor's and the writer's awareness that the book's success is due to its adherence to the rules for writing travel literature, yet typical rhetorical strategies are applied here in such a way as 'not to undercut but to bolster a writer's authority' (McAllister 1988, 18). Blessington, probably well advised by the publisher and already more confident than when writing her first travel account, skilfully turns self-justification into self-assertion in her *Journal of a Tour through the Netherlands to Paris, in 1821*.

Blessington's self-confidence when it comes to her publications increased over the years. In *The Idler in Italy* and *The Idler in France*, written in the 1820s but published between 1839 and 1841, she bears no resemblance to the author of the two early travel accounts. Her first publication on her return from the Continent, *Conversations of Lord Byron* (1834), not only revealed her name but was proudly signed by 'the Countess of Blessington', which emphasized the equal status of the great poet and the author. By then Blessington had already gained social recognition, and the publication of her *Conversations* only helped turn her name into 'a brand useful for selling books' (Hawkins 2012, 51). Unlike her two early journals, *The Idler in Italy* and *The Idler in France* are therefore signed 'by the Countess of Blessington'. This change, Schmid argues, was part of her 'literary self-fashioning', grounded on her 'aristocratic status' (Schmid 2013, 123).

Apart from disclosing her title, another self-fashioning and marketing strategy was using engravings as frontispieces to Blessington's books (Hawkins 2012, 71). In the first volume of *The Idler in Italy*, for example, we find the engraving by Frederick Christian Lewis after the portrait drawing by Edwin Landseer (reprinted on the cover of this book). Thanks to her circulating portraits, Blessington had become recognizable to the public as an unparalleled beauty. In consequence, they influenced the reviewers of her works, who assessed Blessington as a 'combined personal, moral, and literary beauty' (ibid., 66). Blessington used her portraits as reminders of the fame gained prior to her journeys, so that her readers would also associate her texts with beauty.

In the *Idlers*, Blessington is more self-assured not only in terms of displaying the authorship of her journals but also in her observance of conventions concerning titles of travel accounts. A title was supposed to express the genre, the account's organisation and its contents. As a novice, Blessington wished her early accounts to be classified by the public as travel writing, and therefore their titles are straightforward. Blessington chose the journal form, since in the eighteenth century it had been a common narrative structure for travel accounts (Batten 1978, 38). Accordingly, all the entries in her accounts follow chronological order, and dates of daily entries are meticulously noted down. In terms of content, in both accounts the word 'tour' is applied, thus informing the reader about the nature of the travels: she completed the circuit, returning to the point of departure (ibid.). Typically, both titles also include

Blessington's destinations as well as the range of dates during which the tour was taken and when the journal was published (Batten 1978, 65–68; Kinsley 2008, 98). As an addition to the title, in the first account the author includes an epigram: 'Let us become acquainted with the beauties of our own country, before we explore those of a foreign land'.[4] This stylistic device is to show the author's appreciation of her homeland. Acting on that advice, she follows the fashion among the upper class – which started in the second half of the eighteenth century – to explore the unknown parts of the British Isles (Batten 1978, 93–94; Korte 2000, 77–81).

Titles of travel accounts were often 'misleading', since, though some writers adhered strictly to the genre, others used the terms only as a sales gimmick (Batten 1978, 37). Blessington's two early accounts have 'suitable' travelogue titles – just appropriate for a novice writer – but the other two show the author's departure from the convention. *The Idler in Italy* and *The Idler in France* are not plainly descriptive titles specifying the details of the journeys (apart from their destination) and indicating their generic affiliation,[5] but rather conceptual ones, imparted with interpretative potential, which provoke readers into thinking about their meaning.

The titles of Blessington's mature accounts concentrate on the traveller rather than on the process of travel.[6] The author may have borrowed the title figure from Samuel Johnson's popular series of essays *The Idler*, published from 1758–60 (Schmid 2013, 146). When her *Idlers* were published, she was no longer an anonymous writer, but a figure of renown who could afford to make such a bold move as to position her accounts in relation to the works by as significant an author as Johnson. The narrator of her account may thus be considered to have identified with Johnson's vision of the idler. One of his critics argues that Johnson created this unpretentious figure in order to reach a broad general audience; nonetheless, even if in a light and playful manner, his purpose was to convey didactic content to his readers (Spector 1997, 181). Blessington's choice of the title was a tactical one as well.

The titles are suggestive of purposeless and pleasurable journeys, and they would have appealed to all those keen on light reading. Given the fact that the timing of the publications coincides with her financial difficulties, Blessington must have wished that the books would sell well. Her choice of the titles also indicates that Blessington identified with the trend of leisure travel, discussed in the introduction of this book. As I demonstrate in the subsequent chapters, the epithet 'idle' characterizes her state of mind, leisure activities and search for the authentic. She devotes a lot of space in the books to her idle contemplations of social, literary and aesthetic issues, among others, which are facilitated by her mode of travel and lifestyle during longer sojourns. Among her favourite leisure pursuits are loitering in art galleries, musing in churches and libraries, sauntering around cities and horseback riding into unknown territories. These activities enable Blessington to go beyond the surface of common tourist attractions.

Nevertheless, the text proper also makes it clear that Blessington is more often prone to industry than indolence and, following Johnson's advice, definitely wishes to provide the reader with not only pleasure but also instruction (Johnson 2013, 49). This is obvious from a confessional overtone of her declarations reappearing in the text, such as: 'I have been idle for the last four days, and have not even opened my journal. One day of idleness, like one sin, is sure to beget another' (*IiI* 1: 324).[7] Notwithstanding such censuring and rather ironic comments on the vice of idleness, it can be observed that Blessington frequently adopts such a disposition deliberately, in order to emphasize that she is not the kind of whirlwind traveller ridiculed by Johnson, who 'guesses the manners of [a town's] inhabitants by the entertainments that his inn offered him' (Johnson 2013, 50). In a manner similar to typical travel titles listing the years spent abroad, Blessington's *Idlers* emphasize the slowness and duration of her journeys (Batten 1978, 67–68). The traveller is not lazy either, since she travels slowly but attentively, and therefore the account of her journeys can be trusted to be accurate and deliberate (ibid., 65). She boasts the luxury of leisure time – definitely a class privilege – which lets her mind 'extend its views', becoming more receptive (Johnson 2013, 49). Even though it happens that because of '*dolce far' niente* [...] the usual motives and incentives to study and usefulness are forgotten' (*IiI* 2: 48), idleness proves the 'method of travelling' enabling her to fully experience and appreciate as well as accurately record the foreign, and thus renders her a 'useful traveller' (Johnson 2013, 50, 52). In fact, analogically to Johnson's, Blessington's *Idler* aimed at attracting an audience but wished that, in the process of reading, the readers would understand the opposite of what the title on the book cover suggested.

It is worth mentioning that Blessington's manifestation of her idle attitude even in the titles was also one of the strategies to mark her social status as a lady. In her study of conduct books published mostly towards the end of the eighteenth century, Sarah Jordan points out that in this period idleness was assigned to upper-class women, yet in an ambiguous manner, since they were 'both required to be leisured and enjoined not to be idle' (2014, 117). Instead of being engaged in any productive work, ladies were expected to be leisure incarnate in order to please their male companions (ibid., 113–14). Nevertheless, by no means was their leisure time to be wasted but used fruitfully, for instance, by gaining accomplishments, supervising household matters and engaging in charitable activities (ibid., 114–15). Ladies' motivation to become accomplished was a problematic issue, since any activity that aimed at self-improvement, naturally to a reasonable extent, such as educational reading and studying, was encouraged; yet those activities that might arise from their wish to be admired were despised (ibid., 116–17). Among the ladies' pursuits mostly disapproved of for involving self-display were taking part in public amusements; showing off artistic talents; and devoting too much attention to polishing manners, social skills, fashions and even the fine arts (ibid., 117). As I will argue throughout this book, Blessington plays with the widely discussed notion of ladies' idleness. At times she depicts herself as incarnating a ladylike ideal of leisure; on other occasions, she treads against the stream by embracing facets of idleness not expected of her rank, yet always in the most genteel manner.

The final element of the title page that is influential in creating the first impression of a book is the name of the publisher. Although the rank of the publishers of the first two journals did not single them out from the crowd (A. and R. Spottiswoode; Longman, Hurst, Rees, Orme, and Brown), Henry Colburn was a well-known and recognizable brand name, which contributed greatly to the success of the *Idlers*. By means of marketing strategies, Colburn created a special aura around the texts, a sort of paratextual packaging to appeal to their potential buyers.

Henry Colburn specialized in publishing travelogues, biographies and, above all, silver fork novels. Having realized that they were a great space to promote books, Colburn launched a number of magazines, such as the *New Monthly Magazine* (1814), the *Literary Gazette* (1817) or the *Athenaeum* (1828), which included advertisements, book reviews and news on forthcoming publications (Melnyk 2002, 4). He became such an expert at puffing up his books that he earned a reputation as 'an unscrupulous promotional genius' (Erickson 1996, 152) and the 'Prince of Puffers' (Sutherland 2014, 136). Colburn was partial to 'people with titles' – he aspired to publish works by aristocrats for the members of their own class (Melnyk 2002, 37; Sutherland 2014, 136).[8] Rubbing shoulders with the aristocracy, he met Lady Blessington, and in the future was to mastermind her literary career (Sutherland 2014, 584).[9] Their cooperation started in 1832 with the publication of *Conversations of Lord Byron*, which was part of a series of Byron biographies written by famous writers and published by Colburn (see Melnyk 2002, 204–5). Having recognized the sales potential of the *Conversations*, Colburn first serialized them in the *New Monthly Magazine* and then published them in a book form in 1834. In this way, Blessington joined the circle of Colburn's titled writers, among whom were Lady Morgan and Charlotte Ann Eaton. Therefore, when *The Idler in Italy* was to be issued in 1839, the author was already recognizable as a writer and traveller to the Continent.

The newly issued *Idler in Italy* was advertised in the *Athenæum* and reviewed in the *New Monthly Magazine* and the *Literary Gazette*. The reviews, very extensive and naturally flattering, abound in opinion-forming statements that convince potential buyers that the text offers value for money, and that they are the readers whom the author had in mind when composing the lines. A reviewer for the *New Monthly Magazine* begins by pointing out the book's fault – namely, the fact that it misleads the reader, since by no means could such a busy traveller be considered an idler. This contrived criticism is followed by numerous positives. The author's wide range of interests is applauded:

> Our fair Journaliser's versatile pen gracefully flies from Politics to Cookery, from Religion to Scenery, from Fashion to the Fine Arts, including Music and the Drama, from illustrations of national character, in humble lives and into hospitals, to the highest society of the realms through which she passed. (*New Monthly Magazine*, March 1839, 418)

The reviewer also enthuses over the author's ideas, which 'are all liberal, unprejudiced, impartial, and breathed with a frankness, free from pretence, display or affectation' (ibid.). The reviewer, aware of the expectations of travel accounts, with these suitably puffy epithets convinces the public of the *Idler*'s authenticity and universality, thus enticing not only the aristocracy but the readers of all walks of life. To the satisfaction of the general public, Blessington's reflections are also claimed to 'please, while they instruct, sober while they elevate' (ibid., 421). In terms of style, the author is appreciated for not applying 'biting satire' when addressing matters of 'public utility' but being governed by 'the feminine spheres of feeling, fancy, taste and wit' (ibid., 423).

In a similar manner, a reviewer for the *Literary Gazette* claims that the author's idleness produces 'so much pleasure' for the world in which 'there is too much toil and too little repose' that her recollections 'must gratify every reader of taste and feeling' (*Literary Gazette*, March 2, 1839, 129). The two reviewers whet the readers' appetites by quoting extensively from the account, concentrating on the passages in which Blessington dwells on 'the distinguished individuals' in whose footsteps she followed or whom she met, including Byron, to whom considerable passages are devoted (*New Monthly Magazine*, March 1839, 419; *Literary Gazette*, 2 March 1839, 129–30).[10]

The reviewer of *The Idler in France* for the *New Monthly Magazine* emphasizes that this is the sequel to *The Idler in Italy*, which was well appreciated and obtained popularity 'speedily' (*New Monthly Magazine*, July 1841, 420). It is guaranteed that these volumes will satisfy both the 'desultory reader' interested only in 'light literature' and those who have visited the same spots and now can have 'their sense of pleasure refreshed' (ibid.). The reader is promised to find in the volumes 'lively anecdote[s]' about Parisian fashionables (ibid.). The review in the *Literary Gazette* is written in the same vein. The writer is applauded for the 'grace, refinement, and delicacy' of her pen (*Literary Gazette*, 19 July 1841, 385).

So persuasive was Colburn's promotion that there was no need for the author to preface the text with her own self-assertive declarations. Within the back matter of the second edition of *The Idler in France* (1842), there is an exhaustive advertisement of Blessington's works published by Colburn, which presents her as a renowned writer of travelogues (Figure 1.1). It notes that *The Idler in Italy* is embellished with the portrait of Lady Blessington. Then it lists thirty locations described in the book, as well as the names of thirty personages whom Blessington sketched, the first three being Byron, Shelley and Moore. The reader is also informed that the third volume of *The Idler in Italy* may be bought separately, since, it can be assumed, it covered particularly attractive destinations, such as Rome and Venice, and could be used as a guidebook to these places. The second advertised work is *Conversations of Lord Byron* (promoted as *The Countess of Blessington's Journal of her Conversations with Lord Byron*), the prestige of which is strengthened by the fact that it is 'uniform' with Thomas Moore's 'Life of Byron' and includes a portrait of Lord Byron. To convince the potential buyer of the quality of Blessington's works, extracts of two very favourable reviews are also added. *The Idler in Italy* was assessed by the *Caledonian Mercury* as 'sparkling with anecdote, and rich in critical remarks on literature, the fine arts', and the *Conversations* were praised as 'beyond all comparison the best thing that has been written on Lord Byron' (*IiF* vol. 2).

The advertisement in *IiF* presents the *Idlers* as authoritative and definitive guidebooks to the most popular destinations in Italy and France, and the author's ambition that they would be considered as such is evident from the tables of contents. Employing an itinerary-based framework, the contents are as long as eight pages (*IiI* vol. 2). In *The Idler in Italy*, the name of each city is capitalized and followed by a detailed catalogue of miscellaneous subjects covered in the book, such as places of interest, personages, customs and works of art. In *The Idler in France*, the table of contents at the back of the second volume is divided into chapters and similar catalogues. The reason for such scrupulosity is to ensure that readers can easily navigate these exhaustive reference books while preparing for their journeys and when already on their way.

In sum, the paratext, approached as a complex of external generic conventions and marketing strategies, may prove a very useful tool in the discussion of the texts, since it situates them in a specific context, otherwise incomprehensible for the readers living in a different time. It is of special assistance

WORKS BY LADY BLESSINGTON,
PUBLISHED BY MR. COLBURN,
To be had of all Booksellers.

I.

THE IDLER IN ITALY.

3 vols. small 8vo. with fine Portrait of Lady Blessington.

N.B. The Third Volume may be had separately.

Among the many other Continental towns and places of celebrity visited by Lady Blessington, and described in this work, are the following:

Rome	Salerno	Fontainebleau
Naples	Pozzuoli	Geneva
Florence	Pæstum	Lausanne
Herculanæum	Mola di Gaetæ	Berne
Pisa	Nocera	Baden
Beneventum	Amalfi	Zurich
Pompeii	Castellamare	Lucerne
Terracina	Leghorn	Nice
Vesuvius	Paris	Genoa
Portici	Rouen	Vienna, &c.

The following will be found among the various distinguished personages of whom Lady Blessington has given sketches in this work:

Byron	Sir W. Gell	The Duke of York
Shelley	Sir W. Drummond	Sir D. Wilkie
Moore	Mr. Trelawny	Countess Guiccioli
Napoleon	W. S. Landor	Prince Borghese
Murat	Duchess of Devonshire	Casimir de la Vigne
Maria Louisa	Lord J. Russell	Baron Denon
Madame L. Bonaparte	Lord W. Russell	Lord Dudley and Ward
Cardinal Gonsalvi	Lord Normanby	Mr. Mathias
De la Martine	Mr. Lister	Lord King
Duchess de St. Leu	Mr. Hamilton	Mr. Herschel, &c.

" The whole work presents an animated and attractive view of modern Italy, sparkling with anecdote, and rich in critical remarks on literature, the fine arts, &c."—*Caledonian Mercury.*

II.

THE COUNTESS OF BLESSINGTON'S JOURNAL OF HER CONVERSATIONS WITH LORD BYRON.

1 vol. 8vo. uniform with Moore's " Life of Byron," and embellished with Portrait of Lord Byron.

" Beyond all comparison the best thing that has been written on Lord Byron—the truest, cleverest, and most pleasing. With all possible delicacy, consideration, and good nature, the true character of Byron is laid open, even to its inmost recesses."—*Spectator.*

Figure 1.1 *Advertisement of works by Lady Blessington published by Mr. Colburn.* Back matter of the second edition of *The Idler in France* (1842, vol. 2). Public domain. Source: http://hdl.handle.net/2027/uc2.ark:/13960/t9f47s236?urlappend=%3Bseq=635

when one is dealing with travel writing, still only 'a loosely defined body of literature' (Hooper and Youngs 2004, 2). What is of utmost importance from my perspective is that the paratext foreshadows the strategies applied by the writer to manoeuvre her identity in her early and mature travel accounts, which I discuss in the following chapters.

Chapter 2

FROM LIFE TO TEXT

I will now discuss those features of the texts themselves that allow for their categorization as nonfictional travel writing. Being a novice traveller and writer, Blessington did not aspire to write her early travel journals strictly in the encyclopaedic tradition established by Joseph Addison's *Remarks on the Several Parts of Italy* (1705), which recorded solely useful and objective observations of foreign lands and displayed a great scope of knowledge. Nevertheless, in her early journals, she adopted some of the received conventions of his age in order to be admitted to the circle of travel writers. The author of *The Idler in France* and *The Idler in Italy* had already been a seasoned traveller and writer. Here Blessington too drew on the practices of the previous age, yet selectively, her goal being predominantly to recount her subjective experience of travel, influenced by her social, national and gender position.

Blessington presented her early travels in the form of a journal – one of the two basic techniques in the eighteenth century, along with letters (Batten 1978, 38). Belonging to the genre of life writing, the travel journal aims at the presentation of 'an individual's own life, thoughts and experiences' (Ożarska 2013a, 15). In the eighteenth century, however, travel accounts that were too autobiographical at the cost of factual details would come into criticism (Batten 1978, 39). Even though this attitude had already become *passé* by the time Blessington published her journals, she nevertheless refrained from revealing too much of herself. At the same time she tried to convince her readers that she was not a 'fireside' traveller and that her accounts were credible (ibid., 76).

The organizational pattern adopted in the journals reflects a diaristic mode of recording travel experience. Typically, the presentation of events is chronological and follows the traveller's itinerary, starting with the departure from London and concluding with a happy return home (*IoW* 1, 84; *NtP* 1, 171). Moreover, the layout of the journals is clearly organized, as entries are regular, relatively short and in most cases indicated by specific dates, including the day of the week. In a manner similar to other writers attempting to achieve 'both temporal and spatial arrangement' (Kinsley 2008, 26), in *A Tour in the Isle of Wight, in the Autumn of 1820* Blessington took great care to link the dates to specific locations. The names of places are printed as centred and capitalized headings preceding entries, in which the journal recalls what Kinsley terms 'cartographic itineraries', which were a popular form of organizing home tours, with the aim of facilitating their navigation (ibid., 34–35).

The narratorial mode also enhances the journals' verisimilitude. A standard first-person narration is used throughout the early journals, with the singular pronoun 'I' being used interchangeably with the plural 'we'. The aim was to emphasize that the female traveller was accompanied by a male chaperone, whose protection she appreciated (*IoW* 60), which was a typical convention among women travel writers in the previous age (Robinson 2001, 18).[1] In terms of style, the entries are written in a manner conveying the character of spontaneous speech utterances. The sentences are complex, longish (even reaching one page in length), full of interjections indicated by various punctuation marks and grammatically inconsistent – for example, beginning as a question and ending as a statement (*IoW* 2). To give an impression of writing on the spot, she resorts to hyperbolic inversions expressing her unrestrained strong emotions (*IoW* 74; *NtP* 22) or meta-comments pointing to her fruitless attempts to verbalize what she has just beheld (*IoW* 11, 56; *NtP* 83). On the other hand, there also appear self-referential statements declaring that she has visited some places but sees no point in detailing them in her journal (*IoW* 3). At times, rather than personalizing the narrative, the author uses an 'abbreviated journal style', characterized by short gerund clauses without the nominative pronouns, in an attempt to be believable, and she also replaces the personal pronoun 'I' with the more distanced plural 'we' (Batten 1978, 40; *IoW* 38; *NtP* 108).

In terms of content, the preface to *Journal of a Tour through the Netherlands to Paris, in 1821* claims that the journal is hardly amusing or instructive, yet this was just a pose of false modesty, since the text proper shows that the writer aimed at both. Thus, her entries constitute matter-of-fact observations of foreign manners, customs and works of art (*NtP* 29, 151–53). There are also passages providing the reader with the measurements, the materials and architectural details of Napoleon's apartments (*NtP* 85–87), and a two-page-long enumeration of books encountered in the Lisle library (*NtP* 35–38), as well as such practicalities of interest to tourists as crossing the Channel (*NtP* 11–12), going through customs (*NtP* 13), finding accommodation (*NtP* 39–40, 149), and obtaining passports (*NtP* 78) or entrance tickets (*NtP* 101–2).

In order to comply with the requirement of the previous age to 'blend pleasure with instruction' (Batten 1978, 25), Blessington intersperses the journals with numerous passages whose primary aim is to amuse readers. Thus, the writer recounts anecdotes concerning famous figures like Napoleon and Josephine (*NtP* 120–22, 124), slips in jokes heard on her way (*IoW* 50) and adds impromptu rhymes evoked by some situations (*IoW* 18; *NtP* 166–67). What is more, in order to divert readers, Blessington relies on the descriptive conventions of the previous age, which may be exemplified by sketches of landscapes, particularly frequent in *A Tour in the Isle of Wight, in the Autumn of 1820*. As I illustrate in Chapter 4, these descriptions are imitative of Gilpin's representations of natural settings, whose sole purpose was to entertain readers (Batten 1978, 29, 75–76, 107).

There is a considerable change in the manner that Blessington described her travels in the mature accounts, compared to the earlier ones. The titles of *The Idler in France* and *The Idler in Italy* are by no means self-explanatory, and there are not any prefaces indicating their genres. It is assumed that they were based on Blessington's authentic diaries, kept during her travels (O'Dwyer 2008, 42), which in their form might have been analogous to the early travel journals. Nevertheless, what distinguishes the *Idlers* from these early journals, even at first glance, is their substantial size. *A Tour in the Isle of Wight* and *Journal of a Tour through the Netherlands to Paris* are modest-looking single-volume books (84 and 171 pages long, respectively), but *The Idler in France* consists of two volumes, amounting to over 600 pages, and *The Idler in Italy* is made up of three volumes, all together well over a thousand pages. This fact indicates a difference not only in the duration of the journeys but also in the writer's aspirations for their artistic form. After all, they were rewritten about ten years after Blessington's return from the Continent, when she had already been recognized as a writer, a fact that influenced the final version of the accounts. In like manner to her contemporaries, at that time Blessington no longer believed that her accounts ought to 'respond to [the reader's] thirst for facts' by 'avoiding the least appearance of fiction and egotism' (Batten 1978, 80–81, 119). In fact, the manifestation of her presence and the eclectic (non-fictional and fictional) status of her texts are the two most distinguishing aspects of the *Idlers*.

In comparison with the early journals, the *Idlers* display the author's increased self-assurance and a broader perspective. First, although here too the narrator follows the itinerary pattern and notes down dates and places, she tends to be neglectful about it, and her entries are by no means regular. Twenty years earlier, she would probably have feared that her readers might attribute this lack of conscientiousness to her failing memory and fear that they would refuse to give credence to her words at all. When writing the mature accounts, she was confident enough to suggest that representing her true experience was more important than abiding by the requirements.[2] This is well illustrated when she informs her readers about what she saw and might have written about, yet, on second thought, decided not to. After sightseeing the antiquities of Nîmes with a cicerone, for example, she notes that she 'might fill several pages and fatigue others as nearly as much as he fatigued [her]; but [she] will have pity on [her] readers and spare them the elaborate details' and, instead, wish them, should they visit the place, 'a tranquil and uninterrupted contemplation' of its antiquities (*IiF* 1: 15). Such self-reflexive comments enable her to display her matter-of-factness, yet at the same time portray her as a commentator who is authoritative enough to decide what her readers shall learn.

Although in the *Idlers* Blessington avoids some of the practices she obeyed in the early journals, she consistently attempts to convince the reader that the life story recounted therein has taken place in reality. Such a requirement for life writing was defined by Lejeune as 'the autobiographical pact' formed between the writer and the reader, which intends that the story told by the former is verifiable and the latter accepts it to be so (Lejeune 1989, 13–14). Blessington's contemporary reviewers, and thus her readers too, had no doubts that the *Idlers* recounted Blessington's authentic travel experiences, owing to biographical evidence present in them.[3]

As I have shown, the paratexts of Blessington's travel accounts provide an insight into the identity of the historical 'I'[4], and some details from her life preceding the story are recorded there. The quoted epigram enables Blessington to be identified as English, and the title pages of the successive journals reveal her social advancement. The preface to *The Journal through the Netherlands to Paris* and the advertisement following *The Idler in France* mention the earlier works by the author that earned her some recognition as a writer. The unveiling of the author's identity in the paratext is valuable, inasmuch as it discloses much about both the narrator and the protagonist. The entrance of the historical 'I' to the text proper is manifested in the table of contents preceding the second volume of *The Idler in Italy*, as the word 'authoress' reappears in four headings – for example, 'Byron Dines with Authoress for the last time' (*IiI* vol. 2).[5]

The internal evidence present in the *Idlers* illustrates the way Blessington inscribed herself in the figures of the narrating 'I' and the narrated 'I'. This may be well illustrated by the influence of the hardships she experienced while on the Continent. Writing entries in such moments, the writer draws the reader's attention to her presence, self-dramatizing her experiences and allowing them to impinge on the text. The most 'terrible blow' to Lady Blessington was her husband's death (*IiF* 2: 97), the presentation of which will suffice to illustrate the point.

There is no mention of the happenings in May 1829. The last recorded comments before the death concern the Blessingtons' arrangements for moving to a new abode, and then 'a chasm of many months' (*IiF* 2: 97) follows. The account is resumed after four months, in September, which, being the month of Blessington's birthday, usually encourages melancholy reflections (*IiI* 1: 20). But this time it is clear that Blessington is deep in mourning, which is of consequence to the narrative flow. The narrator recalls the moment she last 'opened this book' and reflects how her sense of time has changed henceforth. 'How slowly has time passed since! Every hour counted, and each coloured by care; the past turned to with the vain hope of forgetting the present, and the future no longer offering the bright prospect it once unfolded' (*IiF* 2: 97). Indeed, in the following months Blessington would lead a very sedentary lifestyle; 'ill and confined to [her] chamber', she received numerous friends offering their condolences (*IiF* 2: 97, 97–138). Her journal entries are much less frequent, and the account of the next nine months occupies only forty-two pages. Too much occupied with remembering the past, she was not capable of looking forward to the future. The entries resume in May, when the narrator admits that 'indisposition [...] languor and lassitude' have caused her to abandon journalizing, but the first anniversary of her husband's death occasioned reflections on her lack of 'confidence' owing to the death of her husband, 'on whose existence [her] happiness depended' (*IiF* 2: 138–39).

The ideological 'I' situated in the narrative of this period is determined by the convention of travel writing. It may be impossible to tell whether by sharing such confidences with readers she wished to convince them of her true feelings towards Lord Blessington – a fact that was disputed by many people – or whether she was simply assuming the persona of a distressed widow. Whichever is true, the position that is adopted here is that of a woman who, when unchaperoned by her male companion, is afraid to venture into the unknown, which is the convention observed in Blessington's early journals.

Another self-related issue in the narratives is the national standpoint, which evidences that, as Smith and Watson observe, the ideological 'I' is 'multiple and thus potentially conflictual' (2010, 77). The manner of narration is clearly related to the subject's evolving national identity, since the narrator resorts to different strategies when addressing England and Ireland. In her second journal, she confesses, 'I have so much of the natural John Bull feeling about me' (*NtP* 99). The narrator therein apostrophizes England as a mother whom her 'travelled children' appreciate only after visiting other countries (*NtP* 154–55). In a similar manner, when writing about England in the *Idlers*, she tends to assume the pathetic style of an exile 'year[ning] for home' (*IiI* 2: 89):

> No! there is nothing like dear old England! We may love to wonder in other countries; but *that* is our home, the home of our choice, of our affection.
>
> One has read of a lover who left his mistress that he might write to her. It is thus we leave our fatherland, to think of it more fondly, more proudly; and to return to it as the schoolboy does to his mother's arms, after his first separation. (*IiI* 1: 132)

The passage reveals the traveller whose separation from the country only strengthens her attachment to it. Nevertheless, it can be observed that her feelings for England are by no means in direct proportion to her attitude towards her compatriots abroad. Over the course of time, Blessington appears to have grown critical of English tourists to the Continent, as she dissociates herself from them in her travel narratives.[6] On these occasions she assumes the position of the 'Anglo–Italian', characterized by Mary Shelley as having 'many peculiar marks which distinguish him from the mere traveller, or true John Bull' (Shelley 1990, 343).

The narrator's comments on Ireland, in turn, emphasize her social status, yet they also reveal her yearning for the country of her childhood. Only once in the *Idlers* is Ireland rendered as the country of the present; namely, when the writer recollects Lord Blessington's voting for Catholic Emancipation in Ireland in 1829 (*IiF* 2: 64–65). In the passage, the Blessingtons' relation with Ireland is that of superiority. She claims that by going to Ireland and taking part in the vote, Lord Blessington fulfilled his duty towards his Irish liegemen, and that she had granted him her approval. Most often, however, Ireland is presented as the land of the writer's memories (*IiI* 1: 169). She does not miss Ireland as she does England, yet the former disposes her to retrospections and analogies between the countries she visits and Ireland, as if subconsciously she tried to rediscover Ireland in the places to which she travels. On numerous occasions the narrator reflects that the natural beauties (*IiI* 3: 9, 281), people (*IiI* 1: 282–83; *IiI* 2: 189–90, 424), temperaments (*IiI* 2: 325), practices (*IiI* 1: 169; *IiI* 3: 127), language (*IiI* 2: 341) and objects (*IiI* 1: 206, 321, 377) she encounters on her way remind her of those of Ireland. The technique of comparison, usually applied by travel writers in order to help readers visualize the unknown, here evidences Blessington's apparently unintentional attempt to reconnect with the country of her origin. After all, she does not address the Irish in the *Idlers*, but the English, whom she could not have assumed would recognize the analogies.

The persona of an English upper-class woman is the prevailing facet of the ideological 'I' in the text. Contemporary critics tend to be very cautious not to overgeneralize and overestimate the matter of differences between women's and men's mode of writing in terms of stylistics (Bassnett 2002, 240; Foster and Mills 2002, 3). Nonetheless, they also admit that, together with such aspects as the period, nationality and social position, among others, gender does influence the experience of travel (Foster and Mills 2002, 3) and influences travel writing, when it comes to such aspects as 'emphasis', 'selection of material' and 'the relationship between the traveler and the putative reader' (Bassnett 2002, 240). Therefore, it may still be of use to consider Blessington in these terms.

The protagonist is presented in such a way as to emphasize her social status and gender. She travels with her companions, as well as maids and footmen, in three opulent carriages, which are so impressive that one passerby considers them to be not a family but a 'regiment' setting out for war (*IiI* 1: 42), and the proprietors of the inns they arrive at are discomfited to receive 'such guests' (*IiF* 1: 30). Though a little ashamed of being seen to indulge in such extravagance, the countess admits she could not have done without her double-springed sleeping carriage with its library, soft cushions, eiderdown pillows and 'innumerable other little comforts' (*IiI* 1: 43), a comment that reveals her sophisticated feminine predilections. In Part III I expand on the presentation of the countess, for instance in Paris, where she indulges in ladylike activities, such as associating with distinguished personages, attending theatres and operas, contemplating works of art in galleries, and shopping for luxury goods. At times, for example while in Naples, in contrast to such leisure activities, the protagonist is presented as the proper lady of the house, engaged as a hostess of her literary salon, but also preoccupied with household matters, like finding lodgings or hiring servants.

In addition, the narrator's self-reflexive comments assert that, apart from being 'a fine lady' (*IiI* 1: 371), she considers herself as one of 'female travellers' (*IiI* 2: 163), expressing her opinions 'like a woman' does (*IiI* 2: 117). She travels to gain a true experience of the foreign, even if at times it might seem unbecoming for one in her station, for example when she becomes engrossed in the domestic life of Neapolitan peasant women. Picturing herself as immersed in 'the everyday experience', she situates herself among Romantic women travellers (Jones 1997, 498).

Femininity also impinges on the writer's conception of the reader. In a fashion similar to authors of guidebooks, the narrator indirectly addresses her readers when, for instance, recommending destinations, attractions, accommodation or cuisine (*IiI* 2: 8; *IiI* 2: 86–87). In these cases, the readers can be identified as English travellers, both male and female. Nevertheless, when she is concerned with conventionally ladylike topics, such as women's appearance, fashion, marriage customs or family life (*IiI* 2: 311–12), she directs her words specifically to female readers, irrespective of their social status; for example, at one point she turns to 'mammas and nurses' (*IiI* 2: 221–22). Yet, most often she writes for her equals (*IiI* 1: 138, 186) calling them 'fine ladies' or – ironically – 'ye fair dames' (ibid., 254), who might share her interest and be preoccupied with similar matters, such as reconciling family life with self-development:

> Lose not, then, O woman! the precious time afforded you for mental cultivation, in vain and unbecoming clamours for equal rights with men. Those amongst you who perpetrate this sorry folly, inflict the deepest

injury on your sex, by furnishing ground to the other, to deny you the respect to which you are entitled. Be worthy to become the friends as well as companions of your husbands, by qualifying yourselves to share their studies while sweetening their homes. Rejoice that you are saved from the arena of politics, and the arduous efforts compelled by professional life; and that the many hours of uninteresting labour to which men are condemned, are left to you for the acquisition of knowledge, and the fulfillment of duties pregnant with the dearest interests. Soothe their care, reward their toil, secure their peace; and your equality, nay more, your superiority, will be felt, if not acknowledged, by all who owe their felicity to you. (*IiI* 3: 306–7)

The textual evidence discussed so far proves the presence of the historical 'I' within the narratives and the ideological complexity of the narrator. Nevertheless, as I have mentioned and exemplify throughout the book, these texts cannot be read exclusively from the autobiographical angle since, apart from being non-fictional personal narratives in prose, they depend on a number of other forms of writing, including fiction. Thus, they may well support the point of contemporary theorists arguing for an eclectic nature of travel writing. For example, Korte understands travel writing as a genre characterized by its 'hybridity and flexibility' (Korte 2000, 9), whereas Borm treats it as a 'variety of texts both predominantly fictional and non-fictional whose main theme is travel' (Borm 2004, 13).[7] The *Idlers* are a case in point.

First of all, apart from relating the personal history of the traveller, the *Idlers* include informative and practical passages as well as observations and reflections on a much wider scope of issues than the early journals did, so they are reminiscent of modern handbooks (Buzard 1993, 69). Moreover, as I demonstrate in the following chapters, the accounts are constituted by numerous discourses of various natures and not only imitate reportorial accounts of places and events. Finally, in describing her journeys, Blessington makes use of fictional strategies typical of specific genres, such as sketches, Gothic romances and fashionable novels.

This proves that, despite their autobiographical character, the *Idlers* were not 'straightforward transcriptions' of her life, to use Mills's words (2003, 35). Even though at the time such literary embellishments were not expected in non-fiction travel writing, they were used by professional writers striving to achieve 'the status of celebrity' (Moroz 2013, 107), which was the case with Blessington. Even if she risked that these passages would cast a shadow of doubt on the credibility of her accounts, the evidence of her ability to endow her texts with literary qualities strengthened her status as a literary celebrity and also guaranteed high saleability.

Chapter 3
FICTIONAL STRATEGIES

Travel writers have always borrowed from the world of fiction. Some of them wrote accounts of travels that were solely fictional, since the travels described never took place (see Adams 1962). Those who travelled and recorded their travels consciously reworked their diaries, applying the same techniques that novelists used, especially when they were novelists themselves (see Moroz 2013, 104–8), as Blessington was. Even at first glance, one notices that, although her texts are conventional in terms of linear narration, moving from place to place, she manipulates the temporality of her journeys. Some stretches of time elicit but brief comments. For instance, when the narrator wishes to spare her readers tedious details of the journey between places (and in consequence make the narration more dynamic), she simply remarks: 'I pass over the hackneyed road from London to Hartford Bridge without comment' (*IoW* 2).[1] In contrast, on other occasions the travel time may be prolonged, for example when the author relates some anecdote concerning the actual location or describes landscapes that are of importance to her. Within Blessington's accounts of longer sojourns in one place, observations and reflections typical of non-fictional travel writing are intersected with passages reminiscent of fictional forms, which is my focus in this chapter.

Blessington authored eleven novels, all of which draw on or follow the pattern of the fashionable novel. Fashionable novels, or silver fork novels, presented the life of the aristocracy during the Regency period and, at least presumably, were written by the members of this class. They were in vogue from the mid-1820s to the 1840s. One of the figures who contributed to their popularity was publisher Henry Colburn, who canonized the writers of the genre in the series *Colburn's Modern Standard Novelists* (1835–41), which included Lady Blessington.

Blessington is known to have used her personal experiences to write her fashionable novels (O'Cinneide 2008, 35). This fact was even used as an argument that the reality depicted therein was verifiable. To give but one example, a reviewer of *The Two Friends*, which depicts the fashionable society of England, France and Italy, observes that 'Lady Blessington has *seen* the world, and is an acute observer of it in the circles in which she has moved' (*Literary*

Gazette, 1835, 69), and claims that she is the right person to represent the life of aristocracy in novels.

Blessington also used the formula of the novel in order to present her personal travel experiences. Given the popularity of the genre, this tactic appears to be by no means surprising. Having her novels adjusted and reprinted according to the requirements of Colburn's series, Blessington might have decided, or might have been asked by the publisher, to rewrite her travel accounts in the same vein as her novels, to guarantee their marketing success. This assumption appears very probable, given the fact that, as I demonstrated in Chapter 1, the *Idlers* were promoted in a way analogous to silver fork novels.

As 'semi-fictionalised portraits of contemporary elite society' (Culley 2014, 133), fashionable novels provided a model that could be easily adopted to Blessington's autobiographical accounts. Throughout her travels, she surrounded herself with the English aristocracy staying abroad, and she also commented on those staying back home. She employs two ways of presenting characters, either giving their full names or using initials followed by dashes. She is very careful about naming the people; thus, when she wishes to ingratiate herself with some of them, she gives their full names and praises their qualities and achievements. This was the case, for instance, with Sir William Drummond, Sir William Gell, Keppel Craven and William Hamilton, whom she befriended while in Naples (*IiI* 2: 206–7). On the other hand, when her comments on the English become critical, bantering or indiscreet, she refrains from giving their full names. As generous as it might seem of her, this was just a stylistic device, which she applied in her novels as well. In silver fork novels, in a manner similar to *romans à clef*, characters represented real persons, even though their surnames were slightly changed or fictitious.[2] Despite having their identities disguised, people were easily recognizable by their acquaintances anyway, as they knew their weaknesses, manners or catch phrases. What is more, writers would frequently include name keys at the end of their novels, thus resolving the mystery; so did Blessington in *Grace Cassidy; or, The Repealers* (Gettman 2010, 64; O'Cinneide 2008, 46–47). The possibility of peeping into the doings of contemporary figures staying abroad would have been tempting for both people of the traveller's social stratum and for middle-class readers, who could entertain the illusion of participating in their fashionable life.

Apart from reporting on members of the contemporary elites, in the accounts of her travels Blessington refers to current happenings, such as political events or incidents of public interest. A few examples will suffice to indicate the analogy with fashionable novels. One current topic is the Irish question, which is exploited in *The Repealers* and appears also in *The Idler in France*, when Blessington comments on her husband's voting for Catholic Emancipation in Ireland in 1829 (*IiF* 2: 64–65). Another example is a detailed account of the July Revolution of 1830 in France, the significance of which I evaluate in Chapter 10. Nevertheless, what English readers of travel literature were particularly interested in were the anecdotes concerning the Emperor Napoleon and his family, which Blessington also included (*IiF* 1: 222; *IiF* 2: 221).[3] Moreover, the writer refers to incidents which, though not of national significance, were reported in newspapers and deeply moved the public of the time. This is best exemplified by her detailed accounts of the awful and sudden demise of the English tourists in Italy in 1824 – Miss Bathurst (*IiI* 2: 320–23) and Mrs and Mr Hunt (*IiI* 2: 421–23).

Miss Rosa Bathurst drowned in the Tiber at the age of seventeen. Blessington recollects seeing the girl two years before as she was coming out of the opera house, fondly embracing her mother and looking 'in the flower of youth and beauty' (*IiI* 2: 320). Then the narrator sets the background, presenting Rosa's family as haunted by misfortune, since years earlier her father disappeared while on a diplomatic mission to Vienna, thus orphaning three children, and his body was never found. What follows is a detailed yet lively narrative of the fatal event, which is rendered melodramatically sensational by the choice of wording. Rosa was spending the winter in Rome under the protection of her aunt and uncle, Lord and Lady Aylmer, who one early spring day took her on a horseback ride along the bank of the Tiber (*IiI* 2: 321). Since the path grew narrower, they decided to turn round, and all of a sudden the horse slipped off the path and fell into the river along with Rosa, who was instantly carried away by the strong current under her guardians' very eyes. By an unfortunate twist of fate, none of them could swim, so 'horror-stricken' they watched her become engulfed in her 'watery grave' (*IiI* 2: 321–22). The writer finally reflects:

> How terrible must have been the return to that home [...], while she – the beloved, whom her protectors would have shielded with anxious care, even from the most genial shower of spring, was sleeping in death, with the yellow waters of the Tiber booming over her beautiful form, and sullying those long and silken tresses, of which those who loved her – and they were many – were so proud [...] How can the fearful tale be told to her mother, who has already pined for years under the mysterious disappearance of her husband? (*IiI* 2: 322–23)

The second incident concerns a couple of lovers on their honeymoon Grand Tour, who fell victim to brutal murder. Here, too, Blessington recalls meeting Caroline and Thomas Hunt in Naples and being struck by their 'youth, personal attractions and fond attachment' (*IiI* 2: 421). Three days later, on their return from Paestum, they were robbed and shot by eighteen ruthless bandits. Apart from the chronological presentation of the events, the writer points to the immediate motive for the murder: when ordered to hand over their belongings, Mr Hunt, a 'spirited young man, was more disposed to offer resistance, than to comply with this demand'. His servant too 'remonstrated with the brigands', whereas his wife, in turn, 'greatly alarmed, entreated him to give them the bag of dollars which was […] beneath their feet' (*IiI* 2: 422). In a manner similar to the former narrative, the writer romanticizes the lovers' death by visualizing how 'Mrs. Hunt, seeing a robber take aim at her husband, threw herself between them, clasping him in her arms, and received two balls, which passed from her person to his, mortally wounding both' (*IiI* 2: 422). Thomas was killed outright; Caroline died the next evening, after hours of suffering from a severe gunshot wound and 'rav[ing] of her husband' deliriously (*IiI* 2: 423–24).

Apart from the fact that the two incidents were subjects of topical interest among members of the upper class, the manner in which they are presented is reminiscent of fashionable novels of the day, which tended to be melodramatic and pathetic in style yet moralistic in tone (Schmid 2013, 159). The heroine of each story is a fine young lady with whom the writer – herself a lady traveller and a wife – identifies. As a guardian to her sister and stepdaughter, she also sympathizes with the victims' relatives. To appear convincing, she uses evocative language, confronting physical beauty and youthful emotionality with tragic death and inconsolable grief, in a manner similar to sensational tabloid newspapers geared towards readers of sentimental dispositions, whose style was copied in silver fork novels. Additionally, fashionable novel plotting is here enriched with the exoticized foreign setting – the treacherous nature and the savage banditti of the South, which, along with the realistic yet melodramatic style, make the narratives resemble Gothic romances.

The two stories are presented from the perspective of an empathetic insider, whose moral tone is nevertheless perceptible. The narrator is by no means judgemental; she does not suggest that Lady and Lord Aylmer's incautious actions might have led to Rosa's death. Nevertheless, the message must have been self-evident, since soon after the *Idlers* went public, Lady Aylmer felt compelled to justify their decisions and to comment that, though described with 'much pathos and feeling', the facts had been misstated by Blessington (quoted in Thistlethwayte 1853, 281). On the other hand, in her tale of the Hunts, the writer discloses the circumstances of the Hunt couple's death, by which she points out their imprudence and ostentatiousness. Here, too, the moral was obvious, especially given the fact that the very case must have been circulating as a cautionary tale, to warn affluent tourists not to display their valuables. Even years later, one guidebook straightforwardly stated that 'Mrs.

Hunt foolishly displayed a case of valuable jewelry at the inn where she passed the night' (Fertridge 1865, 838).

Silver fork novelists attempted to give a detailed account of 'the opulent, leisured fashionable life' of the upper class, at the same time moralizing about 'the wickedness of such a life' (O'Cinneide 2008, 47). This was by no means an easy task for the writers who represented the very lifestyle. The golden mean could be achieved by resorting to irony, which Blessington did. This is well illustrated by her account of the English staying in Paris, which I elaborate on in Chapter 10. In a manner similar to the presentation of London in fashionable novels, Paris is here presented in a realist vein. Typically, the writer situates herself among the people of her rank at dinners and parties (*IiI* 1: 86, 242) as well as in such fashionable locations as the Palais Royale (*IiI* 2: 34–36) or the Avenue des Champs-Élysées, and gives details of 'the most extravagant exhibitions of luxury' (*IiI* 2: 37). The writer is not, however, devoid of self-criticism, and thus at times her entries turn moralistic and point to the follies of the upper class. In this they resemble the genre of the sketch, which was the predecessor of the silver fork novel in terms of structure and aesthetic (Sadoff 2012, 107).

In 'The Park' and 'The Italian Opera', two of the four sketches of *The Magic Lantern, or Sketches of Scenes in the Metropolis* (1822), Blessington criticizes London's vacuous pleasures, whereas in the *Idlers* she ridicules the behaviour of men and women of fashion while in Parisian parks, operas and theatres (*IiI* 1: 21). She, for instance, pities 'the promenaders [in the Tuileries Garden who] look as if they only walked there to display their tasteful dresses and persons' (*IiF* 1: 270). To emphasize her satirical intent, the narrator interlards the text with French words in italics: 'The women eye each other as they pass, and can tell at a glance whether their respective *chapeaux* have come from the *atelier* of Herbault, or the less *recherché magasin des modes* of some more humble *modistes*' (*IiF* 1: 270–71). Apart from the snobbish mannerisms of the aristocracy, she condemns the impropriety of their conduct. For example, she cannot resist relating a scuffle that she witnessed between 'two ladies – *gentlewomen*', who against their will 'were brought in close contact' and 'from remonstrances proceeded to murmurs, not only 'loud but deep,' and from murmurs […] to violent pushing, and, at length, to blows' (*IiF* 1: 314–15). In a similar manner, the narrator depicts another pet activity – shopping sprees – which I take up in Chapter 10.

In her travel accounts, Blessington transfers the realm of fashionable London to the Continent, and apart from the universal vices of the aristocracy, she comments on the behaviours that she believes are unbecoming to English ladies and gentlemen travelling abroad. While in Naples, she expresses her dissatisfaction with the fact that an English lady known for her appreciation of the arts could have been as vain as to erect a funeral monument to her lap dog next to that of Virgil (*IiI* 2: 227–28). Another example is that of 'a very fat, elderly Englishman' on a sedan chair whom Blessington encountered while ascending Vesuvius (*IiI* 2: 369). The writer is critical of the John Bull–like tourist's preconception of the Neapolitans as foolish and dirty thieves (*IiI* 2: 369–71) and of his motivation to see the sights – 'the desire to surprise, or silence our neighbours' – when, in reality, 'panting and exhausted, he used a considerable portion of the breath he could so little spare, in uttering exclamations of anger at his own folly in attempting such as ascent' (*IiI* 2: 370). Not only does the passage function as a comic relief in an otherwise typical account of the event, but it is also an occasion for Blessington to express her disapproval of the ignorance, snobbishness and hypocrisy of many a 'piteous' English tourist on the Continent (*IiI* 2: 369).

Interestingly enough, the English are presented in a similar manner in Blessington's fashionable novels that are set on the Continent, such as *The Two Friends* (1835) and *Strathern; or, Life at Home and Abroad* (1845). In the latter, for instance, the character Louisa, when talking to her mother, expresses indignation over the lifestyle of the English staying in Rome:

> I dislike nothing in the Eternal City but the balls, dinners, and *soirées* introduced into it by our compatriots, who seem to forget they are not in London, and pursue the same dull and heartless round, of what they misname pleasure, that they follow there. (Blessington 1845, 1: 129)

In particular, the mother and daughter are critical of card-playing as improper for ladies, who pursue it merely out of boredom (Blessington 1845, 1: 130). It is especially incomprehensible for those on the journey, which offers numerous sources of enduring and praiseworthy enjoyment, among others 'the contemplation of nature […], the vast mine of literature […], the study of the fine arts' (Blessington 1845, 1: 132).

From the perspective of her contemporary readers, the most appealing story that Blessington included in the *Idlers* was definitely that of Lord Byron. The poet, whose career, scandalous life and adventures were reported in all European newspapers, was cut out to be a protagonist of a fashionable novel. Therefore, it comes as no surprise that novelists would impart traces of the Byronic hero to their characters, the best example of which was Edward Bulwer-Lytton's *Pelham* (1828). Though she had already devoted a separate book to Byron, Blessington used him in her travel accounts, but in a manner analogous to her usage in the silver fork novelists.[4]

The *Idlers* are interspersed with loose narratives concerning Lord Byron that show affinity with 'the dandy novel', a subcategory of the fashionable novel drawing on the tradition of the picaresque romance and the Bildungsroman (Rosa 1964, 78).⁵

Blessington traces the poet's entrance into the fashionable society of London (*LiF* 2: 109), his youthful attempts to make a name for himself as the speaker in the House of Lords, as well as his early career as a poet (*LiI* 2: 81). She also recounts Byron's controversial separation from his wife and his subsequent adventures on the Continent. She describes the poet's stay in Geneva, where he befriended Shelley and formed an insouciant habit of sailing in most challenging weather (*LiI* 1: 89–90), as well as the time spent in Venice at Palazzo Mocenigo, which she characterizes as the period of his 'indulgence of the habits', 'low amours, and reckless associations' as well as other 'evil-doings' (*LiI* 3: 128–29). In spite of being 'a dark spot' in his life, Venice was also where Byron formed 'the last, and only real attachment', with the Countess Guiccioli (*LiI* 3: 131).

The story of their love affair, in turn, unrolls in a manner reminiscent of the 'society novel', concentrating more on a female heroine and emphasizing family relationships (Kendra 2003, 61–63). Teresa, a beautiful sixteen-year-old girl, was forced by her father, Count Gamba, to marry Alessandro, Count Guiccioli. Although fabulously wealthy, Count Guiccioli was forty-four years Teresa's senior and a two-time divorcée, so very soon it turned out to be an 'ill-assorted marriage'. Nevertheless, a few months later the family moved to Venice, where by sheer accident 'the fair young bride' encountered Lord Byron. She instantly fell in love with the poet, who reciprocated her feelings. Having lived in seclusion until then, she was stupefied by the fact that the hero entered her life and followed her back to Ravenna. Torn between obedience to her father and passion for Byron, Teresa resolved to separate from her husband, despite the risk of being excluded from Italian society. Eventually, she received the pope's consent to leave Count Guiccioli on condition that she should remain in the custody of her family, with whom, for political reasons, she had to move first to Pisa and then to Genoa, where she was followed by Byron and where their love continued in secret (*LiI* 2: 46–50).

In the account of Teresa's acquaintance with Byron while in Genoa,⁶ Blessington provides her readers with an explicit characterization of the poet, which reveals his dandyish nature. She begins with a four-page description of the poet's 'highly-prepossessing' appearance, literally presented from his 'well-shaped' head to his 'deformed' foot, as well as his manners, described as 'graceful, animated, and cordial' but 'too gay, too flippant for a poet' (*LiI* 1: 393–96). Throughout the next 100 pages, the narrator encourages her readers to draw their own inferences about the poet through his speech, behaviour and their mutual interactions.

Byron acts in a gentleman-like and cordial manner (*IiI* 1: 393, 397), but, on the other hand, he is flippant and lacking dignity. His looks (*IiI* 1: 395), voice (*IiI* 1: 396) and manners are described as 'womanly' (*IiI* 2: 18), and indeed he is so preoccupied with his appearance that he would cancel his meetings due to 'a wart on his face' that made him unpresentable (*IiI* 2: 26). The poet may become melancholic, detached, supercilious, attentive to his own feelings and negligent of those of others (*IiI* 2: 52), yet at the same time he is 'desirous to be popular' (*IiI* 2: 32), desperately needing the audience to admire and listen to him (*IiI* 2: 5). When opposed, he reacts with the annoyance and sulkiness 'of a spoilt child' (*IiI* 2: 76). Byron fits Rosa's model of 'the intelligent dandy' (Rosa 1964, 22, 71), since he is a witty and shrewd conversationalist (*IiI* 1: 399), a great admirer of books and arts (*IiI* 2: 30) and just 'the way-ward child of genius' (*IiI* 2: 51).

From the pages of *The Idler in Italy*, a fully developed protagonist with more facets than 'a picaresque rogue' (Rosa 1964, 9) and a dandyish lover emerges. In her depiction of the poet one year before his death, Blessington also captures the dandy whose experiences have led him to maturity, self-criticism and disillusionment with London's fashionable high life, which he once aspired to enter. In a manner similar to her *Conversations of Lord Byron*, the narrator lets her protagonist speak for himself in the *Idler*. Whenever she turns to indirect speech, there is a sense that the poet discloses something of himself, that behind the mask of an aloof dandy there is a person 'capable of gentle and fond affection' (*IiI* 2: 60), who is not only the protagonist of love stories but also of an unhappy marriage, a motif that reappears in fashionable novels as well. Blessington emphasizes that, despite their separation, the poet 'continually leads the conversation to Lady Byron', whose feelings Byron denies having ever attempted to hurt. The poet even asks Blessington to use her influence to procure his wife's portrait for him.

The narrator lets Byron criticize the vices of their nation, and of the members of their class in particular. It is well exemplified by her recollections of the poet's resentful reflections on the public's reaction to his separation from his wife: 'Byron attributes the insults he received to a false system of morality in England, which condemned him without proof, and intruded itself into a domestic disagreement' (*IiI* 2: 79). As a counterbalance to the accusations of their countrymen, Blessington sketches the scene in which the poet, with a trembling voice, expresses his standpoint:

> '[Lady Byron] has been too long accustomed to the happiness of a daily, hourly communion with our child', said he, 'to admit of any interruption to it, without being made wretched; while I' – and he looked more sad than I had ever observed him to do before – 'have never known

this blessing, have never heard the sound of Ada's voice, never seen her smile, or felt the pressure of her lip', – his voice became tremulous – 'and can therefore better resign a comfort often pined for, but never enjoyed'. (*IiI* 2: 58)

Another situation that Blessington recalls is when in reply to her own observations of the poet's insensibility to most beautiful views, he sarcastically declared: 'I hate cant of every kind, and the cant of the love of nature as much as any other' (*IiI* 2: 17), thus alluding to the English vice of affectation and posturing. Byron expresses disappointment with his countrymen also when asked about his reason for going to Greece (knowing he would die there): 'A grassy bed in Greece, and a grey stone to mark the spot, would please me more than a marble tomb in Westminster Abbey' (*IiI* 2: 79).

Bitterness, cynicism and disillusionment are typical traces of a dandy type, which Blessington imparted to her protagonist, thus revealing her own feelings towards her countrymen. Much as in her *Conversations*, in the *Idlers* Byron 'becomes the mouthpiece for [Blessington's] own opinions' (Cronin 2002, 24–25). After all, they were both ostracized by members of an aristocracy infected by hypocrisy and scandalmongering. She could have well become the heroine of her story, yet she decided to foreground Byron so that she herself could stay in the shadows while taking up problems that concerned her life as well.[7]

***

Part I of this book has shown that Blessington was a self-conscious travel writer, capable of inscribing particular visions of herself by maneuvering between modes of writing and genres. I have argued that even though in both the early journals and the *Idlers* an autobiographical mode of narration is adopted so that she would be perceived as an authentic traveller and a credible writer, there are considerable differences between the texts. In the anonymous texts, the priority is to appear as an unassuming novice, a goal that is attained by the adherence to the established literary conventions and the current publishing practices as to women's travel writing. On the other hand, the narrator of the *Idlers* exploited a number of marketing strategies to mediate her status, gained prior to the journeys, and the image of an upper-class woman traveller abiding by the emerging Victorian rules of propriety, searching for a true experience of the foreign, yet still longing for England.

I have also pointed out that the *Idlers* promote Blessington as a versatile writer, since the books draw on both fictional and non-fictional forms. Her informative and instructive entries reveal her to be a reliable and knowledgeable guide for tourists, whereas the passages modelled on the genre of the fashionable novel render her an expert on the life of the upper class and on its intriguing representative – Lord Byron. They also expose her as a critic of national vices and of English tourists' manners. Most importantly, however, embellishing her travel texts with artistic devices enables her to foreground her writing capabilities, thus confirming her status as a literary celebrity and promoting her as an author of readable books.

Part II
IMAGES

Chapter 4
NATURAL SCENERIES

In her study of women travel writers and the language of aesthetics, Elizabeth Bohls points out that at the turn of the eighteenth century the search for a perfect view became the priority of British travellers to the Continent. She notes that in order to develop proper taste in landscaping, one needed to have 'a high degree of literacy, an acquaintance with writings on aesthetics and works of literature; access to paintings, or at least engravings; and the mobility to examine and compare different views' (Bohls 1995, 66). As the titles of her two most extensive travel accounts, *The Idler in Italy* and *The Idler in France*, suggest, Blessington wished to be perceived as a scenic traveller enjoying the luxury of leisure time, which enabled her to appreciate the scenery of the foreign countries. Though she refrained from admitting it openly in the preface to the journal, she had the same aim when on her home tour of the Isle of Wight.[1]

The scenic tour was not only a travel practice but also a genre of writing (see Bohls 1995, 66). Thus, when travel writers found scenery they had searched for, they would attempt to paint it with their words. However, as Chloe Chard observes, they tended to admit that words fail to translate to the reader 'the dramatic intensity' of what the eye experienced (Chard 1999, 84). Accordingly, when Blessington records the moment in which she pauses to contemplate the view, she frequently doubts her ability 'to do justice to it by description' (*IoW* 56). On such occasions she is tempted to draw analogies between the arts of painting and writing. Once she helplessly exclaims: 'What a picture is now spread before me, and how poor, how colourless are words to paint it!' (*IiI* 2: 193). Later on she continues this train of thought:

> How incapable are words to paint impressive scenes so as to array them with all their features and peculiarities before the mental vision of another! And almost as feeble are they in representing the sentiments and reflections which spectacles engender. That which is easily effected by ill-executed picture, or slight drawing, language generally fails to achieve. How vain then are all attempts at description! (*IiI* 2: 289)

Each time, however, despite the claimed inability, the writer makes an attempt to illustrate the scene.[2] Then she stops the narrative flow of the text and creates her 'word-paintings'.[3] The painterly effect of her landscape descriptions is attempted by means of vivid language and a careful choice of words. The account of the Isle of Wight abounds in such 'picturesque' scenes.[4] Bonchurch Landslips, for example, is depicted in similes – the hills are 'green as emerald, and ornamented with flocks of sheep, white as unstained snow' (*IoW* 46); while the range of hills 'in the back ground [...], sprinkled with patches of wood, completed the picture' viewed from the footpath to Wootton Bridge (*IoW* 27).

What constitutes a frame of reference for the descriptions of landscapes and cityscapes are the writer's preconceptions about the places visited, formed by well-known paintings. When she feels incapable of illustrating the scene, she often compares it to something that has already been depicted. That is what Blessington usually does on her arrival to a new place; for example, looking out of a church window while in Vicenza, she records beholding 'a landscape that forcibly reminded [her] of those charming ones of Claude Loraine; so bright, so glowing, yet so tender were the hues of the objects that composed it (*IiI* 3: 220).[5]

For a scenic tourist, the ability to associate and compare the real view with its artistic representations was one of the chief pleasures. To use Payne Knight's words, 'The spectator, having his mind enriched with the embellishments of the painter and the poet, applies them, by the spontaneous association of ideas, to the natural objects presented to his eye, which thus acquire ideal and imaginary beauties' (Knight 1806, 154). His predecessor, Joseph Addison, in his essays *The Pleasures of the Imagination* (published in the *Spectator* in 1711), claims that the eponymous pleasures of the imagination arise 'from visible objects [...] when we call up their ideas into our minds by paintings, statues, or descriptions' (Addison 1828, 2). In their experience of nature, British travellers would conjure up the landscapes by the three seventeenth-century landscape painters – Claude Lorrain, Gaspar Poussin and Salvator Rosa. As a matter of fact, the travellers were very familiar with the Continental scenery long before setting off on their journeys. This is because English estate holders would model their landscape gardens on scenes by the three painters. A number of artists would go to Italy in order to copy their frescoes, and affluent tourists would seek opportunities to buy their works and bring them back home (Brand 1957, 137–38). Thus it was only natural that, when finally reaching their destination and facing some overwhelming scene, travellers would compare it to the vision of the place already formed in their imagination. For example, before describing the view over Salerno, Blessington observes, 'It was among the wild and romantic scenery in the vicinity of La Cava, that Salvator Rosa and Poussin studied nature in her grandest and most picturesque forms, and several of the subjects of their pictures may be here discovered' (*IiI* 2: 333).[6]

To be considered a landscape connoisseur meant having the ability to identify the set of landscape patterns established by the artists and to follow the guidelines developed by theorists. Such instructions were provided by, among others, William Gilpin in his *Three Essays: On Picturesque Beauty; On Picturesque Travel; and On Sketching Landscapes* (first published in 1792), which contains a series of lessons on viewing and capturing picturesque scenery on paper. To him, the correct perception of landscape is dependent on a particular way of looking at it. He defines the objects of picturesque value as those 'capable of being illustrated by painting' (Gilpin 1794, 3). Thus a landscape is to be approached in the same way as a work of art: 'We examine what would amend the composition: how little is wanting to reduce it to the rules of our art' (ibid.). In other words, viewers need to act as if they were in an art gallery and as if, instead of the scenery, they examined some painting or statue. Consequently, the scene must be looked at from a correct distance, particular viewpoint and perspective. This is how Gilpin describes the procedure:

> The whole view was pleasing from various stands: but to make it picturesque by gaining a good foreground, we were obliged to change our station backward & forward, till we had obtained the right one. Two large trees, which we met with, were of great assistance to us. (quoted in Barrell 1972, 5)

Following Gilpin's instructions, when approaching some city or region for the first time, Blessington assumed an advantageous position, usually on the summit of a hill. Before arriving in Naples, for example, she ordered her postilion to pause on the brow of a steep hill so that she might 'gaze on the beautiful panorama' before her (*IiI* 2: 191–92). At the Hill of Cassel she was even assisted by a large telescope, which provided her with a view of 'thirty-two-fortified towns, and three hundred villages' (*NtP* 21).[7] A high viewpoint is, as Barrell observes, also the basic rule in Claude Lorrain's paintings. The vantage point, he writes, is to be high enough 'for a distant horizon to appear above any rising ground between it and the viewpoint'(Barrell 1972, 7–8). Thanks to the effect of depth, 'the eye, attracted by an area of light usually set just below the horizon, travels immediately towards it over a long and often steeply contoured stretch of intervening land' (ibid., 8). Sketching the panorama of Naples from mountainous Caprera, Blessington first draws the readers' attention to the blue waters of the bay and of the sea which 'mingle with the azure sky in the distant horizon' (*IiI* 2: 395). Only then does she write about Naples's 'cupolas, steeples, and minarets' that bound the view on one side, and the islands of Ischia and Procida on the other (*IiI* 2: 395).[8] These elements on both sides, tinted with darker colours, constitute a kind of side flats (the coulisses) framing the landscape behind them. This recalls a typical Claudian composition, which is arranged into lateral bands, indicated by successive elements or contours of different colours (Barrell 1972, 11). Such tonal division may also be observed in Blessington's description of the view between Toulon and Frejus:

> I have never seen a more picturesque scene than was here presented to me. The blue waters of the Mediterranean, sparkling like sapphire beneath the rays of the sun, spread themselves out until their hues mingle in the far distant horizon with the fainter blue of the clouds; while innumerable white sails are wafted over their surface, looking like birds skimming some immense lake. When the eye turns to the other side of the picture, snatches of a rich landscape are seen through the different arches of the ruins, which are festooned with ivy and drooping wreaths of wild flowers. (*IiI* 1: 326)[9]

When analyzing this sketch, one can visualize the foreground consisting of intermingled bands of fairly dark colours – first emerge gray ruins and green vegetation; deeper into the picture there is a layer of white sails stretched along the water; then comes the band of sapphire sea suffused with yellow sunlight, and the final plane is the fainter blue of the clouds in the horizon. The depiction is but a simplified version of the Claudian composition,[10] but the balance between lighter and darker tones can be easily recognized, as well as the fact that the writer first leads the reader's 'eye' vertically towards the penultimate sunlit band. Only then does she draw their attention back to the details in the foreground.

As shown above, the effect of a picturesque composition is achieved to a great extent by applying contrasting colours and lights. In the passage above, Blessington uses the palette of Claude's favourite colours – different shades of blues, greens and grays. In yet another sketch, she exploits the Claudian effect of various tints of sunlight. Going along the coast of Mergellina at twilight,[11] she thus illustrates what she sees:

> What a succession of beautiful views, each acquiring new charms from the changes in the atmosphere. From a *golden hue*, in which the skies, sea, and promontories were steeped in a *yellow light*, like some of those pictures by Claude Lorraine, on which the eye delights to dwell, they changed *to a tint of deep glowing rose*; and then deepened into *purple*, which gave the whole scene the effect of being viewed through a *coloured glass*. (*IiI* 2: 199, emphasis added)

In demonstrating such a variety and changeability of colours and lights, Blessington clearly refers to the effect of the so-called Claude glass (or black mirror), a device popular among artists, travellers and connoisseurs of landscape in the late eighteenth and early nineteenth centuries. Carried in hand, it was used to examine the landscape with one's back to the real view. The device was a dark-tinted convex mirror, which not only condensed and diminished the reflected piece of scenery (thus abstracting it from its surroundings), but also reduced and simplified the colours and tonal range of scenes, giving them, in consequence, a painterly quality characteristic of Claude Lorrain (Ward 2008, 107).[12] Another optical instrument, often confused with the former one, was Claude Lorrain glasses (or filters), which, as Gilpin explains, were 'combined of two or three different colours; and if the hues are well sorted, they give the objects of nature a soft, mellow tinge, like the colouring of that master' (Gilpin 1808, 124).[13] The function of Claude Lorrain glasses was to produce a number of interpenetrating colours, the effect of which is well illustrated in the passage above.

Not only colours and lights, but also some topographical features were indispensable to the effect of a picturesque composition. In his instructions on how to create sketches, both visual and verbal, Gilpin pays great attention to details. Thus a proper composition needed to consist of a series of intermingled elements such as trees, rocks, broken ground, woods, rivers, lakes, plains, valleys, mountains and distances (Gilpin 1794, 42). To satisfy these compositional demands, one should, if necessary, even rearrange the elements of the real view. An artist, Gilpin writes, 'may throw down a cottage' or 'he may even turn the course of a road, or a river, a few yards on this side, or that. These trivial alterations may greatly add to the beauty of his composition' (Gilpin 1788, 28–29). Though a trace of irony may be detected in these words, they would be treated seriously by a person who aspired to be an arbiter of taste. Blessington's first view of a place is thus often presented as an enumeration of such fixed elements. Salerno, for example, unites 'all the charms of woods, rocks, and mountains, with dilapidated castles, watch–towers, churches, and convents [...]. In one part may be seen the ruins of a fortress, crowning a mountain which lifts its bleak front on high; while all beneath it is glowing with the richest vegetation' (*IiI* 2: 331).

In the very same excerpt, however, she goes beyond Claude's harmonious compositions with the coulisse, fixed elements and bands of lights. Instead, the eye is here instinctively led towards the ruined fortress overgrown with foliage in the lateral part of the picture. In this she appears to be more indebted to the style of Salvator Rosa.

For Rosa, creating a structured composition was by no means a priority. Unlike Claude, he did not paint extended vistas but rather enclosed scenes, and he focused on individual objects, often awkward and imperfect (Barrell 1972, 51). Claude and Poussin created idealized Arcadian landscapes, with mythological figures and classicist buildings, whereas Rosa chose mysterious spots like remote coasts, wild mountain regions or barren lands, which he peopled with bandits and outlaws. Thus, judged by classical criteria, his landscapes were usually recognized as 'strange' or even 'savage'. Nevertheless, Lady Morgan in her biography of the painter, points out that they gained in popularity in the early nineteenth century, along with the growing appeal for 'romantic' scenery (Morgan 1824, *passim*). As Brand notes, at that time the picturesque, attractive for its universal visual qualities, was gradually outshined by the 'romantic', which appealed to the imagination and sensitivity of the individual (Brand 1957, 169).

Romantic scenes were those that aroused a wide range of intense and often contradictory emotions. While at the Pitti Palace in Florence, Blessington notes down her reflections on Rosa's paintings, emphasizing their ambiguous character:

> Salvator Rosa's genius led him to paint only the terrible or the sublime. There is no landscape of his that does not exemplify this fact; for even in his representations of inanimate nature, some stupendous rock, yawning abyss, or blasted tree, produces this effect, even when the banditti, which he loved to introduce in them, are omitted. This propensity to paint the terrible or sublime, may be traced to have had its origin in the haunts he frequented in his youth, where Nature wore her wildest aspect, and where banditti were not unseldom seen; adding a fearful though a picturesque effect to the composition. (*IiI* 1: 136–37)

Here she identifies the contrasting elements in Rosa's works. His figures of banditti appearing in gloomy rocky settings are at the same time fearful and charming. His nature is wild but also impressive. The subject matter of his landscapes is either the terrible or the sublime, or both at the same time.[14] Juxtaposing these two notions, Blessington invokes Burke who, in *A Philosophical Enquiry into the Origin of Our Ideas of the Sublime and the Beautiful* (originally published in 1757), claims that terror is in fact the source of the sublime:

> Whatever is fitted in any sort to excite the ideas of pain and danger, that is to say, whatever is in any sort terrible, or is conversant about terrible objects, or operates in a manner analogous to terror, is a source of the *sublime*; that is, it is productive of the strongest emotion which the mind is capable of feeling. (Burke 1792, 47)

During her travels, Blessington intentionally searches for such circumstances that would arouse strong emotions. For instance, when going from Siena to Radifocani she chooses the route which she describes as 'created to be the abode of banditti', and she appears disappointed that she eventually does not encounter them on her way (*IiI* 2: 160). Nevertheless, the desire for intense sensation is best exemplified by her attraction to overwhelming waves, inaccessible rocks, and bottomless chasms, which was only typical of the travellers of her time (Eco 2004, 282). When on the Isle of Wight, Blessington goes to the now-destroyed Blackgang Chine (Figure 4.1), the impressions of which she recollects by means of the most evocative language:

> Here were seen the works of God in all their native *grandeur*; the ocean in *resplendent* majesty, spreading its *vast expanse* as far as the eye could reach; *unbounded* […]. Mountains of rocks, whose *stupendous heights* appear *inaccessible* […]. [T]he celebrated Black Gang Chine [seems] to frown with *terrific grandeur*, and threatens the traveller with destruction […]. Not a bush is to be seen on any part of the *mouldering* precipice, to soften its *wild aspect* […]. *Large masses of rock* are scattered about, and some single ones, of *gigantic* appearance […] remind one of the battle of the *Titans*. (*IoW* 56–57, emphasis added)

Figure 4.1 Samuel Bradshaw (fl. 1832–1880), *The Undercliff, Isle of Wight, as seen after passing the church of St. Lawrence, on the way to Black Gang* (after William Leighton Leitch). Lithograph. © National Trust Images.

With such overstatements, she may have referred to Burke's observation that greatness of dimension and height as well as rugged and broken surfaces are productive of the most striking effect (Burke 1792, 107–8).

When recounting her stay in southern Italy, Blessington uses another vision very popular among Romantic writers – that of ominous volcanoes. Describing Vesuvius from its peak, she contemplates the destructive power of nature:

> This *vast and yawning* abyss was *sending up a dense smoke*, and many parts of it bore evidence to the *smouldering fire* concealed beneath its surface, by emitting *small though lurid flames*. When viewing this immense gulf, and reflecting on the destruction it has occasioned, overwhelming cities and towns, and laying waste the most fertile and beautiful lands, it is impossible not to feel a *sentiment of awe*; and one cannot divest oneself, at least I could not, of a presentiment that in this *smouldering* crater, I beheld the engine of future destruction to the enchanting country around. (*IiI* 2: 372–73, emphasis added)

The gazer is struck by the ghastly appearance of the crater abyss – its immensity, its dense smoke and glowing flames – but also by the extent of the land wasted by its power. Like the previous one, this vision is structured by Burke's category of dimension, but also of strong light and sombre colours, which, among other circumstances, he believed aroused sublimity (Burke 1792, 81). The viewer's possible responses to the sublime power range, according to Burke, from astonishment and awe to reverence and respect (ibid., 219). Blessington admits to experiencing a sense of awe, but what is also perceptible here is the feeling of potential danger. The way she visualizes Vesuvius is suggestive of Salvator Rosa's representation of the crater of Etna. Blessington's desire to investigate the mysteries of unpredictable nature may be compared to Empedocles venturing into the unknown. The difference is that, unlike Empedocles, she is not going to fall into the depths of the precipice.[15] This is the essence of Burkean sublimity: despite feeling a sense of insecurity, viewers encountering some threatening circumstances are still able to derive peculiar pleasure by keeping their distance. Only thus can the threat be mitigated. The feeling of terror can only produce 'a sort of delightful horror, a sort of tranquillity tinged with terror' when it is considered but not experienced (Burke 1792, 218–19). Even in such circumstances, however, Blessington manifests her capability to maintain aesthetic distance, which only a person of taste would do.

So that she would not let herself be too carried away, she averts her gaze from the volcano crater and, instead, enthuses over the view from its summit:

With what delight does the eye turn from the contemplation of the fearful and yawning crater, to dwell on the *glowing* picture seen from the summit of Vesuvius! The *bright blue* sea, on whose *glassy* bosom innumerable white sails are flitting, like *snowy-pinioned* birds; the vine-clad hills and *fertile* Campania, with the *undulating line* of the coast reaching out like a crescent towards each end of the Bay; the Isle of Caprea, shielding it from the rude winds or waves of the ocean; and Naples descending to the extreme edge of the shore, as if to lave her terraced palaces in its *pellucid waters*. The promontory of Misenum lifts its head to the right, and the high land of Sorento bounds the left; Nisida, Procida, and Ischia are seen rising from the *calm* bosom of the sea like islands called into life by the wand of *enchantment*; and all this *lovely* scenery is bathed in an atmosphere so *transparent*, and canopied by a sky so *heavenly blue*, that it looks as if it were indeed, what the Neapolitans proclaim Naples to be, 'A piece of Paradise dropped on Earth.' (*IiI* 2: 376–77, emphasis added)

What she beholds is a Paradise-like scene. The colours she uses are clean and mild, almost transparent – 'pellucid waters', 'heavenly blue sky', 'snowy-pinioned birds'. The surfaces are no longer rugged but delicate and smooth – 'undulating waves', 'the calm bosom of the sea' and the crescent-like coast. There are no sharp angles breaking the view. Each part of the scene is blended with the other parts. The hills fade away into Campania, which mixes with the shore, which melts into the sea, which, in turn, blends with the sky. Delicacy, smoothness, soft colours and an unbroken continuity are some of the qualities Burke considers essential to the effect of beauty (Burke 1792, 189–90). The evocative language the writer uses to sketch this idyllic landscape expresses how her disposition has changed into blissfulness and idleness.

In an aesthetic study of place, views, like works of art, should be examined from a distance. And Blessington usually does abide by this rule. At times, however, step by step she positions herself within the landscape she sketches. Instead of participating in guided tours, for example, she often prefers to 'loiter alone' through the city to savour its atmosphere (*IiI* 2: 345) or to explore 'on horse-back' (*IiI* 2: 12) its environs. On one of such trips, she cannot wait to 'escape from the erudite explanations of [her] grave and learned' guide, so that she can 'scramble over wild banks of vineyards, and mounds of earth, in order to explore some tempting-looking court of a building' (*IiI* 2: 284). With such statements she fashions herself as an explorer crossing the boundary separating the foreign and the familiar. They show that the narrator attempts to earn recognition not only as a connoisseur conforming to the aesthetic acknowledged in England, but also as an eyewitness ready to reinterpret its principles if need be.

Such an attitude is well exemplified by the writer's depiction of human beings. Like the idyllic landscapes by Claude or Poussin, Blessington's topography is enriched with local people. However, her treatment of people differs from that of Gilpin, among whose ornaments to the landscape were figures understood as 'moving objects as waggons, and boats, as well as cattle, and men' (Gilpin 1794, 77). In this definition people are not, to use his term, a 'leading subject' characterizing the scene (ibid., 126) but are flocked together with all moving objects, constituting mere structural elements within the composition, whereas in Blessington's word paintings they frequently come to the fore. This is well exemplified in the following passage:

> No description can render justice to the beauty of the scenery between Amalfi and Castellammare, one moment offering views of the blue Mediterranean, seen sparkling over the groves and vineyards, between it and the mountains, and the next showing a convent-crowned eminence, rising from a mass of wood, or ruined fortress standing on some bold projection of rock. The hamlets through which we passed were exceedingly picturesque. Each had its fountain, round which groups of women were filling their *classically shaped water jugs*, singing, laughing, and chatting the while; *their dark hair rolled* like those of the *antique female statues*, and their *scanty drapery* revealing just enough of their figures to give them the appearance of having furnished the *models*, of the *rural-nymphs* we see in some of the pictures of the old masters. They saluted us gracefully, offered some of the sparkling water [...]; and exchanged smiles and pleasantries. (*IiI* 2: 353–54, emphasis added)

What we have here is another typical picturesque landscape with mountains, a mass of wood and ruins. This time, however, Blessington seems more interested in people than their natural environment. She abandons the position of a detached observer on the hill; instead, she approaches the human community and fixes her gaze on the young women gathered around the fountain. Describing the women, Blessington, instead of the picturesque, invokes the qualities of the beautiful, such as smoothness, delicacy and gracefulness, which Burke identified with the feminine, and which were epitomized by the statue of Venus de' Medici (Burke 1972, 193).[16] The women's ideal physique, scanty drapery dresses, dark rolled hair and graceful movements remind Blessington of 'antique female statues', corresponding with the presented fountain and classically shaped water jugs.[17] Quintessentially feminine, they might well, Blessington states, pose for paintings of rural nymphs. Such a representation would appeal to most upper- and middle-class English women of the Romantic era who strived for the Burkean ideal of femininity, to be conceived as erotically desirable, sensual but also fragile (Mellor 1993, 109).

Even though Blessington still keeps her aesthetic distance and perceives the women in a manner similar to the way she perceives paintings and statues in the gallery, she appears to be immersed in their everyday life. They may resemble works of art, but they are human beings – tangible and passionate. They are caught up half-naked, working, chatting and enjoying themselves. Her concentration on human figures is even more apparent in the following passage:

> A very interesting and picturesque group are assembled beneath my window, consisting of the united families of the two gardeners [...]. The children are all touching and kissing the new-born infant, the grandmother cautioning them not to be too rough in their caresses; and the mother, with no symptom of recent illness [...] is partaking of her usual evening repast. All seem in high glee, and I am told that tomorrow she will resume her customary occupations, as if nothing particular has occurred [...]. I should say [...] that the Italian peasantry are a very affectionate race. (*IiI* 2: 291)

If the previous sketch concentrated on the landscape as such, only touching upon human figures, this excerpt certainly gives precedence to the represented people. Although the people are still observed from a privileged position (viewed from above) and conceptualized within the framework of aesthetic discourses, being a 'picturesque group', Blessington's treatment of this rustic family is opposite to Gilpin's. Blessington is clearly engrossed in their domestic life. She empathizes with the loving family and sympathizes with the mother, who has to resume her duties soon after the birth of her baby. Thus she seems to assert that the ability to appreciate such authentic scenes is as much part of taste as the ability to examine works of art.

When making human beings the meaningful elements of her word paintings, the writer goes beyond the Gilpinian manner of portraying scenery. She then questions the idea of aesthetic disinterestedness, which Ruskin many years later would define as 'the lower picturesque', practised by those who are 'incapable of acute sympathy with others' as opposed to 'the higher picturesque' (Ruskin 1869, 9–10). For Blessington, this everyday experience is what in fact makes the landscape complete.[18]

Chapter 5

RUINS AND EDIFICES

Throughout the discussion of Blessington's landscapes, I underlined her ambition to be counted among the leisured class, considered capable of appreciating the scenery and eligible to form authoritative judgements on it, owing to their expertise in aesthetics and the visual arts. At times, however, she registers her spontaneous responses to the encountered views, too, thus marking yet another trend in the aesthetic discourse of the early nineteenth century, which also characterizes her representations of architecture and art.

Along with the increased democratization of travel, artistic appreciation of the countries visited became a widespread phenomenon, not limited to the aristocratic class and gradually lacking in authenticity. This, however, as Maureen McCue observes, gave rise to an alternative trend – that is, the emergence of 'an aristocracy of taste', formed by those gifted with a 'refined sensibility and an innate ability to perceive and respond to beauty and genius' (McCue 2014, 77). Unlike technical scholarly knowledge, the innate capability for genuine and creative appreciation of art could not be acquired from conventional sources like guidebooks, and characterized exceptional individuals such as poets, among whom was Lord Byron (ibid., 78), and others who were inspired by them followed in the same vein. This chapter demonstrates how Blessington maneuvred between manifestations of her technical knowledge, penchant for antiquarianism and archaeology, on the one hand, and her spontaneous responsiveness and emotionalism, on the other, when visualizing architecture.[1]

Approaching architectural forms, Blessington, as she does with landscapes, subconsciously searches for the views ingrained upon her 'mind's eye' by seventeenth-century landscape artists. When in Spoleto, she enthuses over a picturesque aqueduct which, 'seen spanning a rich country', reminds her of 'one of those fine pictures of Claude Lorraine or the Poussins, who delighted to represent them' (*IiI* 3: 13).[2] Like the painters, in her sketches Blessington demonstrates a special liking for dilapidated and mouldering buildings and monuments falling into ruin, which often constitute the central point of the depicted view.[3] This is mainly because of their picture-like qualities. As Gilpin expressed it, 'Among all the objects of art, the picturesque eye is perhaps most inquisitive after the elegant relics of ancient architecture; the ruined tower, the Gothic arch, the remains of castles, and abbeys' (Gilpin 1794, 46). Accordingly, when, for example, depicting the vicinity of Southampton, Blessington concentrates on its medieval abbey: 'Nothing can exceed the beauty of the situation; and the venerable ruin itself presents a most imposing and romantic scene' (*IoW* 6).

Blessington makes use of compositional assets of ruins. They may constitute part of the Claudian coulisse 'spanning' the landscape behind them, as, for example, in her view of Frejus: 'To the right, a fine view of the sea presents itself; and to the left, some remains of Roman buildings, consisting of a pile of broken colonnades' (*IiI* 1: 325).[4] They also may, like ancient castles growing out of mountains in the vicinity of Salerno, form 'a fine back-ground to the picture' (*IiI* 2: 334).[5] In her descriptions she includes such elements as 'broken colonnades' (*IiI* 1: 325), 'pointed arches' (*IiI* 3: 13), 'large blocks scattered around' (*IiI* 3: 249) and a ruined fortress 'crowning the summit of a steep and rocky mountain' (*IiI* 2: 334), which impart a sense of 'ruggedness' to her sketches, the effect of which Gilpin found particularly 'pleasing in painting' (Gilpin 1794, 6–7).[6] What adds much to their picturesque effect are shrubs and ivy adorning edifices and monuments. Describing Carisbrooke Castle near Newport on the Isle of Wight, she observes that the 'building as it now stands is highly picturesque, and the ivy which twines itself so luxuriantly round it, adds much to its beauty' (*IoW* 51).[7]

Apart from reflecting on ruins as elements of surrounding scenery, Blessington at times finds herself interested in their origin and their existence in time.[8] As Brand points out, the interest in classical antiquities, having started in eighteenth century England, persisted well into the next century and concerned not only archaeologists, architects, artists and scholars but also 'ordinary, inexpert tourists' (Brand 1957, 159–60). At times Blessington admits to her 'superficial knowledge' of antiquities (*IiF* 1: 49), thus sympathizing with the readers who might also lack this specialized tuition. Perversely, on other occasions, she reveals her penchant for classical studies. It is documented that before making an excursion, along with her household members, she spent the evening reading and studying what she was going to see (Lovell 1969, 22). She was eager to explore ruined buildings and to follow the progress of archaeological excavations (*IiF* 1: 34; *IiI* 2: 284). She also boasted 'the best cicerone in Italy' – Sir William Gell – who was an acknowledged archaeologist (*IiI* 2: 280).

The writer displays her archaeological and documentary flair especially when she describes her way from Italy towards Paris. It is well exemplified in a passage devoted to the remains of the Triumphal Arch and the Mausoleum of St Rémy. Rather than a picture-like composition, it takes the form of a treatise ten pages long, which constitutes a tangle of architectural terms and classical styles (*IiF* 1: 40–50). The writer also provides a meticulous commentary on the Latin inscription carved on the architrave of its entablature, thus displaying her acquaintance not only with classical architecture but also with the history of Roman civilization. Apart from this 'verbiage of a conscientious cicerone' (*IiF* 1: 15), she also includes detailed ekphrases,[9] like her discussion of bas reliefs on the fronts of the Mausoleum of St Rémy (*IiF* 1: 43–55). This and similar passages, which appear incomprehensible to laymen, are clearly addressed to well-read readers craving more knowledge. The writer attempts to win their recognition as an antiquarian and classical scholar.

Her predilection for ekphrastic renditions of architecture is also apparent when Blessington describes Gothic churches and cathedrals.[10] We can see that throughout her travels, from 1820 to 1830, her accounts of churches and cathedrals evolved as a result of her taste in art maturing over these years. In the beginning, especially as she relates her travels from England through the Netherlands to Paris, she draws heavily on the ancient rhetorical tradition, which was common for travel writing long before the nineteenth century. These are typical ekphrases, providing the readers with facts concerning the location, size, materials used for building the edifice, its architectural style, the name of its builder and its patron saint (Czermińska 2005, 35–46). She thus characterizes the cathedrals of Winchester, Rochester, St Omers, Tournai, as well as of Paris and Amiens. The longest description is that of the Tournai Cathedral, which is 'a magnificent building, in the Saxon style of architecture, and thought to be twelve hundred years old. It is built in the shape of a Roman cross, with three fine entrances; it is five hundred feet long, and one hundred and fifty feet high' (*NtP* 41).[11] As this passage shows, the writer also adheres to convention by meticulously noting all the numbers and measurements. Then she enters the church and shows her readers around its interior, drawing their attention to architectonic structure and listing all the statues, paintings and bas reliefs that she finds worth noting.

Such enumerative and descriptive techniques were typical of encyclopedic travellers of the previous age (Batten 1978, 99). Collecting as much information as possible, Blessington risks bewildering, if not boring, her readers. On the other hand, she thus attempts to convince the readers that she saw the building, which was essential, given the fact that many travel writers described places they had not been to. Assessing the credibility of a travel account solely on the basis of its compliance with the established conventions of travel writing was a common practice among eighteenth-century readers (ibid., 59). Moreover, apart from her trustworthiness, the writer manifests her background knowledge of not only architecture but also of the local history.

When it comes to stylistics, it can be observed that Blessington employs strong epithets when introducing the buildings. The cathedrals in Tournai and Amiens are characterized as 'magnificent' (*NtP* 41, 150), that of Paris is 'venerable' (*NtP* 93), and the style of the cathedral in Siena is 'superb' (*IiI* 2: 151). The practice among travel writers of using such attributes, although they may have expressed their authentic impressions, was also part of the rhetorical convention of commendation. Praising the subject, they justified its description (Czermińska 2005, 37).

Nevertheless, in the course of her travel accounts, one notices that Blessington does not always conform to the eighteenth-century understanding of travel writing as 'an impersonal relating of facts' (Batten 1978, 41). On many occasions, she refuses to adhere to mere facts serving solely an instructive function. Instead, she adopts an attitude of the poetic connoisseur, which Colbert, in turn, terms 'the Romantic imagination', and which assumes the rejection of 'simple objectivity, fancy, or shallow perception' (Colbert 2005, 8). Blessington decides to articulate the personal feelings inspired by a given edifice, and the expressions she uses to do so demonstrate a change in her emotionality as she travels towards the South. The less conventional her language becomes, the more spontaneous it grows. The reader may easily imagine her face flushed with excitement as she beholds the Milan Cathedral for the first time: 'I could not resist hurrying off to see the Duomo, while the servants were unpacking imperials and chaise seats […] Never did I behold so beautiful an edifice' (*IiI* 3: 244–45). Apart from inverted clauses (as above), her enthusiasm is strengthened by the use of hyperbolic language. For instance, whereas the cathedral at Winchester is characterized as just 'well worth of inspection' (*IoW* 4), St Peter's is hyperbolically defined as 'worthy of the Divinity' (*IiI* 2: 170).

Blessington's emotional and reflective attitude also manifests itself in her depictions of buildings falling into decay. The already-quoted antiquarian passage devoted to the Triumphal Arch and the Mausoleum of St Rémy all of a sudden draws to an end, and the writer starts wondering: 'Who could look on these monuments without reflecting on the vanity of mortals […]?' This thoughtful reflection marks a turn towards another understanding of ruins – the fact that they have survived for ages makes one think about the generations long gone and forgotten. The writer concludes the passage with a poem of her authorship in which she continues the same train of thought:

> Who came, like me, to gaze and brood
> Upon it in this lonely spot –
> Their minds with pensive thoughts imbued.
> That heroes could be thus forgot.

Even though 'seasons roll,/ and centuries pass', the buildings 'still unchanged' keep their place, while people 'like shadows in a glass,/ Soon glide away, and leave no trace'. The ruins are to tell a story of people who 'lived – they hoped – they suffered – loved'. Here, the visual aspects of ruins as part of the surrounding landscape are dominated by their emotive potential. As often happens in Romantic texts, the lyrical subject's melancholic mood is intensified by the atmosphere, as 'the wind a requiem sighs,/ And the blue sky above it weeps' (*IiF* 1: 52–55).

Similar reflections accompany the writer when she depicts the Temple of Diana in Nîmes.[12] 'Is not every ruin a history of the fate of generations, which century after century has seen pass away?' she muses. 'I never see a beautiful landscape, a noble ruin, or a glorious fane, without wishing that I could [...] create a sympathy' (*IiF* 1: 25).[13] She is sorry for its lot. It is not only the picture-like qualities of ruined buildings, but also their story that Blessington tries to present to her readers. Thus Blessington again goes beyond the 'heartless' picturesque, and instead enters into a 'communion of heart' with her subject, as John Ruskin would put it (1869, 9). The story of suffering told by the ruined temple seems to be soothed only by nature embracing its walls. The writer metaphorically writes of wild fig trees that 'enwreathe with their luxuriant foliage the opening made by Time, and half conceal the wound inflicted by barbarian hands' (*IiF* 1: 24).

What Blessington also has in common with other writers of the Romantic period is her historiosophical conception of ruins. Such thoughts occur to her particularly when she is gazing on the ruins of Rome, which she calls 'the wrecks of her fallen grandeur', particularly the Coliseum (*IiI* 2: 164–69). She sympathizes with the once-flourishing city, upon which time has wrought destruction (*IiI* 2: 166). At the same time, she is sorry for the nations who will never learn that history repeats itself. To sanction her observations, she quotes from Byron's *Childe Harold*:

> A ruin – yet what ruin! from its mass
> Walls, palaces, half-cities, have been reared;
> [...] Alas! developed, opens the decay,
> When the colossal fabric's form is neared. (*IiI* 2: 167)

Remembering the verses while beholding the Coliseum's 'vastness, its silence, and its decay', tinged by moonlight beams, arouses in her most sublime feelings (*IiI* 2: 167).

Aesthetic sensations mingle with melancholic reflections in Blessington's passages devoted to ancient ruins, while her descriptions of Classical buildings and Gothic cathedrals often combine sensuous and spiritual experience. The aspect conducive to such an effect is the management of light. It is well exemplified by the account of her visit to St Peter's at a time when 'the sun was streaming brilliantly through the gold tinted glass' (*IiI* 2: 170).[14] Burke notes that strong light, 'as that of the sun [...] immediately exerted on the eye [...] overpowers the sense' (Burke 1792, 122–23). The vivid language Blessington uses to describe the scene appeals strongly to the sense of sight: the mosaics glitter with 'prismatic hues'; the edifice, illuminated by the 'glorious orb of day', glows in its 'pristine grandeur'; the fountains in the court of the church throw up their 'silvery showers, to which sunshine lent the brightest rainbow dyes' (*IiI* 2: 170–71). To these there are sound effects added, strengthened by the 'vastness' of the building: the 'crystal waters' fall down with a 'gentle murmur' and break the silence reigning around; 'the pealing organ' sends forth its 'swelling notes', which are echoed through 'the lofty dome' (*IiI* 2: 171–72). Interestingly enough, to illustrate the effect of this visual scene, she refers to the sense of taste and compares it to the most ordinary experience of alcoholic intoxication: 'The eyes drink in the wondrous *coup-d'oeil*, and the mind luxuriates in the delicious draught [...] [St Peter's] excites and elevates almost to ebriety' (*IiI* 2: 171). It is not only the senses, however, but also imagination, 'that most insatiable of all the mental organs', that is 'fully satisfied' by the scene (*IiI* 2: 170–71). She imagines there being the Divinity in the temple whom she calls 'the *Most High*' (*IiI* 2: 170). Such is the result of excessive light in the building but also of its magnitude, which Burke asserts, unlike smallness, makes imagination rise to an 'idea of infinity' (Burke 1792, 115). The effect, of a 'deeply religious nature', is such that Blessington and her companions remain speechless, and their hearts are 'filled with wonder and admiration' (*IiI* 2: 170).

While describing St Peter's, Blessington also enthuses over 'the beauty of its proportions' (*IiI* 2: 170). In her accounts, the aesthetic category of architectural beauty is inextricably linked to the laws of proportion and symmetry. This is the rule formulated by Vitruvius in his treatise *Ten Books on Architecture*, to whom Blessington refers in her accounts (*IiI* 1: 127; *IiI* 3: 218). Sketching ancient temples and Classical buildings, she attempts to capture these qualities, especially referring to colonnades; for example, she praises 'beautiful old columns' of St John's Church in Ravenna (*IiI* 3: 48).[15] Any attempt to disrupt this architectonic harmony comes in for harsh criticism. When describing fragments of antiquity in the cathedral of Siena, she notes that 'a companion has been made to this beautiful column [...] but the modern pillar is so immeasurably inferior' (*IiI* 2: 152).

In her writings Blessington also enthuses over the aesthetic qualities of classically-inspired architecture of the Renaissance, in particular buildings designed by Palladio, whom she recognizes as having 'a praiseworthy desire of beautifying all that he touched' (*IiI* 3: 218). The features of Palladian style that she repeatedly praises are 'the purity of design and elegance of execution' (*IiI* 3: 216). Blessington's enthusiasm for Palladianism locates her still in the aesthetics of the eighteenth century because, as Brand notes, the style came into criticism at the beginning of the new century (Brand 1957, 153). However, she greatly appreciated its practical relevance and the fact that the artist 'understood the application of his art to the erection of dwellings' (*IiI* 3: 218). Her predilection for the aesthetic qualities of his palaces and villas in Vicenza reveals her taste for Italianate house style, for which Palladian buildings would become a model in the mid-nineteenth century.

Blessington adopts quite a different perspective on the category of beauty in architecture when describing the Duomo in Milan. The writer admits that the lightness of the cathedral, the effect of its white facade with pointed 'snowy pinnacles', challenges her conception of a Gothic cathedral as evoking 'solemnity and grandeur' as well as 'a contemplative gravity' (*IiI* 3: 245). Thus she alludes to Burke's observation that 'when the highest degree of the sublime is intended' in buildings, they should not be white but rather of 'sad and fuscous colours' (Burke 1792, 126). Instead, Blessington associates the cathedral with the category of the beautiful. It does not arouse sublime feelings but gives her a lively pleasure (*IiI* 3: 245). To see whether the changing light will influence her perception, she beholds the cathedral both in daylight and at night, as Impressionist painters would do. Whatever the time, it strikes her as 'equally beautiful' (*IiI* 3: 246). Here, she may have drawn on Burke's gendered conception of the beautiful and the sublime, as she imagines the cathedral to be erected by some enamoured monarch to 'emulate the purity and delicate beauty' of his young queen (*IiI* 3: 245). She criticizes those who claim that the Duomo is 'painfully glaring to the eye', accusing them of laying claim to connoisseurship 'by the easiest of all modes, that of finding fault with what pleases the mass' (*IiI* 3: 246). She, instead, chooses to relish the assets of the building.

Quite different is Blessington's response to the cathedrals of Venice, Verona and Siena. She introduces the first two churches, stating that they are 'more curious than beautiful' (*IiI* 3: 112, 236). Then she expands on the idea. The adjective 'curious' conveys a sense of eclecticism and exoticism that is typical of the Italian Gothic. In St Mark's Cathedral, we find a combination of Venetian art with 'the spoils of many countries'; here 'the chaste elegance of Greek chisel' intermingles with 'some gaudy specimen of Byzantine taste' (*IiI* 3: 112). A number of expressions she uses suggest that Blessington finds the place overloaded with such ornamentation. It is '*studded over* with saints and legends' and '*incrusted with* turquoises', there are '*innumerable* columns' and '*numberless* statues *scattered around*' (*IiI* 3: 112–13, emphasis added).[16] The epithet 'curious' also expresses an idea of bizarreness. In fact, Blessington's thoughts go back to the medieval times to which the cathedrals owe their grotesque character. She presents the buildings as medieval bestiaries. The entrance of the Verona cathedral is guarded by two griffins 'of very grim and fierce appearance' (*IiI* 3: 236), and that of Venice is watched over by an equally 'fierce lion rampant' (*IiI* 3: 113). She thus describes the interior of the cathedral in Siena:

> Columns with foliage twined round them, grotesque figures innumerable; allegorical groups resembling the phantasms of a night-mare [...] images of lions tearing lambs [...] saints and sybils being mingled with lions, elephants, and dragons, presenting altogether an incongruous appearance. (*IiI* 2: 154)[17]

For Romantic writers, presenting cathedrals as habitats of frightening animals and hybrid creatures was a way to permeate the vision of Gothic architecture with the aesthetic of grotesque and terror so popular at the time (Czermińska 2005, 134–36).

The grotesque mood of the cathedrals is strengthened by their illumination, especially St Mark's Cathedral, whose most distinctive characteristic is 'the want of light' (*IiI* 3: 112, 113). As a result, the edifice assumes a 'mystical appearance' (*IiI* 3: 112). Unlike many other churches she visited, however, here the use of 'mystical' is not related to religious elevation, but rather to magical practices. Not even once does Blessington mention the atmosphere of prayer. On the contrary, she associates the place with demonic practices of black magic; it reminds her of 'the palace of some necromancer' who is 'forbidden the light of Heaven' (*IiI* 3: 113). She calls the place a 'subterranean dwelling' reminiscent of scenes from Dante's work. She even imagines the winged lion over the main entrance, which is the traditional emblem of St Mark, to be a wizard 'menacing all intruders on his privacy' (ibid.). The obscurity and the 'peculiar' atmosphere of the church, she reflects, may easily fill one with 'awe' (ibid.). She is not specific whether the feeling is more about astonishment or dread, but as Burke reasons, both of them result in a state of sublimity. Astonishment, he writes, 'is that state of the soul, in which all its motions are suspended, with some degree of horror. In this case the mind is [...] entirely filled with its object' (Burke 1792, 79). Standing in the twilight, Blessington cannot think clearly; her vision is blurred and thus her imagination is at work.

Blessington also unlocks the power of her imagination when giving accounts of her visits to Gothic castles, which were another popular architectural topic in the pre-Romantic and Romantic periods. The description of the castle in Dover in the beginning reminds one of a conventional ekphrasis. She visited the edifice because, though a 'dreary pile', it is 'well worthy of observation' (*NtP* 6–7). First, she provides encyclopaedic details and the interior description in a manner she learned from her guide. All of a sudden, however, as if she has realized her reader's real expectations, she relates how, wishing to stop the guide's 'tedious narrative', she asked him 'if there were any ghosts seen about the castle?' (*NtP* 7–8). Blessington evinces a similar interest in East Cowes Castle on the Isle of Wight, which in general 'excites only the most pleasing sensations', but when it comes to its interior, 'no complaint can be urged of any want of the gloom that characterised such buildings. No; here the very genius of dreariness and cold seems to have fixed his seat' (*IoW* 11–13).

In the account of her visit to another castle – the Bracciano Castle in the neighbourhood of Rome – it is possible to detect the influence of the aesthetic of literary Gothic over her writing. It is written in the vein of Gothic romances, 'the perusal of which', Blessington confesses in the *Idler*, 'so often blanched [her] cheek with fear, in the days of [her] early youth' (*IiI* 2: 544), and traces of which can be found in her own novel writing. For example, in *The Two Friends*, the heroine Cecile is taken against her will to live in France with her long-absent father. She is then placed in his empty and decaying mansion, the Hotel de Bethune in Faubourg Saint-Germain, whose furbishings – 'vast and dingy mirrors', 'faded velvet' and 'damask hangings', 'discoloured girandoles', 'cumbrous screens' and the sombre portrait of her grandmother – 'formed a dreary picture'. The building gives Cecile an impression of 'some ruined chateau á la Radcliffe' where she feels like 'a prisoner, about to enter his dungeon' (Blessington 1838: 63).

The Bracciano Castle in the *Idler* is introduced as part of a picturesque landscape composition typical of the genre:

> Placed on a lofty eminence, it commands a boundless prospect on both sides; on one is seen the beautiful lake, with the fine woods that surround its shores and on the other, the picturesque town of Bracciano […] The gothic towers, formed of black lava, stand boldly out in strong relief against the blue sky that surround them, and the whole place forms just such a picture as the pen of Radcliffe delighted to trace. (*IiI* 3: 544)[18]

The castle is presented as a mighty Gothic fortress, but at the same time it is frightening. Thus Blessington follows the convention in which the gloomy scenery foreshadows the upcoming events. This is how Ann Radcliffe seizes her readers' imagination at the beginning of *A Sicilian Romance*:

> As I walked over the loose fragments of stone, […] I recurred, by a natural association of ideas, to the times when these walls […] resounded

with the voices of those whom death had long since swept from the earth. (Radcliffe 2008a, 1)

In the very same manner, Blessington's thoughts turn back to Middle Ages and to the castle's former inhabitants, 'whose romantic life and tragical death form so striking an episode in the history of Tuscany' that they would make an interesting subject for 'dark romances' (*IiI* 3: 544–45). When entered, the castle has a spooky atmosphere about it: 'The fitful blaze of the fire' lights up 'the scowling faces of the tapestry and pictures', and 'massive chairs' of their owners are 'still arranged beneath them' (*IiI* 3: 545). It becomes an ideal location for Blessington and her companions to stay for the night and amuse themselves telling ghost stories by the fire. In these terrifying circumstances, she recollects, Sir William Gell had his nerves 'so much alarmed' that later on he did not dare to sleep in his room alone (*IiI* 3: 546). Blessington alludes here to Burke's characteristic of terror which, though not involving actual danger, seizes imagination and produces 'an unnatural tension and certain violent emotions of the nerves' (Burke 1792, 214). As the writer reflects, any such story 'loses half its terrors, unless told in a feudal castle like this, with every object around appealing to the imagination with irresistible power' (*IiI* 3: 546). The passage demonstrates the writer's attempt at rendering her descriptions of architecture more artistically attractive by applying the techniques typical of Gothic stories. As I exemplify in the following chapter, the writer took a similar stand on the visual aspects of Roman Catholicism.

Chapter 6

SACRED ART AND RELIGIOUS PRACTICES

Over the years spent travelling, Blessington developed a great passion for art. During her first recorded journey, to the Isle of Wight, she was unsure of her critical judgement and thus unwilling to give details of the artwork she beheld (*IoW* 35). Yet later, when in the Netherlands and France, she counted herself among 'the lovers of painting' (*NtP* 39) and devoted considerable attention to depicting works of art (*NtP* 72, 106–8). When setting out on her tour through French and Italian cities, Blessington thus had been predisposed to make the most of their cultural heritage. This anticipation is well reflected when she enthuses over the artistic treasures of Florence: 'Beautiful art! that snatches loveliness from the rude grasp of all-devouring time, and transmits to us the charms that inspired genius to work such prodigies' (*IiI* 2: 121). She spent more than nine months in the city, and the account of the period includes numerous museological entries in which the narrator, already confident in her judgements, approaches works of art as if she were trained as a critic. She appears to be taking her readers for a walk through the city's galleries, providing them with specific information on the works, artistic techniques, styles or motifs as well as offering her own comments on each noteworthy piece.

As I have already shown, religious sites are typical topographical features in Blessington's cityscapes, and their architecture and ornamentation deeply influence her visual sensations. Once churches are entered, their potential becomes even greater, since wandering through them and beholding their murals and carving is like undertaking yet another tour (*NtP* 70). Each niche, side altar and chapel constitutes a scene worth looking at and reflecting on. It is clear from Blessington's reflections that she is attracted to these scenes, but the feelings that accompany her on such occasions are not easily defined.

Generally, in her writings Blessington does not reveal much of her personal religious views.[1] What we know is that she was born into an Irish Catholic family, but, at least in her adult years, her attitude towards religion was never 'formal' and rather 'sentimental' (Lovell 1969, 14). Such is her attraction to religion, which she demonstrates during her travels, especially to Italy. What is of interest to her is the aesthetic potential of Roman Catholicism in relation to its doctrines and practices. During her travels, Blessington underwent a variety of both aesthetic and religious experiences, and the ways she coped with them helped define her own identity. Communing with sacred art was essential to cultivate her taste, and facing Catholic rituals enabled her to affirm her own religious standpoint.

The position Blessington assumes when recollecting her visits to places of worship is neither that of an ardent devotee nor of an undiscriminating tourist, but rather of an art connoisseur. She always takes aesthetic considerations into account when deciding on sites to see. Chapels, churches and cathedrals are definitely highlights on her checklist, but when she describes them no religious fervour is felt. Many a time she adopts a typical ekphrastic attitude towards them. The church of Notre-Dame de Paris, she begins, 'is well worthy of attention: the architecture is extremely fine, nor is the church disfigured by any those disgusting images so conspicuous in the country churches' (*NtP* 95). Having presented the exterior, surroundings and at times the history of the place, she proceeds to describe the interior, paying special attention to its ornamentation.

Blessington avails herself of the opportunity to share her aesthetic impressions with the reader. The cathedral in St Omers is a 'fine building […] with a very beautiful pulpit, and a most splendid organ' and with 'some curious old monuments' (*NtP* 16). She does not hesitate to use negatively loaded words, and thus in her opinion the very same cathedral is 'injured by […] tawdry ornaments', some of which are 'wretchedly and gaudily bedaubed with paint and gilding' (*NtP* 17). She continues her tour through chapels and niches in search of paintings, statues and reliefs worth her notice. Often she just enumerates the canonical artists whose works she encounters without commenting on them,[2] but whenever she finds some highlight that intrigues her, she proceeds to expand on it as if she were a tour guide standing in front of viewers in an art gallery.

This can be well exemplified by the passage about the church of St Etienne in Genoa.[3] It contains a meticulously organized ekphrastic study of the painting by Raphael and his disciple Julio Romano. Blessington first provides her reader with a short history of the painting, thus revealing her acquaintance with critical texts (*IiI* 2: 30–31). Then she sketches the composition so that the reader can view it. We learn that it is clearly divided into two parts. In the lower part, by Julio Romano, we find St Etienne kneeling and looking towards the Saviour painted by Raphael in the upper part; clouds constitute the border between the two. The writer does not hesitate to interpret the scene; thus she finds the saint's face pious yet triumphant, and she observes Christ's benevolent look. Typical of ekphrastic writing, she also expresses her views as to the value of the work. She considers the saint to be 'admirably portrayed', the clouds to be 'too dark for the general effect' and the cherubim to 'impair the beauty' of the scene (*IiI* 2: 31). All in all, she claims that as 'admirable' (*IiI* 2: 31) as each of the two parts may be, 'this discordant union considerably detracts from the perfect harmony of the whole' (*IiI* 2: 32). Evidently, Blessington assumes here the authoritative position of an art critic. Her knowledge entitles her to visualize the painting to her readers. Moreover, at the end of the passage, she frankly admits that it is she herself who decides what her readers shall see. 'The church of St. Etienne contains some other pictures', she concludes, 'but the painting I have noticed prevents one from looking at them' (*IiI* 2: 32). Blessington seems to be convinced that her correct judgement and refined taste qualify her to decide about what her reader should learn.[4] She acts as a cicerone, showing her readers around churches as if they were art galleries and commenting on sacred works of art as if they were exhibits.

As Clare Haynes observes, one of the reasons behind such a secular attitude towards church visiting is the attempt to 'reduce or counter the effects of the experience of religious excess' (Haynes 2010, 204). Nevertheless, in the course of her narratives, apart from giving erudite accounts of artwork, Blessington occasionally draws attention to the moment of perception, as if she wished her readers to consider her not only a knowledgeable guide but also a sensitive aesthete. At one point she even declares that 'Pictures […] are to be felt, and not reasoned upon' (*IiI* 1: 32). And she feels art quite literally. When recollecting her visit to the art gallery of Bologna, she reflects on the act of contemplating religious paintings. She observes a direct connection between mental and physical perception. *The Murder of the Innocents* by Guido Reni, she admits, 'made [her] shudder: its truth of expression, and wonderful spirit […] render a long examination of it too painful to be borne' (*IiI* 3: 300). She continues in the same vein, stressing the excessive degree of pain by comparing it to a more moderate category of pleasure:

> The repetitions of martyrdoms and similar subjects of horror, however admirably represented, give me more pain than the excellence of the art displayed can give me pleasure; and detract considerably from the enjoyment which the contemplation of fine works confers. (*IiI* 3: 300)

The horror of the paintings' subject matter is so tangible that, despite the exceptional quality of their form, she herself feels physical pain and thus cannot possibly relish them.

In a manner similar to landscapes, religious paintings are conducive to emotional effusiveness. Hardly ever, however, do canonical works provoke any ideological comments. Typical of British travel writers of the time, in order to satisfy the refined tastes of her English readers, she does acknowledge their aesthetic significance, but chooses not to discuss their dogmatic content (Haynes 2006, 35). Her approach differs when it comes to non-canonical art. This may be well exemplified by the image of suffering Christ, evoked a number of times in Blessington's accounts.

Usually an anonymous sculpture, the image can be encountered in churches or by the side of the road. Describing the figure, she tends to employ the aesthetic vocabulary of the sublime and refer to Burke's understanding of its sources. She presents the Saviour as wearing 'the crown of thorns on the head' and the Virgin accompanying him has 'a sword plunged through her heart' (*NtP* 27–28). Focusing on blood that is slowly 'trickling down the face', she again seems to concentrate on the idea of bodily pain (*NtP* 28). Despite the fact that Christ's blood is made of 'a piece of wood carved and painted', its 'most glaring colours' excite her imagination and make her think of 'a sanguine spout' (*NtP* 18). The lofty epithets Blessington uses to express her reactions to such naturalistic representation of God clearly refer to Burke's idea of terror: 'This *frightful* representation is *horribly* natural in carving and colouring; and having real draperies, the effect is rendered still more *disagreeable*' (*NtP* 18, emphasis added). She is in a similar emotional state during a number of encounters with sacred art. Thus she admits that Catholic sacred art does have the potential to produce the most striking sublimity.

However, to maintain her composure and not let herself be too carried away by the scene, she promptly adopts a stance of critical detachment. Her unrestrained observations are followed by sober reflections upon the encountered images: 'Those figures […] really alarm the beholder. All such exhibitions must strike the English traveller as being most impious' (*NtP* 28). Reading on in the passage, we realize that the features of the foreign that 'alarm' and 'strike' the observer become points of difference from the familiar:

> We are commanded 'not to make to ourselves any graven image, or the likeness of any thing that is in heaven,' &c.; 'not to bow down to them or worship them,' and with this command given to us, it appears perfectly sacrilegious to see the temples of 'the Most High' crowded with tawdry images. I have heard Catholics say, that those images are placed in churches for the purpose of exciting a livelier interest by the actual representation of the sufferings of our Saviour; but surely it may be argued, that being daily accustomed to behold those representations, the feelings become hardened, and the effect is destroyed. I am sure that the imaginations of even the lowest class, can form a much better conception of the Messiah and his sufferings, than can ever been conveyed to them by the representations given in churches. (*NtP* 28)[5]

The passage takes the form of an ideological debate over religious representation between English Protestants and Catholics. Blessington not only reveals her awareness of differences between the two religious outlooks, but also, by not limiting herself to the presentation of only one point of view, attempts to present herself as an objective travel writer. Nevertheless, the use of pronouns makes it clear which side Blessington is on ('*We* are commanded', 'the command given to *us*'). Despite being of Irish Catholic origin, she inclines towards English Protestants and presents Catholics as others. 'I have heard Catholics say', she says, thus emphasizing she is not one of them. She justly presents the viewpoint of the other that rendering Christ as bleeding and suffering makes him appear more human than divine and thus the viewer may easily sympathize with Christ and empathize with his terror. Then, however, she disagrees entirely with it. She even cites the Second Commandment to appear more convincing. Expressing her own conviction ('*I* am sure'), she identifies with the English prejudice against Catholics' idolatrous reliance on the image of the Saviour.

Blessington is opposed to Catholic idolatry not only ideologically, but also aesthetically. It becomes to her a matter of good taste. Being sensitive to art, she is appalled at such a poor value of religious images. In another place she concludes a similar debate with an ironic statement that 'our neighbours on the Continent make their graven images unlike any thing human or divine' (*NtP* 18). On these occasions Blessington locates horror not only in the content of the artwork but also in its form. Such images, she claims, may only appear convincing to the ignorant and primitive. Thus, as it is implied, what is a source of piety for Catholics fills English Protestants with disgust. These reflections confirm Chloe Chard's observation that in travel writing the aesthetic category of horror is not only used in relation to the spectator's sensitivity but also as a means of defining the foreign (Chard 1983, 11).

As shown by the passages above, when presenting her subjective response to works of art, Blessington often reveals her convictions about the superiority of Protestantism over Catholicism. She may be ideologically and aesthetically dissatisfied with Catholic sacred art; nevertheless, she is never indifferent to it. Catholic representations of the saints, Bible stories and God elicit in her a whole spectrum of emotional states ranging from awe to repulsion.

The sensation of sublimity is created not only by religious ornamentation but also by the atmosphere during celebrations. When visiting the church of Nostra Signora del Monte in Vicenza, she observes the tantalizing power of the Catholic Mass. She is surprised at the devotion of the people present: 'No head was turned, no eye moved, to note the presence of strangers; a total abstraction from earthly objects appeared to pervade those around' (*IiI* 3: 221). Blessington depicts the devotees as being in a state of mystical elation, unaware of being observed by tourists. Thus she claims the possibility of authentic worship during the Catholic Mass, which for the participants may be the source of sublime feelings. She herself, however, is not carried away by such emotions. She remains one of the 'strangers' observing the worshipers who

> kneeling on the pavement with hands clasped, and eyes uplifted, offered admirable studies to the painter. The light, too, falling brightly from the high windows on the kneeling figures, and shedding a sort of glory on the gilded ornaments of the altar, and the white-robed priest who officiated at it, the rays of the sun now playing over some glowing picture, and casting prismatic hues on the marble, gave to the whole scene an indescribable and touching beauty. (*IiI* 3: 220–21)

To emphasize her detachment from the scene, she describes it in a manner analogous to viewing a work of art or a theatrical spectacle. Her comments on lighting, the costume of the priest and the unnaturally motionless poses of the worshipers seem to be taken from some pictorial composition or a theatrical script.[6]

Pictorial and theatrical metaphors are frequent in Blessington's accounts of religious ceremonies. When participating in a high Mass in Bologna, her attention is drawn to the excessive ornamentation of the church, which appears to contain a number of decorated stages: 'the columns and pilasters being covered by draperies, and an abundance of ornaments scattered around the altars' (*IiI* 3: 290). She complains that 'the sacred edifice lost all the solemnity which appertains to one of its antiquity and magnitude; and resembled much more a place arranged for some theatrical exhibition, than a temple prepared to offer homage to the Most High' (*IiI* 3: 290). With such statements, Blessington expresses her conviction that religious occasions require much greater solemnity than theatrical plays.

Even though she is often disappointed with the spiritual aspect of Catholic ceremony, she does not belittle its aesthetic power. On the contrary, she frequently emphasizes the fact that religious events add much to the surrounding landscape. After the Mass in Bologna, she observes the final procession from a distance and enthuses how 'highly picturesque was its effect as it moved along. The gorgeous vestments of the priests […] contrasted with the gay dresses of the Contadini, formed a picture worthy of the glorious pencil of Paul Veronese' (*IiI* 3: 290).[7]

It may be observed that the further to the south Blessington travels, the more appreciative she becomes of a variety of religious experiences, as if her northern decorum yielded to southern sensitivity. Prone towards idleness, she often resigns from visiting churches and taking diligent notes on the encountered artwork, and instead gets closer to local people and lets herself relish the festive atmosphere that often accompanies religious celebration. She thus describes the fête in honour of Madonna in Bologna:

> The morning was ushered in by ringing of bells; and the streets are densely crowded by the people who are come to form the procession and to view it. From the windows of the houses, bright-coloured hangings of tapestry and damask are floating; all the peasants are attired in their holiday apparel, the variety and richness of the colours of which give the streets the appearance of a vast bed of tulips. Flags and banners of every die, and with various symbols, are borne around by white-robed boys, and priests in silvery surplices and cloth of gold vestments. All is excitement and gaiety. – I must lay aside my pen, and go forth to behold the procession leave the church. (*IiI* 3: 289–90)

The way people celebrate religious events in the South is a novelty to Blessington. The solemn character of churches and cathedrals she has visited is here replaced with joyfulness in which she wishes to participate. In order to conjure up the foreignness of Catholic expressiveness to her Protestant readers, she attempts to translate it into an aesthetic discourse by means of some linguistic tropes.[8] As Chard observes, travellers wish to present the foreign as dramatically different from the familiar. What distinguishes the South from northern Europe is its intensity (Chard 1999, 49). Even ordinary aspects of life when attired in an intensified form become extraordinary. In Blessington's account, the streets of Bologna during the fête abound in such a diversity of colours – bright, white, silver and golden – that they are likened to a '*vast bed* of flowers'.[9] The dresses of peasant females during one of the fêtes at Naples present a 'rich *galaxy* of the brightest colours, mingled with ornaments of pearl, coral, and gold' and convey 'the impressions of some vast *bal costumé*' (*IiI* 2: 295, emphasis added). In Genoa, 'the images of Madonna and saints […] are apparelled in the *gayest* dresses […] and are as fine as bright coloured silks, gauzes, tinsel, false stones and flowers, can make them' (*IiI* 2: 90, emphasis added). Metaphors, similes, superlative forms and enumerations impart a sense of drama to otherwise mundane scenes. These tropes leave the readers overwhelmed by the excess of unfamiliar visual sensations, and thus they may easily sympathize with Blessington's confusion and estrangement when, while viewing the procession in Bologna, she is 'inadvertently separated' from her companions, and finds herself 'hurried along by the crowd, hemmed at all sides by a moving mass of strangers, who seemed to eye [her] with much curiosity' (*IiI* 3: 291).

What makes Catholic ritual so different from Protestant ritual is also a mixture of spiritual and aesthetic experience. The festival in Genoa, for instance, is presented by Blessington from two very different perspectives. First she attends an urban procession, which has a very solemn character, with dignified priests presiding over it, with the royal family in 'full dress', 'ladies richly habited' in the windows, 'all the insignia of the Roman catholic religion' borne along and sweet odours of censers (*IiI* 2: 90–91). Then, driven by curiosity, she moves to a neighbouring village on the seashore and encounters a ceremony on the same occasion, but of a very different character. Here she beholds a 'vast number of peasants' mingled with monks and priests. Blessington provides a meticulous description of the women's clothing and ornaments, as if she wanted to bombard her reader with as many details as possible: richly embroidered bodices and white petticoats, hair braided exactly 'as that of an antique statue', earrings nearly descending to their shoulders, chains with crosses and medallions presenting the images of Madonnas and saints, large rings resembling some shields, and colourful shoes with silver buckles (*IiI* 2: 91–92). Thus Blessington redirects the attention of her female readers away from religious matters and onto conventional women's interests. So richly bedecked, the women constitute the main attraction of the event; it is they that become a kind of spectacle. The sacred mingles here with the secular. What is more, she lends an air of pagan exoticism to the procession, which is only reinforced when she compares the look of the worshipers with that of an antique statue.[10] The Catholic insignia of gold and silver present in the urban ceremony are here replaced by omnipresent nature:

> The procession moved along under an arcade of green foliage erected for the occasion, on the sea shore, the waves approaching to its very limit; and their gentle murmur, as they broke on the sand, mingling with the voices of the multitude as they chanted a sonorous hymn. The blue sky above, and the placid, azure sea, by the side of which the procession advanced, with the sunbeams glancing through the open arches of foliage, on the bright colours of the dresses of the priests and women, formed a beautiful picture. (*IiI* 2: 92)

With nature prevailing over the people, the parade is more reminiscent of some ancient pagan practices than a Catholic ceremony. Given her Protestant prejudices, it seems here as if Blessington's fascination with such undoctrinal religious observances resulted from her immersion in the aesthetics of the picturesque. She in fact depicts the scene as a typical pictorial composition, a method she frequently applies when sketching her landscapes, with the blending sounds of murmuring waves and sonorous singing imparting peculiar solemnity to the scene. To these may be added the element of terror, when Blessington states that the charm of the scene is not even detracted from by the ghastly appearance of the monks wearing 'cowls, with holes cut for the eyes, and cross-bones painted on their breasts' and bearing 'grotesque images of saints and martyrs' (*IiI* 2: 92–93). Even though she seems appreciative of the eclectic character of the procession, she admits that it reminds her of 'the old mysteries of the middle ages' (*IiI* 2: 93) by which she designates Catholic ritualism as primitive.

A discrepancy between aesthetic allure and ideological objections may also be seen in Blessington's accounts of miracles. One of the marvellous events typically described by British travellers to Naples was the liquefaction of the blood of Saint Januarius. Blessington devotes over five pages to her observations and also to her reflections on the event. In the very beginning she states that the scene 'presents one of the most extraordinary examples of superstition that it is possible to imagine in the present time, when education has so much dispersed the mists of error and ignorance' (*IiI* 2: 299). With such an introduction she, on the one hand, expresses her repulsion towards primitive religious practices. On the other, however, she excites the reader's curiosity about some extraordinary occurrences to come.

Being critical of the irrational behaviour of the present, she again wishes to emphasize her detached position and thus relates the occasion in terms of a theatrical exhibition. The passage opens with a detailed account of the altar, the paraphernalia and the circumstances of the miracle, which is reminiscent of stage directions. The action starts with the priest holding the veil and 'praying with the utmost fervor and apostrophizing the saint with exclamations, interrupted by his tears and sighs' (*IiI* 2: 300). Then a group of one hundred women also seated at the altar, whose role is to appeal to the saint to consent to the miracle and whose cries are 'really terrific, resembling more the howlings of savages than of Christians', answer the priest (*IiI* 2: 301). This brings to mind the interaction between the actor and the chorus in a Classical tragedy. The allusion seems quite explicit, given the fact that in a footnote Blessington herself observes the similarity between this ceremony and the one witnessed and described by Horace in his *Satires* (*IiI* 2: 303). Around the stage-like altar there are gathered spectators, attentively following all the proceedings. Their reactions are so exuberant that they become part of this peculiar spectacle. 'Men, women and children, now began to weep together; and never previously had I witnessed such an inundation of tears', relates Blessington (*IiI* 2: 302).

As a special favour, Blessington and her companions are allowed to stand very near the grand altar. This position proves very advantageous, as it affords a thorough view of the situation. However, being in the very auditorium also poses a considerable risk of crossing the boundary separating the spectator from the spectacle. This happens to Blessington and her companions when, after an unsuccessful appealing to the saint, the 'savages' begin in chorus 'to direct sundry glances of mingled suspicion and rage against' the English, accusing them of the failure of the liquefaction and demanding that they take off their bonnets and kneel (*IiI* 2: 301). Being scrutinized by the members of the congregation, the English tourists transmute into spectacle. Presenting the spectacle as staring back is, as Chard indicates, yet another strategy for drawing the reader's attention to cultural difference between the foreign and the familiar (Chard 1999, 162). Very soon, however, Blessington regains the authoritative position of the spectator, which she affirms by applying theatrical metaphors. She is struck by the immoderate and irrational behaviour of the congregation, resembling the gullibility of a theatre audience. She clearly dissociates herself from such superstitious practices, concluding rationally that whether the liquefaction is 'effected through the warmth of the hand, or its vicinity to the large candle alluded to, or both, I cannot decide; but I confess I left the spot an unbeliever of the asserted miracle' (*IiI* 2: 304). With this scene, the writer effectively strips Roman Catholicism of its grandeur.[11]

Blessington also applies the language of aesthetics with reference to Roman Catholicism when evoking funeral rituals. While in Viterbo, she witnesses a funeral procession, which she calls 'a singular spectacle' and then visualizes it as if it were a carnival procession (*IiI* 2: 162). The monks and penitents, dressed in 'grey, blue, black and white', mingle with acolytes in white. Their faces are hidden since they are all wearing 'cowls' with holes cut for the eyes; they are also waving banners and carrying gruesome props: 'a human skull or bone in one hand, and a lighted serge in the other'. She characterizes the parade as 'grotesque and disgusting', but she does not know yet what awaits her while at Naples three months later.

There, 'attracted merely by curiosity', Blessington visits rather sinister tourist sites; namely, an open burial vault, which she calls a charnel house, and the subterranean chapels in the Church of Santa Chiara, both holding exhibitions of 'the deceased unhappily disinterred for the occasion' (*IiI* 2: 449). The scenes seemingly work on her imagination, as her language appears at its best when depicting bodies 'mingled together in grisly fellowship' (*IiI* 2: 307): 'Heads, feet, and arms were seen jutting out at different sides […] a number of reptiles were crawling over the dead, and had already commenced preying on them' (*IiI* 2: 308). Relating the occurrences in the 'chamber of death', in turn, she again applies the language of theatricality describing it as a 'ghastly masquerade', with 'the departed' taking a leading role: they are 'attired in the gaudy finery worn when alive' and have their bodies 'supported round the waist by cords' (*IiI* 2: 451–54). Among the bodies, there stands 'a boy of six years old, whose ringlets have been curled for the occasion', and whose 'embroidered shirt-collar' and 'well-polished buttons' contrast with his 'shrunken dark brown chest' and face resembling nothing but 'a sort of mask of discoloured leather' (*IiI* 2: 449–50). Another one is a young woman 'robed in her bridal vest' whose 'hair fell in masses over her face and shadowy form, half veiling the discoloured hue of the visage and the neck, and sweeping over her, as if to conceal the fearful triumph of death over beauty' (*IiI* 2: 450–51).

Blessington is clearly repulsed at the scenes; she reflects, 'Can anything more preposterous be imagined? – nothing, I am quite sure, more disgusting can be beheld' (*IiI* 2: 448). At the sight of the charnel house, her 'soul shuddered, and the mind shrank back' (*IiI* 2: 308); whereas in the chamber of death she is 'nearly overcome by the mingled vapours' and 'the horrors of an exhibition' (*IiI* 2: 454). In a manner similar to Blessington's account of her stay in the Bracciano Castle, the descriptions from Naples reveal her predilection for Gothic aesthetics. The different passages, however, are suggestive of two opposite strains of the Gothic. The former one is reminiscent of Ann Radcliffe's novels of 'terror'; the latter ones, in turn, are founded on the aesthetics of 'horror'. According to Radcliffe's definition, the difference between terror and horror is that 'the first expands the soul and awakens the faculties to a high degree of life; the other contracts, freezes and nearly annihilates them' (Radcliffe 1826, 149). In the light of the passages by Blessington, it can be paraphrased that terror involves spiritual experience captivating one's imagination in anticipation of some threat, while horror is a bodily reaction of disgust to something revolting or horrific that one witnesses. In fact, Blessington's representations of death are very reminiscent of the gory scenes in Matthew Gregory Lewis's *The Monk*, originally published in 1796, which is considered the epitome of horror Gothic romance.[12]

Filled with horror, Blessington claims to have turned her eyes away, yet she continues watching. What is more, later on she also decides to recollect and depict the scenes to her readers. The passages well illustrate a peculiar 'attraction of repulsion'[13] that characterizes Blessington's attitude towards Roman Catholicism. She shudders in revulsion when confronted with ostensible Catholic superstition, paganism, tawdry taste, artificiality and horror, but at the same time derives peculiar pleasure from witnessing and representing them in writing.[14]

***

In Part II of this book, I have argued that participating in the aesthetic discourse characterizing travel writing after 1815 enabled Blessington to strengthen her status as a member of the upper class, with refined tastes and artistic skills equal to those of her male counterparts. Prior to her journeys, Blessington was constantly referred to in terms of feminine beauty, thus becoming an object of aesthetic contemplation. She took advantage of the position not only by using one of her portraits as the frontispiece but mainly by fashioning herself as an expert on beauty throughout the texts. She presents herself as a scenic tourist in search of aesthetic experiences, yet she clearly attempts to distinguish herself from the masses of uncritical and whirlwind English tourists claiming the same purpose. Her leisurely mode of travelling emphasizes not only her privileged social position, but also her inquiring mind and artistic intuition.

Through the analysis of Blessington's participation in aesthetic discourse, I have demonstrated that she enters into dialogue with tradition so as to perform a number of roles. These roles well characterize the tendencies of women travel writers in the first half of the century. The discussed passages indicate that she attempts to be perceived as a professional and authoritative traveller, at times an art critic and landscape connoisseur and on other occasions a classical scholar. She also presents herself as an explorer of the exotic – spontaneous, impressionistic and sympathizing with the foreign. For the most part she is still immersed in the Romantic imagination and reflection over art and history. As dispersed as the images are, they are all reconciled by the fact that she is always an English lady.

Part III
SPACES

Chapter 7

GENOA: BYRON'S COMPANION

In the period following the Napoleonic Wars, the most popular routes from France to Italy were across the Alps.[1] Owing to new roads built over the mountains, the passages became more accessible and were no longer as perilous as in the past. Moreover, the routes appealed to the travellers of the time, who were searching for breathtaking views. For those who kept journals on their way, the Alpine passages were an ideal occasion to vent their emotions, so they awaited the moment impatiently and then showered their readers with effusive descriptions. After her passage from Switzerland to Italy through the Simplon Valley, Anna Jameson hyperbolically records being enclosed by 'gigantic mountains in all their endless variety of fantastic forms' (Jameson 1826, 42). Similarly, Mary Shelley, who took the same route, writes about 'the naked bones of a gigantic world' whose majesty simplicity 'inspired awe' (Shelley 1844, 1: 135).

These are the emotions that Blessington resigned from when deciding not to follow any of the Alpine routes,[2] which is somewhat surprising, given her penchant for sublime views, and which, in consequence, may have appeared impoverishing to *The Idler in Italy*. What she did instead was go along the Grande Corniche and head for 'Genoa the Superb.'[3] Much as the city lures her for its own assets, she confesses that 'being the residence of Lord Byron gives it a still greater attraction' (*IiI* 1: 389). Thus, as I demonstrate here, what she has to offer her readers, instead of stunning mountain views, is the personal life of the poet. In the passages preceding the account of their actual meeting, the writer already whets her readers' appetites for details concerning the poet. In Geneva on 8 October 1822, she tracks Byron's route and relates being rowed on Lake Leman by the same boatman that the poet employed while there. Maurice tells her a number of anecdotes about the poet and shows her the Villa Diodati where Byron used to stay (*IiI* 1: 88–91). In Nice, on 15 March 1823, Blessington observes that in France, 'Byron is much in vogue'; the French regard him as 'a most mysterious character, in which is mingled much of evil and good' (*IiI* 1: 350–51). A range of feelings accompany Blessington on her way to Genoa. On 30 March she admits that she longs to compare Byron with 'the *beau idéal*' she has formed in her mind and to 'judge how far the descriptions given of him are correct' (*IiI* 1: 390). Even though she is afraid he might decline to see her, 'as he has done to many of his acquaintances', she decides not to 'anticipate such an annoyance' (*IiI* 1: 390). On the night preceding their meeting, already in Genoa, Blessington is as exhilarated by the prospect of meeting the poet as most travellers would be by the thought of an Alpine ascent: 'And I am indeed in the same town with Byron! And to-morrow I may, perhaps, behold him! I never before felt the same impatient longing to see any one known to me only by his works' (*IiI* 1: 392).[4]

Having gradually built up the tension, on 1 April 1823, after the climactic encounter, she perversely records: 'I have met Lord Byron; and am disappointed!' After this she wonders, 'Why is it, that on thinking of those portions of his writings that have most delighted me, I cannot figure the man I have seen as their author' (*IiI* 1: 393). So it is, she concludes, 'when we have heard exaggerated accounts of a person; or when, worse still, we have formed a *beau idéal* of him' (*IiI* 1: 393).

The two months the countess spent in Genoa are minutely described in *The Idler in Italy* and even more so in her *Conversations of Lord Byron*. The writer's pet subjects were overshadowed by the accounts of her encounters with the poet.[5] The city of Genoa and its vicinity appeared to be composed of spaces created through their interactions. Three such localities can be distinguished. Lady Blessington and Lord Byron met once in his abode, called Casa Saluzzo, in the village of Albaro. Then, according to her notes, they dined seven times at the Hotel de la Ville in the city centre, where the Blessingtons sojourned. Thirteen times they went for horseback rides about Genoa, mainly to the village of Nervi and its neighbourhood. This makes altogether twenty-one encounters within two months, which means that, on average, they met every third day. The way each of these sites is depicted sheds new light on their relations and discloses something about each of them.

The Casa Saluzzo at Albaro is where they met for the first time. Despite the fact that Byron avoided any contacts with his countrymen, he received Lady and Lord Blessington, as well as her younger sister and Count D'Orsay, with the most cordial hospitality. As we read in *The Idler*, having sent in their visiting cards, Lord Blessington and D'Orsay were promptly received, while the ladies waited in the carriage. After a while, they saw Byron hurrying towards them and bowing very low, and then heard him explain himself in a remorseful tone: 'You must have thought me quite as ill bred and *sauvage* as fame reports […] in having permitted your ladyship to remain a quarter of an hour at my gate' (*IiI* 1: 397). Then, to the surprise of his household members, he gallantly offered Lady Blessington his assistance in descending from the carriage.

Interestingly, there is a major discrepancy between Blessington's account of the encounter and the one by Teresa Guiccioli, the poet's last mistress. As she has it, fearing that the visit might be limited to a mere 'exchange of visiting cards [...] and trite courtesies' between the poet and her husband, Blessington 'brought all her allurements into play' and 'had recourse to a kind of trick' (Guiccioli 2005, 529):

> It was a warm April day. There had been a storm in the offing since the morning. Being already informed about the times when Lord Byron went out, she decided to accompany Lord Blessington to Lord Byron's gate at Albaro in an open carriage. She was thus reckoning, perhaps, on the threatening [...] weather and on Lord Byron's politeness for a further chance of gaining admittance to his house. Her scheme was wholly successful [...]. Could Lord Byron, being a well-bred and humane man, do anything but [...] go and ask the lady and her companions [...] to alight and take shelter in his house? (Guiccioli 2005, 529)[6]

After describing this long-expected and seemingly well-planned ice-breaking moment, Blessington provides her readers with details concerning Lord Byron's appearance; she depicts him as if she described the panorama of a city just entered. With every meeting she was to disclose new facets of the poet.

The second time that Lady Blessington met Lord Byron was at the Hotel de la Ville. Recalling the situation, Blessington emphasizes the fact that it was Byron who proposed to visit them the very next morning, since he could not wait to see them again: 'We had scarcely finished our déjeuné à la fourchette this day when Lord Byron was announced' (*CLB* 8). Byron continued visiting them at the hotel, despite the fact that he tended to shun crowded places (*CLB* 8). At one point Blessington cites his confession: 'If you knew how I detest [being stared at], you would feel how great must be my desire to enjoy the society of my friends at the Hotel de la Ville, when I pay the price of passing through the town, and exposing myself to the gazing multitude on the stairs' (*CLB* 73).

The Blessingtons' drawing room became the site of their interactions, which, as Susanne Schmid points out in her latest study, took the form of a literary salon (Schmid 2013, 127–32). One of the reasons behind such an analogy is the theatrical form of the encounters, which was characteristic of literary salons (ibid., 126–27). I have already discussed the countess's proneness to theatricality in relation to her aestheticizing accounts of religious art and practices. She and her household members are also recorded to have organized amateur theatricals in the privacy of their home (Molloy 1896, 1: 162–66).[7] Also during her social meetings, as Madden recollects, she 'occasionally aimed at something like stage effects' and 'passed off appearances for realities' (Madden 1855, 1: 95).[8] Blessington and Byron's conversations in the drawing room vacillated between, to use Schmid's words, 'speech as performance and speech as search for truth' (Schmid 2013, 127). This happened on the part of not only the poet but also the countess.

In her *Conversations*, Blessington observes Byron's changeability when talking about his personal affairs and feelings, which, she notes, are 'either lamented with an air of melancholy, or dwelt on with playful ridicule, according to the humour he happens to be in' (*CLB* 20). She writes about 'the chameleon-like character or manner of Byron', which misleads his companions to, she supposes, his great satisfaction (*CLB* 72). This well exemplifies Buzard's observation that Byron's 'theatricality became the predominant feature of [his] fame and a key element in the poet's allure for Continental tourists' (Buzard 1993, 116).

Most probably, Byron observed the same facet of character in Lady Blessington. At the time the Blessingtons stayed in Genoa, Byron was writing Canto XVI of his *Don Juan*. As Guiccioli recollects, he attended their dinners because he was seeking inspiration there and, at the time, he was 'especially in need of a heroine' (Guiccioli 2005, 532). Thus she implies that Lady Blessington was a model for Byron's Adeline of Canto XVI. It seems probable that Byron recognized 'the chameleon-like character' in Lady Blessington as well, and that she was the one he had in mind when writing about Adeline 'playing her grand rôle,/ Which she went through as though it were a dance' (Byron 2008, 869).

Jane Stabler, in turn, addresses the theatrical nature of their acquaintance by analyzing the manner in which Blessington presents one of their meeting sites – the hotel balcony (Stabler 2013, 55). She composes a picturesque scene, which constitutes 'a theatrical backdrop to the Blessington/Byron soliloquy', as Stabler calls it (ibid.). Blessington then quotes Byron's speech as if he were the only actor on the scene:

> What an evening, and what a view! Should we ever meet in the dense atmosphere of London, shall we not recall this evening, and the scenery now before us? But, no! most probably there we should not feel as we do here; we should fall into the same heartless, loveless apathy that distinguish[es] one half of our compatriots, or the bustling, impertinent importance to be considered *supreme bon ton* that marks the other. (*CLB* 45–46)

These words full of bitterness might just as well have been uttered by Blessington herself, as they shared the same fate. Surrounded by scandal, they were 'exiled from [their] country by a species of ostracism' (*CLB* 73). They met in this city of exile and this evening were together, watching out for their homeland in the distance. The scene is made even more pathetic by her recalling 'God save the King', which at the time was sung by the crew of an English ship nearby. She reflects that they 'felt at the moment that tie of country which unites all when they meet on a far distant shore' (*CLB* 46).

As in the scene above, in *Conversations* for the most part it is the poet who speaks. Blessington lets him express his thoughts on a number of subjects, ranging from his writing and personal matters to his acquaintances from London society. She comforts him, but at times she demonstrates her wit and challenges him 'by sharp and caustic remarks', the aim of which is, to use Guiccioli's words, 'mak[ing] herself the mentor of a fascinating young man' (Guiccioli 2005, 529, 537). At times they argued about their attitude towards England; once she recollects how he reproved her for 'always thinking of and reasoning on the *English*', and he deliberately attempted to 'vex' her by criticizing all that is English (*CLB* 178), as if he reproached her for wishing she would eventually return there, while he had abandoned the thought altogether.

Apart from spending many hours conversing with her guest in the salon, Blessington also went sightseeing, following Byron's advice that horseback riding was the best means of seeing the country. The poet himself offered to be her 'cicerone in pointing out all the pretty drives and rides about Genoa' (*CLB* 10). The road to Nervi became their favourite promenade (*CLB* 35). The views Blessington depicts are filtered through the poet's eyes. She introduces Nervi in her typical way as 'a village on the sea-coast, most romantically situated, and each turn of the road presenting various and beautiful prospects' (*CLB* 40). She does not expand on her own impressions of the view, however, but instead goes on to present the poet's, who, in turn, 'pointed out the spots [...] with a coldness of expression that was remarkable' (*LiI* 2: 17)[9]. She then lets Byron speak for himself and explain his 'insensibility':

> I suppose you expected me to explode into some enthusiastic exclamations on the sea, the scenery, &c., such as poets [...] are supposed to indulge in; but the truth is, I hate cant of every kind, and the cant of the love of nature as much as any other. (*LiI* 2: 17)

The poet himself becomes an inseparable part of the places described, as in the following extract:

> When I looked on the calm and beautiful blue sea spread out to-day as we rode along, and the fair and fertile country through which we were passing, with the brilliant sky above us, and the musical voice of

Byron sounding in my ears, my spirits felt relieved from the gloom. (*IiI* 2: 18)

Nervi and its neighbourhood became the extended space of their dinner conversations, thus constituting part of Blessington's 'traveling salon' (Schmid 2013, 133). The difference was that their horseback rides were the occasion for them to speak 'without witnesses' (*CLB* 20), and their literary discussions might have evolved into 'intimate tête-a-têtes' (Schmid 2013, 139). Adjacent to the Casa Saluzzo was the villa called 'il Paradiso', to which Byron wished the Blessingtons to move from their hotel in the centre, thus inducing them to prolong their stay in Genoa. On one occasion, we learn, while showing Blessington around the place, Byron wrote an impromptu in which he introduced her as 'the new Eve' for whom 'what mortal would not play the devil?' (Madden 1855, 1: 85). This was one of several poems dedicated to Lady Blessington, which she reciprocated with her own lines, written in an equally intimate vein (*CLB* 149–51). The wilderness of Nervi also encouraged spontaneous behaviour. Whether real feats or just showpieces, her exploits on horseback impressed Lord Byron himself, who, she writes, thought her 'a female Nimrod for managing as fiery a steed so well' (*IiI* 2: 18). The epithet 'a female Nimrod' was the poet's reinterpretation of a manly Amazon. As the Amazons were known for their promiscuity, this gives their exchanges an aura of eroticism.

Blessington's recollections of the rides differ from Guiccioli's account. At one point Blessington recalls that one day, wishing to visit some of Genoese palaces and pictures, she refused to ride with Byron, which 'furnished him with a subject of attack' at their next meeting (*CLB* 31) because, as she explains, 'our giving preference to seeing sights, when we might have passed the hours with him, was not flattering to his vanity' (*CLB* 32). On the other hand, Guiccioli claims that it was Blessington that 'constantly sought [Byron] out' (Guiccioli 2005, 534).

Six weeks after their arrival, the Blessingtons decided to resume their journey and head for Naples. According to Blessington's telling, on hearing the news, the poet reacted with sulkiness and threatened that he would not dine with them again, and when at last the moment of farewell came, 'the tears […] flowed plentifully down his cheeks' (*IiI* 2: 93). In contrast, Guiccioli records that it was Lady Blessington who 'was so moved […] that she had a veritable fit of histerics' (Guiccioli 2005, 540). All in all, the two must have parted as friends, as he presented her with a memento, and she reciprocated (*IiI* 2: 93).

Five years later, at the end of 1828, when Byron was no longer alive, we find Lady Blessington on her way back to Paris. She decided to revisit the city of Genoa[10] and, consequently, cross the border again through the Grande

Corniche, and not through the Alps. This was a sentimental journey. 'How many recollections come crowding on memory at the sight of this place', she reflects, 'In each, and all, Byron bears a prominent part, and everything around me looks so exactly as when he used to be present' (*IiI* 3: 314). During the short stay she retraced the footsteps of the poet, visiting 'all our old and well-remembered haunts' in Genoa (*IiI* 2: 323). In the salon she used to occupy at the Hotel de la Ville, she records being moved by the very same view she beheld while with Byron:

> On the balcony near which I now write *he* has stood conversing with me; the same scene spread out before us, the same blue clouds floating over our heads. So distinctly does the spot recall him to my memory, that I seem again to see his face, that expressive and intelligent countenance; and to hear the sound of that clever, low and musical voice, never more to be heard on earth. (*IiI* 3: 314)

In this dreamy scene, the poet's countenance becomes an integral part of the admired landscape, and all these visual impressions mingle with auditory impressions of the poet's voice.

Blessington also expresses 'a mournful interest in inspecting' the poet's apartments at the Casa Saluzzo (*IiI* 3: 316). While there she takes the very same seat she did during their first encounter and from the window again enjoys the view pointed out earlier by the poet (*IiI* 3: 316). She then spends some time in the chamber previously inaccessible to anyone other than Byron, in which the poet would write his works, including, she recalls, 'all the letters and the poems addressed to me, now in my possession' (*IiI* 3: 317). Despite the fact that at the time he was no longer alive, Byron's memory lived on, and at every turn Blessington found traces of him.[11] This final visit to Genoa followed Blessington's prolonged sojourn in Naples.

Chapter 8

NAPLES: LADY OF THE HOUSE

In Naples, Blessington spent the happiest two and a half years of her life (Clay 1979b, 153). She devoted 283 pages to describing the period in *The Idler in Italy* (vol. 2); in 1979 the pages were published separately as the *Neapolitan Journals* in Elizabeth Clay's edition titled *Lady Blessington at Naples* (Blessington 1979) At the time Naples was considered a place of great natural beauty, benign climate and antiquarian curiosities (Sweet 2012, 67, 164, 192). I touched upon these aspects in the previous chapters dealing with aesthetics. Nonetheless, as Rosemary Sweet points out, Naples, unlike other cities, in the consciousness of most travellers was the place composed of more ephemeral and subjective aspects – that is, 'its people, its ambience, its way of life' (ibid., 164). In this chapter I argue that Blessington's experience of Naples may be characterized as an attempt to appropriate this space according to her English standards, thus keeping its foreignness at a distance, on the one hand, but having a desire to cross its boundaries and surrender to it, on the other.

On her arrival in the city, as is usual when she plans a long sojourn someplace, Blessington instantly becomes preoccupied with house hunting, in order to find a suitable abode for herself and for her family circle. The countess wishes Naples to become a home away from home, since London was not very hospitable to her. Despite being far from England, she cannot free herself from the ideological constraint of pre-Victorian society, according to which the place of a woman was mostly at home. Mary Poovey coined the term 'the Proper Lady' to characterize the feminine ideal that developed in late eighteenth- and early nineteenth-century England (Poovey 1984, ix). Originally aimed at middle-class women, the ideal could easily be extended to all women, notwithstanding their social position, who aspired to live by some specific standards. The proper lady was supposed to be dependent on her husband, decorous and, most pertinently here, domestic. With her devotion to Lord Blessington, her ladylike manners and attempt to become the proper mistress of her new abode, Marguerite Blessington appears suited for the role.

The way Blessington becomes the mistress of the house appears to be a procedure analogous to the process of a traveller's arrival in a new place, as discussed by Eric J. Leed (1991, 85–86). The process, which may take weeks

Figure 8.1 Italian (Neapolitan) School, circa 1800. *Palazzo Belvedere, Naples*. Watercolour and black wash on paper. Courtesy of National Trust Images.

or even months, is made up of several stages. 'Identification' is an indispensable element of arrival. This happens 'as the traveler identifies the place and as the place identifies the species of traveler before its gates' (ibid., 85). For Blessington, house hunting means visiting all the noteworthy residences in the vicinity. Finally, after mapping its immediate territory, Blessington identifies the Palazzo Belvedere (Figure 8.1) as her habitation while in Naples:

> After having looked at half the palaces at Naples and its immediate environs, I have at length engaged the Palazzo Belvedere, at Vomero [...] I long to take possession of it; but, alas! Some days must elapse before it can be made ready for our reception, for it requires so many of the comforts indispensable to an English family. (*IiI* 2: 197–98)

Mutual 'incorporation', which is the next stage, is not possible until a sense of coherence between the traveller and the place has developed (Leed 1991, 85). To receive its new inhabitants, the Palazzo Belvedere requires a number of adjustments to satisfy their English taste. Before they move to the villa, Blessington devotes a good few pages to giving an account of the process of its renovating and furnishing, which Leed calls the procedure of 'appropriation' (ibid., 86).

The manner of the traveller's entry into a place determines his/her newly assumed identity (ibid., 88). In order to establish herself as the rightful mistress of the house, Blessington needs to enter the place properly, which means taking into account not only her own demands but also the domestic order. She does adjust the design of the residence to satisfy her English taste. Nevertheless, she does not attempt to turn the order of the abode upside down and tries to negotiate some of the matters, especially those concerning interpersonal relations. She, for instance, consents to employ Neapolitan servants 'wearing ear-rings' because apart from that detail they 'look as much like London footmen as possible' (*IiI* 2: 205). She also adopts a typically Neapolitan system of domestic economy – she pays the cook weekly for the provisions of repasts. When it comes to interior design, although she replaces all curtains and carpets, she retains Italian paintings, sculptures, porcelain and other ornaments. This way, over time, the residence assumes 'an aspect of English elegance joined to Italian grandeur' (*IiI* 2: 205). Only now can the traveller take possession of the place. The significance of this appropriation is evident in the following extract:

> We have taken possession of our beautiful abode, which now presents a most delightful aspect. O the comfort of finding oneself in a private house, after sojourning for eleven months in hotels! Of being sure of meeting no strangers on the stairs; no intruders in the anterooms; of hearing no slapping of doors; no knocking about trunks and imperials, no cracking of whips of postilions; no vociferations of couriers. (*IiI* 2: 212)[1]

The fact that she attaches such significance to 'finding oneself in a private house' suggests her identification with the ideal of the proper lady. The more she finds the place different from her country, the more she wants to feel at home there. Though a traveller herself, Blessington appears to abhor anything related to travel experience, like strangers, intruders and couriers. She also succeeds in establishing positive relations with the servants, whose qualities and skills she highly appreciates, and who do their best 'not only to meet the wishes of their employers, but to anticipate them' (*IiI* 2: 222). Thus the final phase of arrival takes place: Lady Blessington becomes 'a source of power, good [and] reputation' for the domain, to follow Leed's reasoning (Leed 1991, 88). Having crossed the boundaries of the place, she turns from a stranger into its proprietress.

Nevertheless, Blessington's successful arrival in the place does not end the process of making compromises between the familiar and the foreign. This is well exemplified when the writer eulogizes the assets of Italy that England lacks, which make Italy much more comfortable to live in. Chard points out that this temptation to praise 'the foreign at the expense of the familiar' was typical of travellers to the South (Chard 1999, 43). Nonetheless, in order to appear fair to their homeland, most of them used 'strategies of caution, limiting and qualifying their expressions of delight' (ibid., 44). It happens, for instance, when Blessington enthuses over the mild climate of Naples and immediately afterwards expresses her sadness about not having a proper fireside at the Palazzo Belvedere, since, although they have no need of 'the warmth of the fire', they miss 'the appearance of that truly English focus of comfort, which attracts round its cheerful hearth the domestic circle of a winter's evening' (*IiI* 2: 314–15). The writer lists the attractions of Naples that help her settle in her new abode; nevertheless, she also recollects the advantages of her homeland which, mundane as they may seem, are presented in an elaborate manner. Thus she ensures her readers of her loyalty to the familiar (see Chard 1999, 44). Her prototype of the ideal home is after all England, not the foreign country, and she wishes to conform to the English ideal of the proper lady.

Even though Blessington aspires to the same feminine ideal, her domestic sphere differs from that of typical English middle-class women. This is because Blessington enjoys the luxury of leisure, which allows her to allot considerable time and space to reading, writing and social activities. In his diary, Charles Mathews gives us the gist of how the place influenced the countess: 'Lady B– is more charming than ever. This is the place, with all its associations, to draw out the resources of her mind – to discover the superiority of her talents' (quoted in Lovell 1969, *22*). He describes the drawing room of the Palazzo Belvedere as so organized as to facilitate 'conversations […] upon improving subjects'. As we read in his account,

> In one corner of the large saloon stood Lady Blessington's table, laden with books and writings; Count D'Orsay's in another, equally adorned with literary and artistic litter. Miss Power's and mine completed the arrangement, while Lord Blessington strolled and chatted from one to the other, and then dived into his own sanctum. (quoted in Schmid 2013, 150)

The drawing room appears here so indeterminate that it might as well be part of Blessington's other residences, both on the Continent and in England. This is because what constitutes the space is not furniture, paintings or ornaments but the people who occupy it and its atmosphere of conversation. 'Every participant has his or her own space, but mutual intercourse is possible at all times in an atmosphere of ease', Schmid notes (2013, 151). The fact that the passage was written by Mathews who, though a member of the party, was not related to Lady Blessington and thus would have been capable of unbiased observations, proves that Blessington's salon indeed had this 'ephemeral quality' about it.

Thus the Palazzo Belvedere is not only a fixed location that Blessington appropriates to become her home and where she fulfils herself as the mistress of the house. It also becomes the sphere of learning and social activities, the setting for her 'traveling' salon while she stays in Naples. It constitutes a social sphere that unites the private and the public, especially as the practice of conversation is by no means limited to household members. Blessington's social activities involve being on good terms with Neapolitan notables as well as with the English living in the neighbourhood, whom she regularly invites to her place to dine. Over time, her Neapolitan villa, as do her other Continental residences, becomes the centre of the local social life, just as is the case with her London residences – 10 St James's Square before her journeys and Seamore Place and Gore House after them. The difference is that here, having escaped 'from the closed doors of London to the less confined society of the Continent', she has got much more air to breathe in (Lovell 1969, *25*).

At one point, Blessington thus characterizes her social meetings:

> We meet in my house or one or two others, without the ceremony of a formal invitation; and time flies with incredible rapidity in these pleasant reunions […] Literature, the fine arts, and the peculiar usages of the different countries to which the individuals composing this friendly circle belong, form the usual topics of conversation. Politics are never named, scandal is banished.
>
> These reunions are never dull, and seem to induce a more than ordinary sentiment of good-will between the parties. (*IiI* 2: 492–93)

Even though this particular passage concerns her encounters in Pisa, it also captures the peculiar atmosphere of her literary salon in Naples. To some extent it functions as the French literary salons did, the tradition of which was partially adopted in England, and with which she familiarized herself while staying in Paris. The salonnière invited guests to her place on specific days and led discussions on, among other things, literature and art (Schmid 2013, 3–5). What is distinctive about Blessington's salon is its informal and cosmopolitan character, which is more reminiscent of an Italian 'conversazione'. The host is aware of Continental fashions and attempts to avoid touchy subjects, such as politics and scandal. What is more, as persons of different national backgrounds are invited, the reunions are often multilingual interactions (ibid., 6–7).

Recounting her stay at Naples, Blessington meticulously notes down the names of all persons she meets. 'We have added many individuals to our list of acquaintances here', starts one of the entries (*IiI* 2: 317). She proudly introduces the members of the royal family such as Prince Butera, who is 'among the most fashionable of the Neapolitan fashionables' (*IiI* 2: 223); scholars such as Sir William Drummond, who 'to a profound erudition in classical lore [...] joins a great variety of other knowledge' (*IiI* 2: 255); Sir William Gell, whose 'society is justly appreciated at Naples, and universally sought' (*IiI* 2: 248) and churchmen like the Archbishop of Tarentum, 'so universally beloved by his compatriots, and so much esteemed and respected by ours' (*IiI* 2: 270). The superlatives and epithets she uses to depict their popularity or knowledge raise the prestige not only of her acquaintances but also of Blessington herself, since the more esteemed they appear, the more respected is she who is privileged to befriend them.

The reason Blessington managed to 'acquire' so many highly esteemed acquaintances was her remarkable talent for conversation. Answering those who wondered why anyone would enjoy being in her company, Peter George Patmore retorts: 'The first half-hour of her talk solved the mystery at once. Her genius lay (so to speak) in her tongue' (Patmore 1854, 198). He even compares her to Madame de Staël, claiming that, as a talker, she was 'as acute, as copious, as off-hand, as original, and almost as sparkling, but without a touch of her arrogance, exigence, or pedantry; and with a faculty for listening that is the happiest and most indispensable of all the talents that go to constitute a good talker' (ibid.).

Blessington herself most valued the acquaintance of persons from whom she could learn the art of conversation. At one point she reflects that a major advantage of her stay in Naples is the possibility to enjoy the friendship of Sir William Drummond, 'the treasures of [whose] capacious mind are brought into action in his conversation, which is at once erudite, brilliant, and playful' (*IiI* 2: 255). It 'teems with instruction, so happily conveyed, as to impress itself deeply on the memory' (*IiI* 2: 405). Apparently, she also improves her skills from her reading, as on another occasion, to describe Drummond's way of speaking, she quotes the comment on conversation steering 'from grave to gay, from lively to severe' from Pope's *Essay on Man* (*IiI* 2: 357).

Schmid argues that literary salons function as 'places and non-places' at the same time; in fact, they 'lack a definite space: sociable activities create their own spaces while they last' (2013, 14). Indeed, the Palazzo Belvedere is not the only setting in Naples for Blessington's salon. Adjacent to the villa, there is a laurel grove, which she calls a 'rural theatre'. It is 'formed of trees and plants, the proscenium elevated, and of verdant turf, and the seats of marble; the different rows divided by cut box and ilex' (*IiI* 2: 243). Not only does the spot provide Blessington and her companions with shelter from the daytime heat, but it also becomes a space enabling them to combine their cultural pursuits with relaxation and repast. As she writes, this is one of the 'pleasure-grounds' of the villa where 'flowers, fruit, and iced lemonade are placed, while drawing, working, and reading, occupy the individuals of the circle' (*IiI* 2: 243). Because of its situation, the laurel grove reminds Blessington of an ancient theatre. Another similarity is that it has the same capacity to hold social gatherings. Blessington's salon, which occupies this space, may be thus compared to Greek symposia, which at times occupied such locations. In a manner similar to symposia, Blessington's salon was an institution that encouraged its participants in self-study, artistic activity and disputes, and at the same time was an occasion for feasting and enjoying oneself, often resulting in short, spontaneous poems specifically composed for recitation. Finally, while literary salons were mostly mixed-gender gatherings, Blessington's one was almost exclusively limited to men (not counting the hostess who presided over it) who belonged to cultural and social elite, which is another analogy with symposia.

Unlike the Palazzo Belvedere, the laurel grove is an unconfined space in which Blessington is more exposed to the seductions of the South, such as 'the opportunity to escape familiar strictures and conventions' (Sweet 2012, 164). It is tempting to transgress the morals of the proper lady, whom it ill befits to socialize with men only. In fact, this was the main argument put forward against her by her opponents, mainly women. At the time, self-study and social activities were frequently considered threats to domestic duties. What must have been grist to her critics' mill was the fact that Naples had already earned the reputation of 'a hedonistic, pleasure-seeking city' (ibid., 177). It thus becomes Blessington's site of struggle between her conventionally female desire to tend her family hearth, as the proper lady should do, and her attempt to dissociate from the Victorian ideal of feminine propriety, which hinders her public activities as a salonnière.

Leaving the safe abode of the Palazzo Belvedere to travel around Naples and its environs involves crossing not only topographical but also symbolic boundaries, which, as Chard observes, 'invites various forms of danger and destabilization' (Chard 1999, 11). The places Blessington visits in the company of her household members and Sir William Gell, their erudite cicerone, become peculiar sites of her salon. During such trips they discuss art, architecture, history and local customs, and refer to what has been written about the places. Thus, their excursions are also ideal occasions for self-study and are also the source of material for her writings. Acquiring knowledge about the places, she appropriates them for her own use, and her position is that of a detached observer. At times, however, it is clear that the city steals over her and that she is more prone to enjoy it than to deliberate over it.

This state of mind can be attributed to the image of Naples created in the early nineteenth century, which, Sweet argues, depended on 'a distinctive *atmosphere*, which drew upon a subjective and personal experience of the city' (Sweet 2012, 197). Travellers associated Naples with 'the intangible qualities of leisure, pleasure and sensuality' (ibid.,). Indeed, Blessington herself observes that the 'delicious atmosphere' of the city 'disposes the mind to be pleased' (*IiI* 2: 242). Nevertheless, she also considers this pleasant disposition in terms of risk. For example, at one point she admits that 'idleness, the besetting sin of this place, has taken possession of [her]' (*IiI* 2: 265–66). On another occasion she reflects that Neapolitan '*dolce far' niente*', that is, its sweetness of doing nothing, 'seems to exclude care and sorrow' but also, she fears, 'excludes the grave and sober reflection so essential to the formation of an elevated mind [...]. It engenders a dreamy sort of reverie, during which, the book or the pen is often thrown down, and the *dolce far' niente* is indulged in even by those who, in their native land, have never known its effeminate pleasure' (*IiI* 2: 244). Blessington is clearly aware of the danger of idleness and uselessness that lurks in this land; nonetheless, she cannot resist its allure, since 'to live, is here so positive an enjoyment', she confesses, 'that the usual motives and incentives to study and usefulness are forgotten' (*IiI* 2: 244).

However, it is not only idleness and passive pleasures but also joyful and unrestrained vivacity that Blessington associates with the city (Sweet 2012, 197). This is very visible when she relates her outings in the vicinity of Naples. The picturesque surrounding of Cumae, for example, has 'so soothing an effect on the mind, that one wishes the importunate cicerone, with his impertinent explanations, far away; that the liberty of a solitary ramble, unbroken by his clamorous descriptions, might be enjoyed' (*IiI* 2: 263). The same reflection accompanies her in Pompeii, where she seeks to 'escape from the erudite explanations of [her] grave and learned cicerone, to scramble over wild banks of vineyards, and mounds of earth, in order to explore some tempting-looking court of a building' (*IiI* 2: 284). These two passages abound in words denoting physical freedom and vitality, such as 'liberty', 'ramble', 'escape', 'scramble', 'wild', 'explore' and 'tempting'. They are contrasted with adjectives referring to the studious cicerone, namely, 'importune', 'impertinent', 'clamorous' or 'grave', which, by contrast, carry negative connotations. Blessington's desire to explore the land may be interpreted as her need, at least at times, to both forget about her household matters and succumb to intellectual carelessness.

Though usually more cautious about her wording, on one occasion she strongly juxtaposes Naples's and London's ways of life: 'Nowhere does the stream of life seem to flow as rapidly as here; not like the dense and turbid flood that rushes along Fleet Street and the Strand in London; but a current that sparkles while hurrying on' (*IiI* 2: 266). By means of this aqueous metaphor, Blessington defines Naples in opposition to London. While she associates London with the density and turbidity of the River Thames, which may be interpreted as the city's confining, stifling atmosphere, she compares Naples to the rushing stream of sparkling water, which represents to her gaiety and vivacity. The people she meets in the streets of Naples, she continues, 'expend more of vitality in one day than [many Englishmen] in three' (*IiI* 2: 266).

The Neapolitan way of life is best illustrated when compared to Mount Vesuvius. When describing the *lazzaroni*, the homeless idlers of Naples, she notices that they, 'like their volcanic country, are never in a state of repose. Their gaiety has in it something reckless and fierce; as if the burning lava of their craters had a magnetic influence over their temperaments' (*IiI* 2: 197). Usually presented as the embodiment of all possible dangers associated with Naples (Sweet 2012, 180), here the lazzaroni symbolize the city's unrestrained liveliness, in which she wishes to participate. How different was the tangibility and gaiety of Naples from what she was to find in Rome and Venice – cities of past liveliness and present melancholy.

Chapter 9

ROME AND VENICE: ROMANTIC TRAVELLER

As unique as they are, Rome and Venice share a common territory – their textuality. The cities function not only as real places but also literary spaces made of all that has been written on them. Pfister and Schaff call Venice 'a virtual palimpsest of texts, which have appropriated the place and refashioned it in their own terms throughout the centuries' (Pfister and Schaff 1999, 1), and the same may be said of Rome. On entering the cities, English visitors instantly compare them to the images, verses and statements echoing in their heads. Blessington, too, reflects that the scenes beheld in Venice 'realized some of the descriptions […] read years ago; […] I could have fancied that no change had occurred since the descriptions I referred to were written' (*IiI* 3: 109–10). As I will show, being too deeply immersed in the literary context of the late eighteenth and early nineteenth centuries, Blessington hardly makes an attempt to write the cities again in her account.

No traveller has ever attempted to describe all that Rome offers. Blessington's first nine-day stay in Rome – on her way from Florence to Naples – is described on merely twenty pages and constitutes an essence of what travellers would usually limit themselves to, especially when hurried by the heat and the threat of malaria (*IiI* 2: 178). Blessington typically begins her account of the Eternal City depicting the first view of St Peter's from the hill above Baccano. Even though she assures the reader she was determined not to 'indulge in the enthusiasm peculiar to female travelers', she recollects that, as 'her heart beat quicker', she found it very hard to 'suppress the expressions of delight' rising to her lips. She thus already signals that, much as she may try, she will not be able to resist viewing and describing the city as her predecessors did.

On entering the city, Blessington is struck by the contrast between the deserted Campagna she has traversed and the gaiety of the people flocking in the Corso: 'It was not thus that I wished my first impression of Rome to be taken' (*IiI* 2: 164). Definitely, hers are not the feelings accompanying 'the gay throng' residing in the city, but rather of those British travellers whose recollections are evoked in her 'solemn associations'. As if to manifest her expectations of Rome, she records falling asleep while recalling Byron's lines: 'Oh, Rome! my country! city of the soul!' (*IiI* 2: 165). The next day, when driving around the city, she claims to have experienced the truth of 'these beautiful lines'.

When Blessington went to Rome, the city had already been 'discovered' and extensively described; there was not much to add for her as a travel writer. Though she kept her journal while there, it did not have the representative function traditionally ascribed to travel writing. Quite the opposite; it was reality that was supposed to imitate literature. Blessington's account of her first visit to Rome is set in literary tradition, but she frankly admits that her vision of the city is predominantly created by Byron's *Childe Harold's Pilgrimage*, the text that becomes her guide to Rome. She herself feels incapable of adding anything of her own to that image, since to her 'the mournful contemplations awakened by this wonderful city, are indescribable' (*IiI* 2: 166). She believes that it is only Byron's lines that truly convey the sentiments that accompany 'every feeling mind' contemplating Rome (*IiI* 2: 165–66). Therefore, she follows in Childe Harold's footsteps and experiences the truth of his words whenever beholding the same views.

Ancient Rome is of most interest to Blessington during her first stay in the city. The ruins of Rome are valued for their aesthetic beauty and for their power to inspire existential and historiosophic reflections. When 'gazing on the wrecks' of the city, Blessington visualizes it as Byron's 'lone mother of dead empires', in whose presence one should reflect on the fate of bygone generations rather than indulge in personal grief (*IiI* 2: 165). Such reflections indicate that Blessington involuntarily follows the tradition of the Romantic 'iconography of pleasurable decay' (Koppenfels 1999, 102), which is also the case in her recollections of Venice.

Like many Romantic travellers, Blessington is aware that such mournful reflections are best favoured by moonlight. Therefore, she plans her excursions carefully so as to achieve the same effect that her predecessors did. She goes to the Coliseum at night – 'the true time for viewing it to advantage' (*IiI* 2: 165). The effect of beholding the Coliseum tinged by moonbeams and reading Byron's lines at the same time is 'truly sublime' (*IiI* 2: 167).[1] The power of the vision is such that, despite the mournful reflections, her imagination is seized and, along with her companions, she seems 'impressed with the magic of the scene' (*IiI* 2: 168).

The following passage is as much the expression of admiration of the Coliseum as an occasion to praise the great poet:

> Byron has afforded a better notion of the Coliseum, in his exquisite lines on it in the fourth Canto of Child Harold's Pilgrimage, than all who have written on it, before and since. He gives us the reflections of it, in

the mirror of his own mind, so powerfully, so beautifully depicted, that no one acquainted with our language, or capable of appreciating our poetry, can ever visit the Coliseum without remembering the verses, and feeling their truth. (*IiI* 2: 168)

Such a textual approach to ancient Rome had been characteristic of British travellers since the eighteenth century. Sweet claims that the purpose of viewing the city's ancient monuments was not to understand their true meaning, but rather to recall some famous poem or historical event with which they were associated (Sweet 2012, 109). It is true that for Blessington admiring ancient Rome is a form of intellectual exercise, since what she views exemplifies knowledge gained prior to her arrival in the city. Nevertheless, the power of her sensory experiences, as well as the authenticity of her feelings towards Byron, can hardly be doubted. The act of seeing the Coliseum may be understood as the process of recreating what Byron felt when composing his lines, an experience that is deeply moving to her.

Blessington continues in the same vein when visiting the Pantheon. Immediately after noting the date in her account she quotes two stanzas from Byron's poem and then only adds that 'Byron has left nothing to be said of [the] Pantheon' except by 'matter-of-fact travelers' and antiquaries who might provide its dimensions and history (*IiI* 2: 175). Though I have already shown that at times Blessington herself is such a meticulous writer, providing the reader with all possible details, here she lacks words to convey what she sees and instead makes it clear that she is more interested in learning how the poet represented Rome in his texts: 'I never visit any of the places on which Byron has written, without involuntarily repeating to myself the lines' (*IiI* 2: 175). Even though prior to her arrival Blessington has already learned much about Rome, she is overawed at discovering how the city realizes the poet's artistic vision. Her reaction to ancient Rome differs from that of Anna Jameson, who puts it bluntly that she 'had been, unfortunately, too well prepared by previous reading [...] to be astonished' (Jameson 1826, 141).

Three years later, Blessington was to sojourn in Rome much longer, for seven months, but the account of that stay differs considerably from the first one. This time, just as in Naples and later on in Paris, she describes day-to-day life, concentrating on such matters as house hunting, acquaintances and forms of entertainment. Not even once does she quote Byron, and this is because she does not mention revisiting ancient sights of Rome. When it comes to other places worth seeing, during her first stay in Rome, Blessington resolves to limit her impressions of the Capitol and the Vatican Museums, as she feels that she should examine them in more detail on her return (*IiI* 2: 174, 177). She particularly regrets having looked merely 'en passant' at the works of Raphael.

She thus whets her readers' appetites for descriptions equally as imaginative as those of the Coliseum or St Peter's. Unfortunately, they are in for disappointment, since on her return Blessington does not meet their expectations. I would assume that she might not have read enough on the places prior to her arrival to kindle her imagination as Byron's lines did. This is what happened to Anna Jameson, as she confesses that she is 'totally unprepared' for her visit to the Vatican Museums and 'ha[s] not yet studied the frescos of Raffaelle sufficiently to feel their perfection' (Jameson 1826, 142–43). Seemingly, both of them lack any point of reference, that is, any literary vision of the places with which to compare the reality.

Just as in her first view of Rome, Blessington's entry into Venice is reminiscent of a ritual performed by all its visitors. She describes the route from Padua to Mestre and then her boat trip along the Brenta. As the boat glides over the Grand Canal, she observes the city from a distance just as, among others, Hester Piozzi and Emily, the heroine of Ann Radcliffe's *The Mysteries of Udolpho*, did. The images she records express her immersion in the traditional representations of the city.[2] In her poem included in the account, Blessington thus addresses the city: 'thou hast been/ A marvel, fair creation of romance' (*IiI* 3: 208). Venice is here conceptualized in terms of magical phenomena, which was a trope introduced by Piozzi, who observed the city's power to produce 'an effect like enchantment' (Piozzi 1789, 151). Later on, the same quality would be appreciated by other writers, Blessington among them.[3] Nevertheless, inquisitive travellers penetrating the city would also recognize its other side – the gloomy one – which turned out to be equally appealing to them.

What makes Venice unreal at first sight is its liminal character, as the city is located in between the land and the ocean, a fact that worked on the imaginations of Romantic writers, for whom the city evidenced the triumph of nature and time over human creation. For them, the glorious history of the city was attributed to the protectiveness of the ocean; they presented the city's origin as a mythological tale, according to which Venice was married to the Adriatic and ever since was to be, as Byron puts it in Canto IV of *Childe Harold*,

> a sea Cybele, fresh from ocean
> Rising with her tiara of proud towers
> […] A ruler of the waters and their powers. (Byron 2008, 149)

In her own poem, Blessington applies the same metaphor, identifying Venice with the 'Adriatic Queen' and with the mythological 'Venus risen from ocean.'[4] Both travellers and Venetians themselves wanted to remember the city's past. Blessington recalls her conversation about the 'floating city' with a gondolier, who recounts the very story, since 'those who love her [...] are obliged to look back to the past [...] to gratify our national pride' (*IiI* 3: 137). Venice is presented as mysteriously growing out of the water or, to use Radcliffe's words, its terraces appear to have been 'called out from the ocean by the wand of an enchanter, rather than reared by mortal hands' (Radcliffe 2008b, 175).

Suspended between land and water, the city appears to be a fairyland from dreams when approached by gondola. Anna Jameson feels as if she 'had seen Venice in [her] dreams – as if it were itself the vision of a dream' (Jameson 1826, 68). Similarly, Blessington describes Venice as 'one of those optical illusions presented by a mirage' (*IiI* 3: 101), by which she alludes to the phantasmagoric qualities of the city. The first view of Venice is usually presented as dreamlike, since the travellers tended to arrive in the city in the evening or at night. 'The rich lights and shades of evening' blur Emily's vision, and thus, apart from the material city, she beholds another one mirrored in the water and shimmering with numerous colours (Radcliffe 2008b, 174–75). Blessington has a similar impression when 'a thousand brilliant stars' and 'the lights streaming from the windows' appear like 'golden columns' on the Grand Canal (*IiI* 3: 109). The effect is strengthened by the city's stillness and the silence reigning in the city, which, Blessington believes, 'constitutes [...] one of its greatest charms' (*IiI* 3: 109). The silence is only occasionally broken by passing gondolas, from which 'soft music stole on the ear' (*IiI* 3: 109). Such sweet music, mingling with the sound of oars, makes Emily think herself 'in a fairy scene' (Radcliffe 2008b, 176).

When admiring 'the marvels of this marvellous city' from a gliding gondola, Blessington seems to daydream (*IiI* 3: 105–6). Many writers before and after Blessington would present Venice in a similarly phantasmagoric way. Dickens, who is known to have consulted extensively with Blessington before going to Italy (Hollington and Orestano 2009, xv), compares Venice to 'this strange Dream upon the water' (Dickens 1973, 127).[5] He imagines 'gliding up a street – a phantom street; the houses rising on both sides, from the water [...] [lights] shining from some of these casements, plumbing the depth of the black stream with their reflected rays' (ibid., 119). This is not the only passage reminiscent of Blessington's description. Just as Byron before them, both Blessington and Dickens with their mind's eye behold Shylock passing upon the Rialto Bridge, a view which inspires Blessington to praise Shakespeare's genius (*IiI* 3: 208). During her dream passage through the city, she has some more literary associations; for example, on her way she visits the haunts of her predecessors, Lord Byron and Lady Montagu, on whose lives and works she then reflects in her text (*IiI* 3: 128–34, 153–54).

What renders Venice 'the proper region of the fantastic' (Jameson 1826, 79) is an abundance of impulses that entrance and overwhelm its visitors. The impressions are 'so vivid, yet multiplied [...] that [Blessington's] head ache[s] from the bright chaotic mass' (*IiI* 3: 105). When describing the architecture of St Mark's Square, Piozzi admits her surprise at beholding 'such a cluster of excellence, such a constellation of artificial beauties' (Piozzi 1789, 151). Blessington is equally overwhelmed when she notes that 'the eye is dazzled by the splendor that meets its gaze, and turns from the palace of the Doges, with its dentellated architecture, sculptured balconies, and arabesque galleries, to the church [...] with its mosque-like domes glittering in the sun' (*IiI* 3: 105). In a manner similar to other writers, she is equally confused when beholding the profusion of decorations at the awe-inspiring St Mark's cathedral (*IiI* 3: 112), which Dickens would characterize as 'unreal, fantastic, solemn, inconceivable throughout' (Dickens 1973, 122).

Venice also seems a mere optical illusion in daylight. Blessington beholds the city in the daytime, when its 'domes, spires, cupolas, and towers' glitter in sunbeams (*IiI* 3: 101). The magical effect is here caused not by obscurity but rather by the incredible contrast between the city viewed from a distance and from close up. Blessington is impressed by 'the grandeur of the houses' (*IiI* 3: 101), observed from the Grand Canal, but on approaching them she sinks into sadness, as she realizes they are all falling into ruin;[6] after all, 'the morning light reveals the melancholy alteration' (*IiI* 3: 110). She reflects that 'the palaces looked as if the touch of some envious wizard had caused them to decay' (*IiI* 3: 101). Here she modifies the Romantic metaphor, turning the wizard into an evil sorcerer, bringing destruction to the city. She then proceeds to illustrate the mournful state of the villas: their windows, supported by 'caryatides of exquisite sculptures', are 'blocked up in the rudest manner'; out of the stove pipes protruding from them, emanate 'murky vapours'; whereas 'over balustrades of marble [...] float the unseemly nether garments' (*IiI* 3: 102). The view of the canal is even more saddening, 'for a green opaque slimy substance half-choked its water, sending out most unsavory smell' (*IiI* 3: 102). The humiliating present of the city is emphasized by nature, which creeps over the richly ornamented edifices, leading to their destruction. Blessington visualizes the sea as 'encroach[ing], by slow but sure degrees, on Venice' (*IiI* 3: 135), as if supporting Byron's reflection that 'states fall, arts fade – but nature doth not die' (Byron 2008, 149). The city's melancholic character is epitomized by 'lugubrious' gondolas – coffin-like black boats, which 'looked as if freighted with the dead owners of the half-dismantled palaces' (*IiI* 3: 102). As Romantic writers would do, Blessington thus equates the city's ruinous state with the fragile human condition. Just as ancient Roman ruins did, Venice's 'ruin and desolation' make her think of 'the instability of life' (*IiI* 3: 117). Similar emotions accompany Mary Shelley, whom the view of dilapidated palaces 'struck [...] forcibly' (Shelley 1844, 2: 79), as well as Anna Jameson, who confesses that on approaching the city she became depressed, since its 'splendor faded'; nevertheless, she emphasizes, 'the interest and the wonder grew' (Jameson 1826, 68).

Although at first view Venice appears a fairy country to its visitors, the deeper into the city they venture, the gloomier the city becomes. This is well expressed by Radcliffe, who first fills her heroine's eyes with tears of admiration at the sight of the magical city, only to situate her in Montoni's palace on the Grand Canal, the place of 'confinement and imprisonment', which foreshadows the horrors of Udolpho (Schaff 1999, 89; Radcliffe 2008b, 175–79). Numerous travellers have imparted such 'claustrophobic and horrifying connotations of a setting' (Schaff 1999, 89) when depicting Venice, since, whereas the city centre has been frequently depicted in terms of enchantment, its peripheries have always represented the repressed. One of the places exciting such murky associations is the Bridge of Sighs, which Blessington enters 'involuntarily repeat[ing] Byron's fine line' (*IiI* 3: 124). While the bridge itself brings memories of Byron to her, her expectations of 'the damp and dreary dungeons beneath' are such as those of Gothic romances. 'The heart shudders when the imagination conjures up the misery that this gallery must have witnessed, and the very air seems pregnant with heaviness and sorrow', she recollects (*IiI* 3: 126). Her descriptions may not be as evocative as those of Mary Shelley, who represents the prison as Piranesi-like dungeons with numerous doors, a dark corridor and winding stairs (Shelley 1844, 2: 86–87); nevertheless, the horror of what the countess saw 'satisfied [her] curiosity' (*IiI* 3: 126).

For ages, Venetians have tried to hide from tourists' eyes the unpleasing – cemeteries, quarantine stations, prisons and lunatic asylums – and situate them in the lagoon islands, of which most visitors were oblivious. However, these very places became especially appealing to nineteenth-century writers drawn to Gothic and Romantic aesthetics, for whom Venice represented as much the enchanting as the horrifying. Dickens recollects that when crossing the lagoon by boat towards Venice, 'through the gloom' he discerned an obstruction in the form of 'something black and massive', which, he was informed by the chief rower, was 'a burial place' (Dickens 1973, 119). As I have shown before, Blessington, too, has a penchant for Gothic tourist attractions, such as gloomy castles or subterranean vaults. It is not surprising, therefore, that while in Venice, she visits the island that has always appealed to writers' imagination – namely, San Servolo, with its lunatic asylum.

In his poem *Julian and Maddalo*, Percy Bysshe Shelley describes the San Servolo institution as a 'windowless, deformed, and dreary pile' (2014, 669). The 'broad sun' sinking behind the bell tower symbolizes the 'dark lot' of its inmates. Though Blessington has already been to several mental institutions, she notices that none of them appeared as 'gloomy and cheerless' as this one;

it seems to her to be more planned to 'produce, than to cure or alleviate the maladies' (*IiI* 3: 143). This impression is caused again by the liminal location of the building which is 'bathed by turbid waters, whose sluggish course in summer offers a melancholy image of the stagnant minds of its wretched inmates when in a quiescent state, as does its troubled waves in winter to the violence into which these poor maniacs are but too often hurried' (*IiI* 3: 143).

The horror of the view is intensified by dark lowering clouds 'swept rapidly across the sky' and 'throwing a deep shade over the water' as they approach the island (*IiI* 3: 143). The location functions as a metonym of its inhabitants; just as menacing nature steals over the building, mental illness shuts down the afflicted. When entering the madhouse, Blessington is enthralled by the monstrosity of its inhabitants. She first describes their voices 'sounding gratingly on [her] ears' and ranging 'from the loud bursts of idiotic laughter down to the low murmurs of complaint'. Their eyes are 'wild and wondering', their countenances 'bearing an expression of ferocious malignity that [is] frightful' (*IiI* 3: 144–45).

While the climax of Shelley's poem constitutes a tale of the Ferrarese Maniac, Blessington in her description focuses on a woman who appears as much insane as she is deadly. Her face is 'as pale as that of a corse' and her eyes 'lustrous and flashing with madness' (*IiI* 3: 144–45). Blessington's presentation of the woman's clothing and behaviour makes one think of a kind of spectre. She is wearing a 'loose robe' and is pacing 'rapidly up and down the hall' seeming 'totally insensible' to anyone's presence (*IiI* 3: 145). Dreadful pleasure is what makes Blessington and her companions follow the apparition to her chamber. And Blessington is satisfied, since there she finds the woman 'look[ing] like an inspired sibyl' and playing her instrument in an unearthly way as if 'the voices of spirits were trying to drown those of the storm' (*IiI* 3: 146–47). Equally powerful sensations, though of a very different provenance, awaited her in Paris.[7]

Chapter 10
PARIS: WRITER OF FASHION AND REVOLUTION

On her arrival in Paris in 1828, Blessington notes down: 'The woman who wishes to be a philosopher must avoid Paris!' (*IiF* 1: 64–65).[1] Thus she marks a change in her interests after years spent in Italy. 'The gay indifference of fashionable Paris', as Sadleir puts it (1947, 104), would have offered a pleasing contrast after her stays in the unsettling cities of Rome and Venice, and in Genoa, then a city of mournful associations. At the time she must have already had in view her return to England, and thus from then on she devotes much more attention to what would most appeal to her female readers, as if she were trying to win the favour of the English ladies, who had excluded her from their company and sympathy. Paris could help her to gain the position of a 'woman of Fashion […] Fashion of the highest kind', as Benjamin Haydon called her seven years later (quoted in Lovell 1969, 107–8). In *The Idler in France*, as well as in *Journal of a Tour through the Netherlands to Paris, in 1821*, Blessington sketches a fashionable map of Paris, recording all the places a woman of the world should visit.

It is also her manner of writing that changes during her stay in Paris. As Sadleir observes, once she leaves Rome and arrives in Paris, Blessington's 'diary regains something of the old serenity and discursiveness' (Sadleir 1947, 104). When browsing the table of contents, one notices numerous entries interspersed throughout the account of the city, which are reminiscent of recurring columns in a womanly magazine (such as the *Lady's Magazine*). Her manner of writing changes along with her changing perceptions of the city, since each place opens up new discursive spaces. Blessington's Paris is made of various modes of life, and so her relation is a compilation of various language modes and genres. It is best exemplified in the entries for July 1830, when she changes her style from that of a columnist describing Paris as the city of fashion into that of a journalist reporting it as the city of revolution.

Parisian circles were an indispensable part of the city's *beau monde* and would have been of interest to fine ladies. The Blessingtons were admitted to leading salons and they also invited guests to their place – the Hôtel Maréchal Ney, situated in the heart of Paris, near the Seine and the Tuileries Garden. The luxurious residence was visited by 'a vast number of guests, foreign princes and princesses, dukes and duchesses, counts and countesses, English ambassadors and men of title' (Molloy 1896, 1: 233). Rubbing shoulders with such personages, the countess could easily perfect her social and conversational skills. While she was learning herself, Blessington instructed her readers. A number of her entries take the form of a conduct book on Parisian sociability. 'Parisian society is very exclusive, and is divided into small coteries, into which a stranger finds it difficult to become initiated' (*IiF* 1: 267), we learn. She concentrates on the practice of salons run by 'certain ladies of distinction': once a week each lady invites to her place a group of acquaintances; no other lady interferes with the arrangements by organizing her own meeting at the same time. In consequence, the members of a given circle are continually 'in each other's society' (*IiF* 1: 268).

Blessington expands on the art of conversation, which is here 'the aim and object of society' (*IiF* 1: 188). She observes that in France conversation is 'an art successfully studied; to excel in which, not only much natural talent is required, but great fluency and a happy choice of words are indispensable' (*IiF* 1: 332). She advises her 'fair compatriots' to follow Frenchwomen's example on how to devote time to 'superficial acquisition of a versatility of knowledge', so that they may 'converse fluently on various subjects' (*IiF* 1: 333), instead of concentrating on their own pursuits, as she believes English women do. The main topics discussed at these meetings are 'literature, the fine arts and the general occurrences of the day' (*IiF* 1: 112). Avoidance of 'ill-natured remarks' but also 'a ceremoniousness of manners' and 'deferential respect from the men towards the women' are the main principles of conversation (*IiF* 1: 112).

One can observe and practice French manners and style of life not only when meeting at salons but also while walking in Parisian parks and gardens, which Blessington frequently reports doing. Her strolls in the Tuileries Garden, the Bois de Boulogne and the Luxembourg Garden, as well as the Avenue des Champs-Élysées, also become occasions to reflect on fashion, one of her pet subjects at the time. Blessington writes, 'Here Fashion is a despot, and no one dreams of evading its dictates' (*IiF* 1: 68). She observes that 'the promenaders look as if they only walked […] to display their tasteful dresses and persons' (*IiF* 1: 270). While walking in the parks, women 'eye each other', and it is visible that 'the beauty of a woman […] excites less envy in the minds of her own sex in France, than does the possession of a fine Cashmere' (*IiF* 1: 270–71).

Paris was far ahead of Italian cities when it came to fashion, and Blessington had no choice but to live up to its standards. On entering the city, she admits that 'everything belonging to [her] toilette is to be changed', since 'what the *modistes* of Italy declared to be *la dernière mode de Paris* is so old as to be forgotten here', and therefore, she immediately engages 'in the momentous occupation of shopping' (*IiF* 1: 64–65). The statement is by no means ironic, as she regularly takes tours through 'the houses of the *marchandes de modes* considered the most *recherché* at Paris' (*IiF* 1: 67). The noticeable profusion of French phrases betrays her cosmopolitan aspirations and enhances her authoritative position as a lady of fashion. Then she notes down the names of the shops and streets where she has bought her hats, gloves and fabrics. Sometimes she just goes window shopping; for example, when loitering through the Palais Royal and admiring exhibited bijouterie (*NtP* 108–9, 138). She reports being an idler in the fashionable Parisian streets, but is also a guide to her female readers. In her fashion columns, she provides them with information on prices, the quality of products and instructs them, somewhat ironically, how to develop impeccable taste: 'Be wise, then, ye young and fair, and if, as I suspect, your object be to please the Lords of the Creation, let your dress, in summer, be snowy-white muslin' (*IiF* 1: 186).

Her shopping sprees become an occasion to comment on marital issues, too, which might also be of interest to her readers. Some of the passages parody the manner of popular eighteenth-century conduct books. They provide mock-guidelines for wives, but also husbands, concerning their behaviour in social situations, such as shopping. She shows the differences between English and French marriage customs and advises honeymooners in Paris:

> Beware, O ye uxorious husbands! how ye bring your youthful brides to the dangerous atmosphere of Paris, while yet in that paradise of fools ycleped the honey-moon, ere you have learned to curve your brows into a frown, or to lengthen your visages at the sight of a long bill. (*IiF* 1: 69)

The parodic effect of such mockingly authoritative passages is achieved by an ironically lofty style with numerous archaic forms and pathetic expressions, by which she alludes to the language of old books of advice. She also invokes traditional rules of propriety and words of warning ('"beneath the roses fierce Repentance rears her snaky crest" in form of a bill'[2]). The epithets she uses to describe Paris (its 'dangerous atmosphere', 'paradise of fools', 'intoxicating city') perversely address common associations with moral corruption and hedonism (*IiF* 1: 69–70). In this way Blessington attempts to present Paris in line with its traditional representations while ridiculing them at the same time.

Among the places Blessington regularly attends are theatres and operas. She then devotes several pages to relate the occasions, providing the readers with the names of the theatres and most popular actors, as well as giving instructions concerning dress code and describing theatrical tastes. She devotes the most space to the descriptions of plays themselves, which take the form of reviews in which she summarizes the plot and pronounces her own judgements on various aspects of the play – acting, costumes, music and stage scenery. On one occasion she goes to *Henry III* to see one of the most popular actresses of the time perform on the stage. Though disappointed with the play herself, Blessington offers a well-balanced review to her readers:

> The crowd brought on the stage in *Henry III.*, though it adds to the splendour of the scenic effect, produces the confusion in the plot, as does also the vast number of names and titles introduced during the scenes, which fatigue the attention and defy the memory of the spectators [...] *Henry III.* has the most brilliant success, and, in despite of some faults, is full of genius, and the language is vigorous. Perhaps its very faults are attributed to an excess, rather than to a want, of power. (*IiF* 1: 313–14)

Blessington also devotes a lot of attention to the audience. Once she remarks, 'The Parisians are, I find, as addicted to staring as the English; for many wear the glasses levelled at [one of the celebrities]' (*IiF* 1: 157). She admits that she too, from her box 'in the centre of the house', observes the most distinguished persons present, whom she then introduces to her readers (*IiF* 1: 84, 323). She describes manners and reactions of the audience and tells anecdotes about incidents of improper behaviour (*IiF* 1: 314).

None of the places is visited by Blessington as often as the Louvre. She counts up being there 'at least thirty times', and this is the first place she goes to on her arrival in Paris in 1821. Bewildered by the multitude of rooms, she resolves to 'devote an hour or two to the Louvre every day' (*NtP* 92–93), and she soaks up the place's atmosphere, enjoying it more and more every day (*NtP* 97). Her walks through the museum galleries and in its gardens provoke essayistic reflections in her journal. On one occasion she 'lounges through a group of statues' and contemplates the beauty of their physiognomies and the calmness of their expressions (*IiF* 1: 280). In her musings, she lets herself be driven by emotions; for example, when meditating on the artists, she observes:

> There is something that stirs the soul and elevates the feelings, in gazing on these glorious productions of master minds [...]. What dreams must have been theirs, who thus portrayed all that the imagination can fancy of beautiful and sublime! How must their hearts have throbbed as the glowing images grew beneath their pencils, and a foretaste of the immortality they were laboring for was granted. (*IiI* 1: 32)

Unlike her role in other fragments in which she fashions herself as an art critic, here Blessington appeals to readers who have not necessarily studied art history and for whom paintings 'are to be felt, and not reasoned upon' (*IiI* 1: 32). Indeed, the thinker that emerges from the passage is mawkishly sentimental. Notwithstanding that fact, Blessington's passing remarks deserve a note of appreciation for, as Madden puts it, 'hav[ing] the merit of those short and memorable sayings, which get the name of maxims and apothegms' (Madden 1855, 1: 77). This is well exemplified when she observes that 'fine music, fine sculpture, and fine pictures gain by long acquaintance' (*IiI* 1: 31). The ability to combine anecdotal sketches of Parisian life along with 'brilliant and deep' reflections and with 'the *spirituel* of observant acumen' was appreciated by her reviewer in the magazine *The Mirror of Literature, Amusement and Instruction*, who assessed *The Idler in France* as 'rich beyond any other book of the season' (*Mirror of Literature* 1841, 28). The magazine regarded Blessington as a cosmopolitan and a seasoned authority and cited her commentaries on Parisian fashion, conversation, manners and opera (ibid., 26–31).

Paris also facilitated manifestations of Blessington's character traits that had not been revealed in her travel accounts until then. They were not only her femininity or witty irony but also depressive moods, especially as her style of writing changed considerably after her husband's sudden and unexpected death in May 1829, when she confined herself to the house and lost interest in the pettiness of city life (*IiF* 2: 97–98). In July 1830, in turn, four months before she was to leave Paris, for the first time during her Continental travels, history was happening before her eyes, and thus an opportunity occurred to present to her readers the writer's engagement in the current affairs of the city. Paris in the nineteenth century was, after all, as much the city of revolution as the city of fashion.

On the first day of the July Revolution (27 July 1830), she witnessed the change that Paris underwent – from the fashionable centre of the world to the revolutionary zone. 'Never did so great a change take place in the aspect of a city in so few hours!' she reflects, and then continues:

> Yesterday a business of life flowed on in its usual current. The bees and the drones of this vast hive were buzzing about, and the butterflies of fashion were expanding their gay wings in the sunshine. To-day the industrious and orderly seem frightened from their usual occupations, and scarcely a person of those termed fashionable is to be seen. (*IiF* 2: 150–51)

She compares the society of Paris to carefree butterflies and orderly bees and the city to a colourful and sunlit meadow. All of a sudden this vision is contrasted with 'the sound of firing', people 'rushing wildly through the streets', 'several persons […] killed by the military' and 'the mob [demolishing and breaking] into the shops' (*IiF* 2: 152).

The 'three glorious days' of the July Revolution are meticulously reported in the text. Usually neglectful about such details, this time she notes dates and thus combines the city's history with her own. She observes military mobilization and reports the main occurrences, linking them to particular places and streets of the city (*IiF* 2: 167). She positions herself close to the events, either observing them right from her window or driving through the streets.³ She is also informed about the course of the revolution by other eyewitnesses – her servants and acquaintances (*IiF* 2: 154). Blessington's account is a factual documentation of the actual events in Paris at the time. However, the manner in which this revolutionary city is portrayed does not at all pretend to be objective; it is presented from her feminine point of view.

Blessington clearly attempts to touch an emotional nerve in her female readers, and accordingly, tension gradually builds up in her entries. After the first day of 'confusion and alarm' (*IiF* 2: 152), she reflects: 'All now seems quiet, so I will go to bed. Heaven only knows if to-morrow night we may be allowed to seek our pillows in safety' (*IiF* 2: 158). The following morning, on 28 July, she learns about barricades erected during the night and observes the bodies of those killed on the previous day displayed on 'the streets in order to excite still more the angry feelings of the people' (*IiF* 2: 158). To appeal to her readers' imagination, she compares these events to 'the fearful and memorable Revolution of former days' (*IiF* 2: 158–59).

On the second day, Blessington finds herself in the centre of the revolutionary city. She ventures into the very streets where the main events happen, an act that is not expected of a woman. She presents herself as performing a 'manly' role demanding courage and self-confidence. Seemingly, this is her greatest adventure ever, as she continuously boasts about her courage: 'I shall begin to consider myself half a heroine, after an exploit I performed this evening' (*IiI* 2: 170). Entering the public (revolutionary) sphere, Blessington risks being seen as rejecting the domestic ideology she supports on other occasions. Yet, all along, she makes sure she observes the proprieties expected of her as an English lady, as if in accord with the tendency among women travel writers to, as Frawley observes, 'satisfy the demands of a public simultaneously attracted to adventure but expecting and exacting the domestic' (Frawley 1994, 129).

Blessington's manner of writing is reminiscent of nineteenth-century Parisian urban narratives which, as Priscilla Ferguson observes, concentrated on the experience of the revolution: 'Revolution on the street, revolution on the page – the two were inevitably found together' (Ferguson 1994, 4). To represent her tangible contact with the urban space, Blessington applies vocabulary designating movement along the streets: having 'sallied forth' and 'traversed' a short distance, she 'arrived at the barricade' which seemed insurmountable, and she was about to 'retrace [her] steps', but on hearing shouts approaching, she in the end 'clambered up' the barricade (*IiF* 2: 170–71). She also notes down the names of the streets she takes and the buildings she passes:

> I left the Rue d'Anjou, and had reached the Rue Verte, when I heard the report of guns, and saw a party of soldiers attacking the barracks [...] I retraced my steps as hastily as possible, fear lending swiftness to my feet, and returned to the Rue de Matignon by the Faubourg du Roule and the Rue St. Honoré. (*IiF* 2: 204)

Blessington is an idler, an urban rambler exploring the streets of Paris, attuning herself to its revolutionary reality and seeking adventure. Yet she is not a flâneur – a spontaneous, free, anonymous observer of the Parisian streets. First of all, she does not amble through the city without purpose, but makes her way straight to the hotel where her friend stays. She thus explains the purpose of her expedition: 'I do not think I should have risked it, had I not known how much my excellent friend [...] stood in need of consolation' (*IiF* 2: 200). She seems confident that such a motivation, probably unreasonable to men, would be perfectly understandable to her more empathic women readers. Second, she is not walking on her own but is accompanied by her male servant. She must have been aware that it would be very inappropriate for a woman to walk through the streets on her own. This is because of the popular dialectical reasoning in the nineteenth century, according to which a female counterpart to 'the male stroller's alienated self' was 'the figure of the fallen woman, the woman of the streets' (Nord 1995, 2–3). This is the reason she cannot explore the city without being noticed. She does make an attempt to conceal her aristocratic status by attiring herself 'as simpl[y] as possible' (*IiF* 2: 170), but, notwithstanding her disguise, she still stands out from the crowd as she is a woman and is attended by her footman, 'this symbol of aristocracy' (*IiF* 2: 178).

In nineteenth-century narratives of urban experience, Deborah Nord argues, a male flâneur 'required anonymity and the camouflage of the crowd to move with impunity and to exercise the privilege of the gaze', while 'the too-noticeable female stroller could never enjoy that position' (Nord 1995, 4). Being aware that her femininity and class expose her to the curiosity of the crowd, Blessington does not even attempt to melt into it. On the contrary, she looks upon herself as 'a woman and a stranger [...] in the streets, on foot, in a city declared to be in a stage of a siege' (*IiF* 2: 172). While on her way she shuns people, perceiving them as a threat. The words she uses to designate them have negative connotations: 'mob', 'stragglers' (*IiF* 2: 167, 171). The people lack any distinctive features, being part of the revolutionary masses. Even though Blessington's intention is to observe the revolutionaries by herself, so that her readers would perceive her as a credible reporter, in this situation she feels it is the revolutionaries who are staring back at her.

The streets occupied by revolutionaries are presented by Blessington as a wild zone where no rules apply. Like Naples, it is a city of boundaries, which she either chooses to cross or not – the walls between her peaceful home and the revolutionary city, the limits of her courage and the boundaries of propriety. She positions herself in both physical and moral danger, since Parisian streets were believed to welcome transgressions. Nevertheless, Blessington does not enjoy the freedom and sticks to her ideals. She relates a scene that implies sexual impropriety against her: on her way she encounters 'ill-dressed and riotous men' who are watching her and holding a cord across the street so that she could not pass, laughing, daring her to 'leap over the barrier' while still drawing the rope higher (*IiF* 2: 176–77). Typical of nineteenth-century women's travel writing, sexual attack is not verbalized here, but instead 'it constitutes a presence which makes itself felt by its absence' (Foster and Mills 2002, 173–74). This is because, as Foster and Mills argue, 'the fault would lie with the woman herself if she reported the fear of sexual impropriety, and would perhaps draw attention to the problematic nature of her travelling' (ibid.). Though the circumstances might appear dubious, Blessington cannot be accused of provoking the situation. She proudly relates how she pre-empted what could have happened. Though already trembling, Blessington thus reacts to the men's 'rude mirth': 'I felt sure Frenchmen would not compel me to such an unfeminine exertion, or give me cause to tell my compatriots when I returned to England that deference to women no longer existed in France' (*IiF* 2: 177).

The way she deals with the situation reinforces her respectability, since she presents herself as able to use her self-confidence, lady-like manners and her national identity to avoid sexual attack. This is emphasized when she recalls the men's answer: 'Let her pass! let her pass! [...] she is courageous and she speaks rightly. *Vive les Anglaises! Vive les Anglaises!*' (*IiF* 2: 177). Only after having the door closed after her, does she confess, 'Now that I find myself once more within the sanctuary of my home, I am surprised at my own courage in having ventured to pass through the streets' (*IiF* 2: 200). In the end, the aim of presenting herself as crossing a boundary into the immoral public sphere is to manifest her alignment to the position of the English moral paragon. She is conscious of the facet of Paris as a city of excess and moral transgression, and she needs to beware, as it might destroy her hard-earned position. This, however, does not stop her from at least alluding to the danger, since the more destabilizing the city appears to her readers, the more willingly they might come to appreciate the appropriateness of her conduct. Just as in Naples, here Blessington is a tourist for whom, to use Chard's words, 'travel is a form of personal adventure, holding out the promise of a discovery or realisation of the self through the exploration of the other', but who manages 'to keep the more dangerous and destabilizing aspects of the encounter with the foreign at bay' (Chard 1999, 11).

***

Part III of this book has illustrated the relation between Blessington's created selves and the cities she visited and represented in her texts. This relation is two-sided. On the one hand, it is the cities of unique character that influence their visitors and impart to them their own peculiar identity. This is what happens during her stay in Rome, Venice and Paris. Of all Italian cities, Rome and Venice are the ones with the 'strongest imaginative associations' (Sweet 2012, 199). Blessington seems well prepared for what she encounters there, yet they still stupefy her. They are the cities of glorious past and ruinous present, which both disappoint her and meet her expectations (*IiI* 3: 102–3). From Blessington's depictions of Venice and Rome emerges a truly Romantic traveller and writer, who both draws on the literary tradition and becomes part of it. In turn, Paris's cultural identity as a city of fashion helps Blessington to win recognition among her countrymen back in London. Relating her stay in Paris, Blessington presents herself as a lady of fashion and a journal columnist, thus satisfying the demands of the public desirous of learning about the Parisian *beau monde.*

On the other hand, each city may stand for something different for each traveller and, as Frawley argues, women's travel accounts in particular 'were less studies of place […] than studies of woman's position in the foreign place' (Frawley 1994, 104). Blessington's accounts of Genoa, Naples and to some extent Paris are the projection of her personal experiences as well as aspirations. This time it is she as a writer who encodes the cities so that they would give her 'unique opportunities for personal identification' (Schlaeger 1999, 63). Genoa is presented by Blessington as an exceptional city in which all typical sightseeing sites are outshined by the places associated with Lord Byron. Blessington assumes the position of a guide to the poet's haunts as well as his companion, not to say a soulmate. In Naples, she experiences that the city indeed possesses 'a dangerous frisson combined with seductive beauty' (Sweet 2012, 164). Altogether, however, she manages to appropriate this space and combine the English ideal of the proper lady of the house with her ambition to enter the public sphere by becoming a salonnière. In this respect, Blessington's rendition of Naples may be compared with that of Paris, which is the city giving her a true sense of adventure, as she participates in its history, happening before her eyes.

CONCLUSION

The catalyst for this book was the conviction that Marguerite Blessington merited scholarly attention as a travel writer. In the introductory survey of the literature on Blessington, I indicated that even though the author herself has been revived in recent years, and her writing and editorial activity have become of interest to scholars, her travel texts have been largely neglected. *The Idler in Italy* and *The Idler in France* have been appreciated as sources of information on the writer's life; however, they have not yet been thoroughly discussed as literary texts. What is more, *A Tour in the Isle of Wight, in the Autumn of 1820* and *Journal of a Tour through the Netherlands to Paris, in 1821* have been almost completely ignored. This book thus offered the first detailed analysis of Blessington's all four travel accounts, which represent the transitional period between the 1820s and the 1840s, reflecting both Romantic ideas and the pre-Victorian reality of England.

Ann R. Hawkins observes that 'Blessington's problem in the complicated world of London society was to find a stance or a series of personae that would allow her a place to speak' (Hawkins 2003a). Even though her travel accounts maintain the appearance of personal journalizing, clearly Blessington was composing them with her London readers in mind. In this book, I have claimed that travel experience and travel writing offered Blessington endless opportunities to reshape her public personae. In the writer's own words: 'We are all influenced by the scene in which we find ourselves placed; and like the chameleon, whose body assumes the hue of whatever is near it, our minds borrow a colour from the objects that surround us' (*IiI* 3: 174).

Such a self-reflexive and bold statement nevertheless would have been unthinkable on the threshold of her travel experiences. In the chapters making up Part I of this book, I indicated a clear demarcation line between *A Tour in the Isle of Wight, in the Autumn of 1820* and *Journal of a Tour through the Netherlands to Paris, in 1821*, on the one hand, and *The Idler in Italy* and *The Idler in France*, published almost 20 years later, on the other. The paratexts and texts proper of Blessington's two early travel accounts reveal her endeavours to be admitted to the circle of travel writers, which was not easy, since she was a novice and a woman. Therefore, she resolved to abide by the recognized conventions of the previous century, which was the only way to convince her potential readers of the truthfulness of her accounts. One of the conventions was adopting the form of the autobiographical journal without bringing herself to the forefront. Moreover, she adopted such common practices among women writers as admitting, justifying and apologizing for the 'amateurish' character of her texts. Nevertheless, in *Journal of a Tour through the Netherlands to Paris, in 1821* the writer's self-justification becomes a subtle means of self-assertion, and she hints at both instructive and pleasurable qualities of her text, the blending of which was an ambition of eighteenth-century travel writers. From the journals a proper female traveller, chaperoned by her male companion, emerges, one who traditionally follows the beaten Continental path, but who also assumes the position of a picturesque traveller on the home tour.

In contrast, the author of the *Idlers* was no longer an aspiring author but a well-established writer and a cultural celebrity. In their paratexts there are a number of techniques geared towards profiting from Blessington's iconic position. From the texts proper, in turn, an author emerges who has become much more self-assured in terms of her manner of writing, and who only selectively abides by the received conventions of travel writing. The writer follows the pattern of the nonfictional travel account and aspires to both instruct and entertain the reader; however, unlike her writing in her early journals, she manifests their autobiographical character, by which she foregrounds her self as impinging on her travels and travel writing. In the *Idlers*, Blessington makes the best of the potential of travel writing to facilitate self-promotion. Her status is reinforced with each volume of the *Idlers* and extolled with every strategy she employs, among which is her exploitation of the fictional formula of the fashionable novel.

Following the guidelines of the then-popular fashionable novel, Blessington manifests her writing skills and enhances her social identity by proving that she thoroughly knows the life of the upper class. Moreover, taking advantage of this literary genre, Blessington renders her travel accounts more enjoyable by taking up some of the popular plots and characters, and thus increasing the readership of her accounts among novel readers. Making Byron a protagonist of her narrative and building a story around their acquaintance was a particularly well-thought marketing strategy, since not only did it enliven the account but also, in a manner similar to the poet's own texts, gave the readers 'a brief span of participation, of imaginary companionship' with the poet (Schmid 2002, 80). Finally, just as fashionable novels did, the fiction-like sections of the *Idlers* provide readers with instructions by dealing with the problems of contemporary society, with the difference that here, rather than moral misdeeds, Blessington condemns the vices of the English as well as improper behaviours and attitudes of English travellers to the Continent. Characterizing her writing and publishing practices, O'Cinneide observes that the fact that Blessington was excluded by the members of her own class made it easier for her to take a broader look and address the problems of the whole nation when approaching seemingly individual matters (O'Cinneide 2008, 4, 59).

Lovell observes that Blessington's books became for her 'a very special means of communication' with her countrymen, providing her with the only way of convincing them of 'what she really was: a woman of education, refinement, taste, and very high moral standards' (Lovell 1969, *20*). This idea served as a point of departure for the chapters constituting Part II of the book. Blessington's travel accounts include a number of passages which I called word paintings. Sketching landscapes with words, the writer demonstrates her proficiency at aesthetic conventions so acknowledged by her countrymen. Moreover, she frequently refers to the landscape painters most acclaimed at the time and seems to have modelled her descriptions on their paintings, so that her readers would appreciate the artistic value of her travel texts.

My readings of Blessington's picture-like passages demonstrated the writer's attempt to represent herself as an artistically literate travel writer with a proper taste in landscape. Nevertheless, I also pointed out that at times she goes beyond the conventions of the Gilpinian picturesque and is drawn more towards the Romantic aesthetic of the terrible and the sublime, which appeal more to imagination and sensitivity. I further argued that when depicting the scenery of southern Italy, the writer both shows an inclination towards the language of Burkean beauty and reveals her appreciation of the local people as adding to the aesthetic value of her word paintings.

I also discerned the writer's wavering between several standpoints in the passages devoted to architecture. In a manner similar to her depictions of natural scenery, in some excerpts she assumes the role of a learned connoisseur and a matter-of-fact classical scholar attempting to share her specialist knowledge of architecture but also convincing the readers of her credibility by means of detailed ekphrases. On other occasions, however, when writing about architecture and its remains she reveals her inclination towards Romantic connoisseurship. When depicting ancient ruins, Classical and Gothic architecture she refers to the categories of the beautiful and the sublime and is prone to spontaneous writing and artistic expressionism, since they evoke in her not only aesthetic but also spiritual sensations.

Blessington's preoccupation with aesthetic matters is also apparent in the way she visualizes the sacred art and religious practices of the foreign countries. As a rule, the writer approaches Roman Catholicism from a typical English standpoint. She treats Italian religious art as an epitome of high culture and wishes to make the most of it. On the other hand, she is confirmed in her anti-Catholic views when it comes to doctrines and practices. Interestingly, though Irish Catholic by birth, she uses Catholicism to assert her assumed identity as

English. As a consequence, on many occasions she feels compelled to assume the position of a detached observer so that her state of aesthetic elation would not transform into a spiritual one. In order to distance herself from Catholic ritualism, the writer foregrounds its performative – that is, unnatural – character. Her uneasiness concerning various aspects of Roman Catholicism does not stop Blessington from dwelling on them, and the feelings that accompany her vacillate between attraction and aversion.

In responding to the visual, Blessington attempts to unite taste with sensibility. She manifests her awareness of aesthetic discourses prevailing in the late eighteenth and early nineteenth centuries. She enters into a dialogue with them and incorporates their rules to demonstrate her refined taste, equal to that of her male counterparts, and thus appeal to her English readership. Her sensibility, in turn, emerges when she draws on the aesthetic of the Gothic romance, but it also manifests itself each time she goes beyond the above-mentioned conventions. It happens when she spontaneously enthuses over landscapes, sympathizes with foreigners, ponders over ancient ruins, is moved by sacred art, and when she searches for the Romantic, the exhilarating and the spiritual.

In each of the chapters of Part III, I argued that Blessington exploited popular visions of Continental cities so that her readers would have particular associations with her. I pointed out that the choice of Genoa – the last Italian residence of Byron before his death – as the first thoroughly described Italian city was deliberate, since Blessington was able to capitalize on her position as 'Byron's Boswell', which she had gained thanks to her famous *Conversations of Lord Byron*. In her recollections of the city, she adopts the same strategy of 'trading on the name of Byron', as Lovell puts it (1969, 95). The city is represented through their relationship – the narrator gives details of the poet, yet what she records of him refers also to her. Thus the reader is being convinced that Blessington was not only Byron's biographer but a highly regarded intimate, the privilege enjoyed by but a few of his countrymen, even if she at times distances herself from his critical views of England.

For Blessington, England remained the main point of reference throughout her travels, a fact that I underlined in the analysis of her recollection of Naples. This time the city is represented as a space that the traveller assumes in accordance with her English standards. She records the process of establishing herself as the proper English lady of her Italian house, thus manifesting her attachment to the emerging Victorian ideals of feminine propriety and domesticity. I also argued that the narrator inscribed within the account of Naples is constructed as an 'Anglo–Italian' and a salonnière. Namely, she appreciates the unconfined lifestyle of the foreigners, takes interest in those belonging to lower classes, yet surrounds herself with the most distinguished ones and aligns herself with their intellectual openness.

Whereas in Naples Blessington is disposed to foreground her social and cultural personae, Rome and Venice offer her the experience of a literary tourist and participation in their intertextual constitution as a travel writer. I demonstrated that Rome turns out to be beyond Blessington's writing capabilities; she cannot view and reflect on it differently than by continuously referring to Byron's visions of the city. The narrator follows in Childe Harold's footsteps and assumes the same role of a melancholic Romantic standing among the ancient ruins. Venice, in turn, inspires in her a whole spectrum of ideas; here she herself becomes an artist searching for and reflecting on the city's magic, which impinged on the imagination of innumerable artists before and after her. She thus manifests not only her immersion in the literary tradition but also her becoming part of it.

Finally, I argued that Paris is recorded as a city in which Blessington balanced between the public and private spheres of her life. Taking advantage of the city's cosmopolitan character, she represents herself as a lady of fashion, salonnière and participant in cultural and sociable gatherings. Recollecting her husband's death, in turn, she assumes the position of an exemplary wife, confined to her house to bewail her loss. Then, during the revolution, she plays the role of an adventuress, venturing out in the city, yet within the boundaries of English propriety. In terms of the manner of writing, the narrator is mostly constructed as a journalist providing her readers with the news of the fashionable world, instructing them in French manners and reporting on the course of the revolution.

The point worth mentioning in this place concerns the relation between Blessington's representations of foreign cities and her national identity, which, though not straightforward, is implicit throughout the accounts. One of the consequences of travel is a re-evaluation of one's national identity and thus one's attitude towards the homeland. Born in Ireland, Blessington spent most of her adult life in England, and therefore this country becomes her point of reference. When leaving England, she records being filled with sadness at 'quitting home for indefinite period' (*IiI* 1: 1), yet what she also felt was resentment towards her countrymen. Blessington's acquaintance with Byron reinforced these feelings. In a way, she shared with him the fate of an exile, especially as he, too, remained in the shade of scandal, which their countrymen refused to forget. Nevertheless, they both could not resist the compulsion to dwell on the circles of English society, their common acquaintances as well as enemies. Naples is defined in relation to London, as she manages to appropriate the city to such an extent that it feels like home to her. On the other hand, the city offered spontaneous freedom to her, which she had been forbidden in London, and thus she might thrive there as a salonnière, surrounded by those who esteemed her. Recounting her stay in Rome and then in Venice, in turn, Blessington leans towards a greater appreciation of her country, as she is indebted to the English literary tradition that enriched her experience of the cities; through her writing, she wishes to be numbered among the English Romantics. In Paris, the last city before her return to London, Blessington attempts to appeal to English ladies, who, after all, ostracized her the most, in order to win their recognition. Notwithstanding her efforts, she dreads that 'in England [she] shall have again to acquire the hard lesson of resignation' (*IiF* 2: 249).

The author's self-fashioning in travel writing may be approached from various perspectives. This book dealt predominantly with social and cultural aspects of identity, also drawing on issues of nationality and femininity. I traced Blessington's predilection for constructing diverse images of herself through her travel writing, depending on the circumstances she found herself in. The early travel journals foreground the personae of a chaperoned woman traveller and a novice writer because these facets would allow her admission to the genre of travel writing, whereas the mature travel narratives present her to the public as indeed the most gorgeous lady on the tour and a seasoned travel writer with the purpose of solidifying her position as a celebrity.

I attempted to show that Blessington's travel texts well represent the reality of travel writing in the period in question. The writer assumes a number of personae in each text by many means, such as constructing the narrator in a particular way, balancing between authenticity and fiction, exploiting diverse literary genres, engaging in dominant aesthetic discourses, responding to other travel texts and following the contemporary trends in tourism. Therefore, the texts reflect the evolution of the travel writing genre in the first half of the nineteenth century from predominantly non-personal travel accounts aiming at pleasurable instruction to multifaceted texts geared towards promoting their authors. As this book evidenced, the indefinable and mutable form of travel writing only favoured Blessington's self-fashioning.

It was the texts themselves that suggested the directions of my argument, and in consequence some issues turned out to be beyond its scope. This book clearly diverged from some dominant tendencies in feminist criticism of women's travel writing, though it did approach the texts as authored by a woman when indicating the extent to which they were governed by literary conventions as well as by social and cultural proprieties. When it comes to national aspects, I argued throughout that Blessington identifies herself as English; therefore, the relation between her Irish origin and her travel experience was only touched upon here. These issues may pose new possibilities for future studies. I hope that this book has set an example of a new critical look at Blessington's literary output, and that the texts discussed herein will no longer be omitted from the studies of women's travel writings.

NOTES

Preface

1. As we learn, for example, from George Barnett Smith's *Women of Renown. Nineteenth Century Studies*, Blessington's travel books were far more successful than her novels (Smith 1893, 77).
2. It is worth mentioning that the first volume of *The Idler in Italy* covers the journey from Dover to Genoa through France, and the two volumes of *The Idler in France*, except for the first 60 pages of the first volume, are devoted exclusively to Paris.
3. Though, as Hawkins and Kraver observe, in the 1861 edition of the book Chorley's tone changes to 'sympathetic' (Hawkins and Kraver 2005, ix). Hawkins also points out that Blessington's contemporaries would learn about her mostly from gossipy articles in magazines and mentions in publications by other personalities (Hawkins 2012, 51).
4. A moderate contribution to the field was made by Edith Clay and Sir Harold Acton, who wrote a short preface (Clay 1979a, 9–19) and introduction (Acton 1979, 3–8) to the 1979 edition of Blessington's *Neapolitan Journals*.
5. The chapter devoted to Blessington is entitled 'Travels of a Lady of Fashion: The Literary Career of Lady Blessington (1789–1849)'.
6. A note on Blessington is also included in Volume 5 of *The Field Day Anthology of Irish Writing* by Angela Bourke (2002, 893–94) and *The Longman Companion to Victorian Fiction* by John Sutherland (2014, 69–70). Blessington's only novel republished in our times is *The Victims of Society*, preceded by a comprehensive introduction by Ann R. Hawkins and Jeraldine Kraver (2005).
7. This text has been the subject of study for Richard Cronin in *Romantic Victorians. English Literature, 1824–1840* (2002, 21–26) and James Soderholm in *Fantasy, Forgery, and the Byron Legend* (1996, 132–62).
8. Blessington's silver fork novels are also discussed by Alison Adburgham in Chapter XVII of *Silver Fork Society. Fashionable Life and Literature from 1814 to 1840* (2012).
9. Schmid's study was preceded by the work of Prudence Hannay (1980), who also concentrated on Blessington's salons.
10. Hawkins's texts that are referred to here are the following (in chronological order): '"Formed with Curious Skill": Blessington's Negotiation of the "Poetess" in *Flowers of Loveliness*' (2003a); 'Marguerite, Countess of Blessington, and L. E. L. (Letitia Elizabeth Landon): Evidence of a Friendship' (2003b); and 'Marketing Gender and Nationalism: Blessington's *Gems of Beauty/L'Écrin* and the Mid-Century Book Trade' (2005).
11. She is also listed among women writers in *Travel Writing and the Female Imaginary* (Fortunati et al. 2001, 8), and D. C. Woodcox comments on her travel writing in *British*

Travel Writers, 1837–1875: Victorian Period (1996, 50–54). However, Blessington is not included in such recent publications devoted to women's travel writing as Kathryn Walchester's '*Our Own Fair Italy*': *Nineteenth Century Women's Travel Writing and Italy 1800– 1844* (2007) or Clare Broome Saunders's *Women, Travel Writing and Truth* (2014).

12 See the chapter 'Frances Trollope, Lady Blessington and French Salon Culture' (Pauk 2008, 71–127).
13 By way of explanation, Florence, which would otherwise merit attention in this context, is not included here, as Blessington's pursuit there was mostly the appreciation of art and the cultivation of her taste, and I address these issues in Part II. Paris is the only non-Italian city covered in this part since, during her eight-year journey on the Continent, Blessington spent six years in Italy and only two in France.

Introduction

1 As John Pemble observes, by the end of the nineteenth century more women than men traveled to southern Europe (Pemble 1988, 77).
2 Scholars such as Chloe Chard point out that the idea of the Grand Tour lasted well into the1830s (Chard 1999, 11).
3 Mary Shelley mentions this in the essay 'The English in Italy' (1990, 342) and in her *Rambles in Germany and Italy* (1844, 1: vii). Anna Jameson even set herself the goal of reading only in Italian while there (Brand 1957, 18).
4 Barbara Pauk observes that Trollope's actual experiences may have differed from their representation in the text (Pauk 2011, 258–59).
5 To read more on Costello's travels and travel writing, see Saunders 2015, 137–62.
6 As Barbara Korte suggests, since the eighteenth century the enjoyment of landscape had been the main reason for making home tours (Korte 2000, 77).
7 In the same vein, 20 years later, Frances Trollope wrote of the air of 'picturesque perfection' that the Italian women have about them (Trollope 1842, 245–46).
8 For instance, women writers would resort to the same self-protective strategies as their predecessors (McAllister 1988, 9), which is well exemplified by the preface to Marianne Bailie's *First Impressions on a Tour upon the Continent in the Summer of 1818* (1819, v–viii).
9 This is what Kathryn Walchester, among others, points out in women's writing about Italy in the first half of the nineteenth century (see Walchester 2007, 22–24). In any case, contemporary critics have been very careful about categorizing women's travel writing throughout history, because of countless divergences in the authors' life situations and travel destinations (Bassnett 2002, 228, 239)
10 Travel writers frequently express the point when commencing their accounts; see, for example, Frances Trollope's *A Visit to Italy* (1842, 1–2) or Mary Shelley's *Rambles* (1844, 1: vii–viii, x).
11 It was particularly useful in the case of texts dealing with Italy – the most often described destination – for example, Catherine Taylor's *Letters from Italy to a Younger Sister* (1840).
12 In doing so they were greatly inspired by Germaine de Staël's *Corinne, or Italy* (1807).
13 In contrast, in *A Visit to Italy* Trollope follows the personal mode, as in the preface she expresses her intention 'to gossip a little about this Italy' (1842, 1, 2).
14 The title of *The Wild Irish Girl* was exposed on the book's cover to lure the readers. I will expand on Colburn's techniques of promoting his publications in Chapter 1. He also published Anna Jameson's *Diary of an Ennuyée* in 1826.

15 *Paris and the Parisians* (1836) was published by Richard Bentley, who continued Colburn's profitable business. Its title page included the information about Trollope's previous travel writings.
16 In the latest biography, Matoff refers to Blessington's baptism certificate to prove that she was born in 1788 (Matoff 2016, 11). In the past, Blessington's date of birth was unclear, and her biographers and critics listed the date as 1788, 1789 or 1790.
17 That Lady Blessington had been to Paris at least once before the Continental journey is evidenced in her travel account (*NtP* 117–19).
18 According to some sources, it was 1816 when they met for the first time (Smith 1893, 51; Clay 1979b, 152).
19 'Smelfungus' was Tobias Smollett's derogatory nickname invented by Laurence Sterne, who first used it in his *A Sentimental Journey through France and Italy*, published in 1768 (Sterne 2002, 37). Sterne criticized Smollett for his highly irritating complaints about France and Italy (expressed in his *Travels through France and Italy* from 1766). Ever since, the name was used generically to refer to travellers prone to complaints and dissatisfaction.
20 This we find out from Sadleir (1947, 52, 55). In *The Idler in Italy* there is no mention of Count D'Orsay joining their household.
21 In Naples the Blessingtons' household was joined by another member – Charles James Mathews, Lady Blessington's friend's son. During their stay in Naples, Lord Blessington went to London and Ireland and brought Charles with him. The countess does not mention it in her account. What she does mention is that in May 1824 they received the news of Lord Byron's death (*IiI* 2: 379).
22 Madden recorded their arrival in Rome in December (Madden 1855, 1: 125), whereas Molloy in November 1827 (Molloy 1896, 1: 208). Lady Blessington wrote evasively: "ROME.– Arrived from Florence last night […] (*IiI* 2: 517).
23 At the time Hortense bore the title of the Duchess de Saint–Leu, and Jerome the title of the Prince of Montfort.
24 In Queen Hortense's house Blessington also talked for the first time to Countess Guiccioli (*IiI* 2: 563).
25 When leaving Rome she visited the graves of Sir William Drummond, Shelley and Keats.
26 A number of insinuating texts appeared in a London newspaper called the *Age* (see Molloy 1896, 1: 253, 258–59; Sadleir 1947, 118–19)
27 The journey back to London is not recorded by Blessington and not mentioned by her biographers either.
28 The case in question was the assumed romance of Lady Blessington with Count D'Orsay, which was rumoured to have forced Harriet to abandon her husband in 1831.
29 The two-volume *Works of Lady Blessington* was published in Philadelphia in 1838 and was followed by other publications by German and French publishers.
30 It was within the property of the Duke and Duchess de Gramont, her friends. In 1852, Count D'Orsay was buried next to her in the same vault.

Chapter 1: Paratexts

1 Blessington was identified as the author of the journal in John Martin's *Bibliographical Catalogue of Privately Printed Books* (Martin 1854, 299), as well as in Robert Harding

Evans's *Catalogue of the curious, choice and valuable library of the late Sir Francis Freeling, Bart. F.S.A.* (1836, 95). Blessington corresponded with Sir Francis Freeling and presented him with her books, which she inscribed.

2   In the text proper she writes, for instance: 'I would advise the traveler, who studies his accommodation on this road, to make his arrangements so as to […] sleep at Lisle' (*NtP* 39). The statement suggests that she considered the possibility that some travelers might use her journal as a preparatory guide.

3   Batten's claim is that in the first decades of the nineteenth century there were either purely entertaining travel accounts or instructive travel guides (Batten 1978, 29–30).

4   I have not managed to identify Blessington's source for the epigram – *Hints to Travellers*.

5   They do not reveal the time of the journeys, supposedly not to draw readers' attention to the fact that the gap between the tours and the publication of the accounts is about ten years (Schmid 2013, 146).

6   Maria H. Frawley acknowledges in her study that it was Marguerite Blessington who made the persona of an idle traveller 'popular in 1839 with the publication of *The Idler in Italy*' (Frawley 1994, 49, 82). In the same vein, Giuliana Bruno writes that 'a tradition of idleness was established by Marguerite, Countess of Blessington' (Bruno 2007, 388). Frances Elliot wrote in the same manner and might have modelled the title of her travel account – *The Diary of an Idle Woman in Italy* (1871) – on Blessington's account. The notion of idleness in Blessington's *Idlers* will be discussed later on.

7   Blessington repeats an almost identical confession in the second volume, in which, furthermore, there are numerous comments on idleness when she describes Naples, and her attitude towards this disposition is not always the same (*IiI* 2: 119).

8   'He was aiming for the aristocratic Mayfair carriage trade. He played on his customers' perceived snobbery by offering memoirs authored by members of their own class' (Melnyk 2002, 37).

9   They knew each other from her salon. Other writers asked Blessington to intercede for them with Colburn.

10 The reviewers also cite Blessington's sketches of Parisian fashions and Neapolitan customs, which would be of interest to the general public (*New Monthly Magazine* March 1839, 420; *Literary Gazette* March 2 1839, 130–31).

Chapter 2: From Life to Text

1   At one point she also typically criticizes 'certain romantic ladies' for 'their solitary rambles in search of adventures' (*IoW* 60–61).

2   This is what Mary Shelley did in her *Rambles*, writing: 'A date or reference may be put down; but during a voyage, I am at first too interested, and then too tired; and at night, on arriving, I confess, supper and the ceremonial of retiring to rest, are exertions almost too much for me: I cannot do more' (Shelley 1844, 1: 155). As Ożarska argues, this passage is illustrative of Shelley's tendency to 'challenge' generic requirements (Ożarska 2013b, 40).

3   However, the writer is very elusive about some of her travel companions and family matters, the revelation of which would have left her open to criticism.

4   The concepts of the historical 'I' (the writer), the narrating 'I' (the narrator), the narrated 'I' (the protagonist) and the ideological 'I' (culturally determined personhood) are used here in accord with Smith and Watson (2010, 72–78). The ideological 'I' is a particularly relevant notion for this book, as it, in a way, conceptualizes my general

objectives. As Smith and Watson argue, 'Historical and ideological notions of the person provide cultural ways of understanding the material location of subjectivity, the relationship of the person to particular others and to a collectivity of others [...]; the importance of social location; the motivations for human actions' (2010, 76). Even when I do not invoke the term itself, so as not to overtheorize, I am in fact addressing Blessington's ideological 'I' whenever I comment on the way she fashions her identity through writing.
5 Three out of the four headings concern Lord Byron.
6 At one point, for example, she quotes three anecdotes 'detailing the ignorance of these [her] compatriots', and comments that she has met 'innumerable' Englishmen like these ones (*IiI* 2: 465–66).
7 Borm also distinguishes the genre of the travel book as a non-fictional travel account. He defines it as 'any narrative characterized by a non-fiction dominant that relates (almost always) in the first person a journey or journeys that the reader supposes to have taken place in reality while assuming or presupposing that author, narrator, and principal character are but one or identical' (Borm 2004, 17).

Chapter 3: Fictional Strategies

1 See also, for example, *IiF* 1: 1.
2 For instance, in Blessington's *The Repealers*, the Countess of Jersey is given the name of the Countess of Guernsey.
3 To read on the popularity of the theme, see Labbe (2010, 48).
4 The techniques of the novelist were useful to reconcile the poet's contradictory facets, and, just as in her *Conversations*, she is capable of representing him as the one who was at the same time admired and laughed at (Cronin 2002, 23–24).
5 Following Matthew Whiting Rosa, April Kendra distinguishes between two subcategories of the silver fork novel – the masculine 'dandy novel' and the feminine 'society novel' (Kendra 2003, 59–60).
6 The account of Blessington's stay in Genoa is discussed in detail in Chapter 7.
7 Blessington's choice is unlike, for example, that of Anna Jameson, who turned herself into the protagonist of her *Diary of an Ennuyée*, which helped her establish herself as a celebrity (Orr 1998, 10). That Blessington did not want to be the protagonist of her own story is evidenced by the fact that she hardly ever mentions another dandy accompanying her – Count D'Orsay – with whom readers would surely connect her.

Chapter 4: Natural Sceneries

1 This is suggested by such passages as the following: 'I should have enjoyed the voyage very much; but a cold autumnal breeze is a bad auxiliary to the picturesque [...]. To enjoy fine scenery, fine weather is an absolute requisite' (*IoW* 7). I believe it is worth noting here that the characters of Blessington's fashionable novels who travel, either in Britain or on the Continent, are also presented as scenic travellers. When they encounter admirable scenery, the action is halted and the narrator presents the view they behold, which influences their state of mind. Scenes from *The Repealers*, whose characters travel to Ireland (Blessington 1838, 302), and from *The Two Friends*, during the characters' stay in Italy may serve as examples (ibid., 25, 42, 52).

2 Before depicting her first view of Marseilles, Blessington defines travelling as 'multiplying enjoyment, by furnishing a succession of new objects' (*IiI* 1: 311), these being landscapes and townscapes, which she then paints with her words. In her book *Atlas of Emotion: Journeys in Art, Architecture, and Film*, Giuliana Bruno lists Blessington among the writers whose manner of visualizing space is so 'descriptively graphic' that it is reminiscent of 'filmic observation' (2002, 83).
3 'Word paintings', as Rhoda Flaxman puts it, are 'frozen moments' of the narrative, which produce the 'painting effect' (Flaxman 1987, 9).
4 Blessington's attempt to be conceived of as a picturesque traveller is here manifested by the recurrence of the words 'picture' and 'picturesque' in the aesthetic context, on average, every seven pages (*IoW* 27, 29, 33, 41, 45, 47, 51, 54–55, 57, 63, 77, 78).
5 Other examples: *IoW* 56; *IiI* 3: 221, 219–20, 289. This is in accord with Edmund Burke's conviction that poetry and rhetoric 'do not succeed in exact description so well as painting does' (Burke 1792, 172).
6 Compare with *IiI* 3: 13.
7 Compare with *IiI* 2: 110–11.
8 Compare with *IiI* 2: 92–93.
9 Compare with *IoW* 27, 29, 45–46; *IiI* 1: 330–31; *IiI* 2: 94.
10 Claude distinguishes five layers, while Gilpin notes only three of them.
11 Twilight and dawn are Blessington's favourite times of the day to illustrate, as they are for most landscape painters.
12 Blessington uses the device as a metaphor for youth in her novel *The Victims of Society*: 'For youth resembles a Claude Lorraine glass, which imparts to all objects its own beautiful tint' (Blessington 2005, 108).
13 The instrument consisted of a number of coloured filters attached to and turning on one centre.
14 Blessington would have encountered similar images in the Gothic romances of Ann Radcliffe, who was also indebted to Salvador Rosa's aesthetic. In *The Mysteries of Udolpho*, one landscape sketch ends with the following remark: 'It was such a scene as *Salvator* would have chosen [...] [the heroine's father St Aubert] almost expected to see banditti start from behind some projecting rock' (Radcliffe 2008b, 30).
15 Still, she cannot stop herself from recounting a story of a traveller who did jump into the crater, an act that she justifies with a proverb: '*Vedi Napoli and poi muori*' (*IiI* 2: 376).
16 Blessington identifies the figure of Venus de' Medici as a feminine ideal, too (*IiI* 2: 114).
17 The same may be said about the human figures in Claude's or Poussin's landscapes, who are fashioned like classical statues.
18 This chapter is a developed and modified version of the article 'Pictures from Southern Italy: *Lady Blessington's Neapolitan Journals, 1823–1826*' (Lipska 2012, 299–307).

Chapter 5: Ruins and Edifices

1 At the time when Blessington commenced her travels, it was mostly Greek and Gothic architecture that captivated the attention of British travellers to the South (Brand 1957, 153).
2 Compare with *IiI* 3: 220, 223.
3 See, for example, Claude Lorrain's *An Italianate Evening Landscape with a Shepherd and His Flock by a Ruined Aqueduct* and J. M. W. Turner's *Interior of Tintern Abbey*.

4 Compare with Claude Lorrain's *Landscape with Draughtsman Sketching Ruins*. She then continues: 'When the eye turns to the other side of the Picture, snatches of a rich landscape are seen through the different arches of the ruins, which are festooned with ivy and drooping wreaths of wild flowers' (*IiI* 1: 326).
5 Compare with Salvator Rosa's *Italianate River Landscape with Figures Before Ruins*.
6 Burke, too, appreciates 'rugged and broken' surfaces of objects. He, in turn, along with their 'greatness of dimension' considers ruins to be productive of the sublime (Burke 1792, 107–8). The ruggedness is one of many qualities that differentiates beauty from the great: 'beauty should be smooth and polished; the great, rugged and negligent' (ibid., 202).
7 Compare with Gilpin 1789, 24.
8 When wandering through the ruins of Cumae in the vicinity of Naples, Blessington admits that her 'mind is divided between present classical associations of the past, and admiration for the beauty of the scenery' (*IiI* 2: 262).
9 Thus the writers applied ekphrasis in its inclusive sense, as a rhetorical device used to depict 'all types of subject matter' (Webb 2009, 3).
10 As Lovell attests, Lady Blessington was a 'confirmed cathedral examiner' (1969, *19*). On arriving in a new town or a city, Blessington usually first headed for its sacred buildings and then wrote down her observations and reflections. See, for example, *NtP* 4, 51.
11 Compare with *IiI* 3: 221, 272.
12 Królikiewicz observes that aesthetic reflection on ruins has always been accompanied by philosophical and historiosophical deliberations (Królikiewicz 1993, 9–10).
13 The same feelings accompany Blessington when she visits the ruined palaces of Venice: 'We invest inanimate objects undergoing this inevitable fate, with a large portion of that sympathy experienced for human being exposed to it' (*IiI* 3: 117). Compare with *IiF* 1: 25–26, 51; *IiI* 3: 2, 101–2.
14 Compare with *IiI* 3: 220. When concentrating on the function of light in Gothic cathedrals, Blessington emphasises the role of stained glass windows; see, for example, the writer's description of one of the churches in Avignon (*IiI* 1: 228).
15 Compare with *IiF* 1: 43; *IiI* 2: 324.
16 When in Siena, she has the same impression: 'The profusion of decoration [in the cathedral] [...] serves rather to distract than to gratify the attention of the beholder' (*IiI* 2: 154).
17 Compare with Victor Hugo's preface to *Cromwell*: '[Grotesque] affixes its mark on the façades of cathedrals, frames its hells and purgatories in the ogive arches of great doorways, portrays them in brilliant hues on window-glass, exhibits its monsters, its bull-dogs, its imps about capitals, along friezes, on the edges of roofs' (Hugo 2004).
18 Compare with Radcliffe's introduction to *A Sicilian Romance*: '[The castle] stands in the centre of a small bay, and upon a gentle acclivity, which, on one side, slopes towards the sea, and on the other, rises into an eminence crowned by dark woods' (Radcliffe 2008a, 1).

Chapter 6: Sacred Art and Religious Practices

1 She meditates on religion in her anonymous poem *Rambles in Waltham Forest*, and in *The Idler in Italy* she once reflects: 'Without the blessed hope held out to us by religion, how fearful would be the prospect of a dreamless and eternal sleep in the cold dark grave!' (*IiI* 3: 302). She might have had similar views on religion to Byron's, as in *Conversations* she records him saying: 'I seldom talk about religion, but I feel it, perhaps, more than those who do. I speak to you on this topic freely, because I know you will neither laugh at me, nor enter into a controversy with me' (*CLB* 69). Regarding her relation

to Catholicism, O'Dwyer points out that Blessington's 'role of Irishwoman was left behind in Ireland, together with the religion of her youth' (2008, 45).
2. For example: 'The churches of Vicenza are numerous, but I have only visited the cathedral and the Corona. The first contains many good pictures by Montagna, Maganza, Zelotti, and Liberi: and the second has an admirable work from the pencil of my favourite, Paolo Veronese, as well as clever pictures by Giovanni Bellini, and Montagna' (*IiI* 3: 219).
3. Using a French version of the name in this context is rather surprising but also illustrative of Blessington's lack of consistency in naming. To avoid confusion, I follow her choices, which means that certain names are given in French, others in the original and some in English translation.
4. Compare with *NtP* 95–96; *IiI* 3: 313.
5. Compare with *NtP* 17, 33.
6. Compare with 'we witnessed one of those exhibitions so common in Italy; where the enthusiasm and passionate warmth of the preachers, so frequently lead them to overstep to propriety of their calling. The matter of the sermon and manner of this expounder of the Roman Catholic Faith, were truly surprising' (*IiI* 2: 363).
7. Compare with *IiF* 1: 57; *IiI* 3: 288.
8. For example, hyperbole, excess and foreign vocabulary (Chard 1999, 4).
9. The same metaphor is used in other places as well, e.g. *IiI* 2: 295. About Genoa she writes that it is 'dressed for a religious festival to-day' (*IiI* 2: 90).
10. In another place she compares the procession with 'the triumphant entry of a Roman conqueror [...] or some of the processions in Pagan worship' (*IiI* 2: 91).
11. In Salerno, after she is shown the broken column in which the blood of St Matthew is believed to flow, she asserts: 'This seeming miracle, so easily explained by the merest tyro in acoustics, it would be here considered nothing short of sacrilege to question; and when one sees the uses to which superstition can be applied, it is easy to perceive why science finds so little encouragement among the priesthood of the Roman Catholic religion.' (*IiI* 2: 340). To read more on Blessington's representation of Roman Catholic saints from yet another perspective, see Fisher 2012, 34–35; 41–43.
12. Take the following scene, for instance: Lorenzo beheld 'a Creature stretched upon a bed of straw, so wretched, so emaciated, so pale, that he doubted to think her Woman [...]. Her long dishevelled hair fell in disorder over her face, and almost entirely concealed it. One wasted Arm hung listlessly upon a tattered rug which covered her convulsed and shivering limbs' (Lewis 2008, 363).
13. 'Attraction by repulsion' is the phrase used by John Forster, Dickens's friend and biographer, which was to express the writer's peculiar pleasure derived from describing death scenes.
14. An earlier version of this chapter has been published as 'Between Attraction and Aversion: Roman Catholicism in Marguerite Blessington's Travel Accounts' (Lipska 2014, 45–59).

Chapter 7: Genoa: Byron's Companion

1. Traditionally, there were two ways to cross the frontier between the south of France and Italy – travelling by boat or crossing the Alps (Black 2010, 12–13).

2   Blessington does mention the Alps on several occasions, usually making them an element of the background to complete her pictorial compositions (*IiI* 1: 102,107, 331; *IiI* 3: 241; *IiI* 3: 283–84).
3   Genoa was a natural stop for those who travelled by sea from the south of France. From Genoa they might continue by sea towards Livorno (Leghorn), to avoid the hardships of the Ligurian mountains, and then towards Florence or Rome.
4   Compare with Mary Shelley's expectations of the Alpine passage: 'I desired to enjoy to the full the sublime scenery of this grand pass' (Shelley 1844, 1: 134). In the passage Blessington concentrates on the sense of sight as if she expected some incredible view.
5   As Sadleir notices, there are some discrepancies between Lady Blessington's account of her acquaintance with Lord Byron and the versions by other people, such as Henry Fox or Byron himself (Sadleir 1947, 60, 63–64).
6   Naturally, Guiccioli's account must have been as biased as Blessington's, given the fact that, as Byron wrote in one of his letters, at the time she 'was seized with a furious fit of Italian jealousy' (Byron to Lady Hardy, 17 May 1823; quoted in Guiccioli 2005, 530, n. 8). Interestingly enough, despite Guiccioli's unfavourable presentation of Lady Blessington, the two became close friends in later years.
7   Molloy records Mathews's letter, in which he recollects that during one of such theatricals the countess 'was dressed as an old lady, in an embroidered silk gown, a cap, and a quantity of curls in front, powdered' (Molloy 1896, 1: 163).
8   Madden also wrote: 'She must become an actress there, she must adapt her manners, fashion her ideas, accommodate her conversation to the taste, tone of thought, and turn of mind, of every individual around her' (Madden 1855, 1: 244). In her 'Night Thought Book' of 1834–35, Blessington herself noted: 'The great majority of men are actors, who preferred an assumed part to that which Nature had assigned them. They seek to be something, or to appear something they are not, and even stoop to the affectation of defects rather than display real estimable qualities which belong to them' (quoted in *CLB* 144 n. 2).
9   On another occasion she writes that Byron 'failed not to point [the views] out, but in very sober terms, never allowing any thing like enthusiasm in his expressions, though many of the views might have excited it' (*CLB* 40).
10 In December 1826, Blessington passed through Genoa while moving from Florence to Pisa (*IiI* 2: 480–83).
11 It was most telling when at one point, while walking along the city's streets, she came across a girl whom she immediately recognized as Byron's daughter Ada (*IiI* 3: 315–16).

Chapter 8: Naples: Lady of the House

1   For similar descriptions, see *IiI* 1: 517–20; *IiF* 1: 89–91, 97–105; *IiF* 2: 76–78.

Chapter 9: Rome and Venice: Romantic Traveller

1   The characters of Blessington's fashionable novels who travel to Rome are also placed at the Coliseum, lit up by moonbeams so that they can feel the magic of the spot. See, for example, *Strathern* (Blessington 1845, 2: 254–55).

2 In what follows only textual associations are addressed; I have discussed the visual ones in the previous chapters on art and architecture. It is worth mentioning, however, that, just as Piozzi's and Shelley's, Blessington's ideas of Venice are much influenced by Canaletto's paintings (*IiI*, 3: 103; Piozzi 1789, 150; Shelley 1844, 2: 84). On the other hand, her vision of the city was not confined to Canaletto's imagery, which is suggested by the following passage: 'Venice *more than realizes my expectations*, though they were highly excited by all that I had read, and by the pictures of Canaletti [sic] [...] I remember, many years ago, when a fine Canaletti hung in one of the rooms I occupied, that I used to long when my eyes dwelt on it, to see Venice, and compare the original with the copy' (*IiI* 3: 103, emphasis added).
3 Radcliffe's Venice is summoned from the ocean by the 'the wand of an enchanter' (Radcliffe 2008b, 175), while Byron's is struck with 'the enchanter's wand'. For Mary Shelley it is an 'enchanted ground' (1844, 2: 82).
4 Compare also with Mary Shelley's metaphor: 'I beheld the domes and towers of the queen of Ocean rise from the waves' (Shelley 1844, 2: 79).
5 Dickens also used his letters to Lady Blessington while composing *Pictures from Italy* (Paroissien 1973, 28–29).
6 Anna Jameson also experiences a whole range of emotions; she writes that 'pleasure and wonder are tinged with a melancholy interest; and while the imagination is excited, the spirits are depressed' (Jameson 1826, 68).
7 An earlier version of this chapter is forthcoming in the journal *Studia Anglica Posnaniensia* as '"Solemn associations": Rome, Venice and Romantic textuality in Marguerite Blessington's *Idler in Italy*' (Lipska, forthcoming).

Chapter 10: Paris: Writer of Fashion and Revolution

1 Blessington expresses the same idea in an earlier account of her stay in the city: 'I am every day more and more convinced that there is much less rational enjoyment of life in Paris than in London. Here the people are continually out, and seem to live in the open air, so that there can be but little time for reading, and none for study' (*NtP* 136).
2 The lines are quoted from James Thomson's 1728 *The Seasons* (*Spring*, l. 996).
3 See *IiF* 2: 150, 154, 161, 162, 164–65, 168, 187–88.

BIBLIOGRAPHY

Primary Sources

Addison, Joseph. (1711) 1828. *Essays on the Pleasures of the Imagination*. Antwerp: Duverger.
Bailie, Marianne. 1819. *First Impressions on a Tour upon the Continent in the Summer of 1818*. London: John Murray.
[Blessington, Marguerite]. 1822. *A Tour in the Isle of Wight, in the Autumn of 1820*. [*IoW*] London: A. and R. Spottiswoode.
———. 1822. *Journal of a Tour through the Netherlands to Paris, in 1821*. [*NtP*] London: Longman, Hurst, Rees, Orme, and Brown.
———. 1822. *Sketches and Fragments*. London: Longman, Hurst, Rees, Orme, and Brown.
———. 1822. *The Magic Lantern; or, Sketches of Scenes in the Metropolis*. London: Longman, Hurst, Rees, Orme, and Brown.
Blessington, Marguerite. 1838. *The Works of Lady Blessington*. Vol. 1. Philadelphia: E. L. Carey and A. Hart.
———. 1839–40. *The Idler in Italy*. [*IiI*] 3 vols. London: Henry Colburn.
———. 1841–42. *The Idler in France*. [*IiF*] 2 vols. London: Henry Colburn.
———. 1845. *Strathern; or, Life at Home and Abroad*. 4 vols. London: Henry Colburn.
———. (1834) 1969. *Lady Blessington's Conversations of Lord Byron*, edited by Ernest J. Lovell, Jr. Princeton: Princeton University Press.
———. (1837) 2005. *The Victims of Society*, edited by Ann R. Hawkins and Jeraldine R. Kraver. In *Silver Fork Novels, 1826–1841*, general editor Harriet Devine Jump. Vol. 4. London: Pickering & Chatto.
———. 1979. *Lady Blessington at Naples*, edited by Edith Clay. London: Hamish Hamilton.
Brockedon, William. 1829. *Illustrations of the Passes of the Alps, by which Italy Communicates with France, Switzerland, and Germany*. Vol. 2. London: Printed for the Author.
Burke, Edmund. (1757) 1792. *A Philosophical Inquiry into the Origin of our Ideas of the Sublime and Beautiful*. Basel: J. J. Tourneisen.
Byron, George Gordon, Lord. 2008. *The Major Works*, edited by Jerome J. McGann. Oxford: Oxford University Press.
Chorley, Henry F. 1838. *The Authors of England*. London: Charles Tilt.
Costello, Louisa Stuart. 1845. *The Falls, Lakes and Mountains of North Wales*. London: Longman, Brown, Green and Longmans.
Dickens, Charles. (1846) 1973. *Pictures from Italy*, introduction and notes by David Paroissien. London: Andre Deutsch.
Eastlake, Elizabeth. 1845. 'Lady Travellers'. *Quarterly Review* 76, 98–137. http://digital.library.upenn.edu/women/eastlake/quarterly/travellers.html.

Eaton, Charlotte Ann. 1817. *Narrative of a Residence in Belgium during the Campaign of 1815; and of a Visit to the Field of Waterloo, by an Englishwoman*. London: John Murray.

———. 1820. *Rome in the Nineteenth Century*. 3 vols. Edinburgh: James Ballantyne.

Elliot, Frances. 1871. *The Diary of an Idle Woman in Italy*. 2 vols. London: Chapman and Hall.

Evans, Robert Harding. 1836. *Catalogue of the Curious, Choice and Valuable Library of the Late Sir Francis Freeling, Bart. F.S.A*. London: W. Nicol.

Fertridge, William Pembroke. 1865. *Harper's Hand-Book for Travellers in Europe and the East*. New York: Harper and Brothers Publishers.

Gilpin, William. 1788. *Observations, Relative Chiefly to Picturesque Beauty, Made in the Year 1772, on Several Parts of England; Particularly the Mountains, and Lakes of Cumberland and Westmoreland*. London: Printed for R. Blamire.

———. 1789. *Observations on the River Wye, and Several Parts of South Wales, &c: Relative Chiefly to Picturesque Beauty*. London: Printed for R. Blamire.

———. 1794. *Three Essays: On Picturesque Beauty; On Picturesque Travel; and On Sketching Landscapes: To Which is Added a Poem, On Landscape Painting*. London: Printed for R. Blamire.

———. 1808. *Observations on Several Parts of Great Britain: Particularly the High-Lands of Scotland, Relative Chiefly to Picturesque Beauty, Made in the Year 1776*. London: Printed for T. Cadell and W. Davies.

Graham, Maria. 1820. *Three Months Passed in the Mountains East of Rome, During the Year 1819*. London: Longman, Hurst, Rees, Orme and Brown.

Guiccioli, Teresa. 2005. *Lord Byron's Life in Italy*, translated by Michael Rees, edited by Peter Cochran. Cranbury, NJ: Associated University Presses.

Hugo, Victor. (1827) 2004. 'Preface to *Cromwell*'. In *The Project Gutenberg EBook of Prefaces and Prologues to Famous Books*, edited by Charles W. Eliot. http://www.gutenberg.org/files/13182/13182-8.txt.

Jameson, Anna Brownell. 1826. *Diary of an Ennuyée*. London: Henry Colburn.

Johnson, Samuel. (1758–60) 2013. *Papers from the Idler*. Cambridge: Cambridge University Press.

Knight, Richard Payne. 1806. *An Analytical Inquiry into the Principles of Taste*. London: Luke Hansard.

Leslie, Doris. 1976. *Notorious Lady: The Life and Times of the Countess of Blessington*. London: William Heinemann.

Lewis, Matthew Gregory. (1796) 2008. *The Monk*, edited by Emma McEvoy. Oxford: Oxford University Press.

Literary Gazette; and Journal of Belles Lettres, Arts, Sciences, Etc. 1835. London: James Moyes.

Literary Gazette; and Journal of Belles Lettres, Arts, Sciences, Etc. 1839. London: Moyes and Barclay.

Literary Gazette; and Journal of Belles Lettres, Arts, Sciences, Etc. 1841. London: Moyes and Barclay.

Madden, Richard Robert. 1855. *The Literary Life and Correspondence of the Countess of Blessington*, 3 vols. London: T. C. Newby.

Martin, John. 1854. *Bibliographical Catalogue of Privately Printed Books*. London: Woodfall and Kinder.

Mirror of Literature, Amusement and Instruction. 1841. Vol. 38. London: Hugh Cunningham.

Molloy, J. Fitzgerald. 1896. *The Most Gorgeous Lady Blessington*. 2 vols. London: Downey.

Morgan, Lady (Sydney Owenson).1817. *France*. London: Saunders and Otley.

———. 1821. *Italy*. London: Henry Colburn.

———. 1824. *The Life and Times of Salvator Rosa*. London: Henry Colburn.

Morrison, Alfred (ed.). 1895. *The Collection of Autograph Letters and Historical Documents (Second Series 1882–1893): The Blessington Papers*. London: Privately published.
New Monthly Magazine and Humorist. 1839, edited by Theodore Hook. London: Henry Colburn.
New Monthly Magazine and Humorist. 1841, edited by Theodore Hook. London: Henry Colburn.
Patmore, P. G. 1854. *My Friends and Acquaintance*. Vol. 1. London: Saunders and Otley.
Piozzi, Hester Lynch. 1789. *Observations and Reflections Made in the Course of a Journey Through France, Italy, and Germany*. Vol. 1. London: Printed for A. Strahan and T. Cadell.
Power, Margaret. 1850. 'Memoir of Lady Blessington'. In *Country Quarters* by Marguerite Blessington, 1–7. Paris: A. and W. Galignani.
Radcliffe, Ann. 1826. 'On the Supernatural in Poetry'. *The New Monthly Magazine* 16, 145–52.
———. (1790) 2008a. *A Sicilian Romance*, edited by Alison Milbank. Oxford: Oxford University Press.
———. (1794) 2008b. *The Mysteries of Udolpho*, edited by Bonamy Dobrée, introduction and notes by Terry Castle. Oxford: Oxford University Press.
Review of *The Idler in Italy*. 1839. *The Athenaeum. Journal of Literature, Science, and the Fine Arts. From January to December*, 165–68. London: Printed for James Holmes.
Ruskin, John. 1869. *Modern Painters Part IV*. New York: Wiley.
Shelley, Mary. 1844. *Rambles in Germany and Italy, in 1840, 1842, and 1843*. 2 vols. London: Edward Moxon.
———. (1826) 1990. 'The English in Italy'. In *The Mary Shelley Reader*, edited by Betty T. Bennett and Charles E. Robinson, 341–57. New York and Oxford: Oxford University Press.
Shelley, Percy Bysshe. 2014. *The Poems of Shelley*, edited by Kelvin Everest and Geoffrey Matthews. Vol. 2. New York: Routledge.
Smith, George Barnett. 1893. *Women of Renown. Nineteenth Century Studies*. London: W. H. Allen.
Starke, Mariana. 1820. *Travels on the Continent*. London: John Murray.
———. 1836. *Travels in Europe*. Paris: Galignani.
Sterne, Laurence. (1768). 2002. *A Sentimental Journey through France and Italy and Continuation of the Bramine's Journal*, edited by Melvyn New and W. G. Day. Gainesville: University Press of Florida.
Strutt, Elizabeth. 1828. *A Spinster's Tour of France, the States of Genoa, &c*. London: Longman.
Taylor, Catherine. 1840. *Letters from Italy to a Younger Sister*. London: John Murray.
Thistlethwayte, Tryphena. 1853. *Memoirs and Correspondence of Dr. H. Bathurst, Bishop of Norwich*. London: Richard Bentley.
Thomson, James. (1735). *The Four Seasons and Other Poems. By James Thomson*. London: J. Millan, and A. Millar. http://quod.lib.umich.edu/e/ecco/004810089.0001.000/1:20?rgn=div1;view=toc
Trollope, Frances. 1836. *Paris and Parisians*. Vol. 1. London: Richard Bentley.
———. 1842. *A Visit to Italy*. Vol. 1. London: Richard Bentley.
Wordsworth, Dorothy. 1874. *Recollections of a Tour Made in Scotland A.D. 1803*, edited by J. C. Shairp. New York: G. P. Putnam.
Yates, Ashton, Mrs. [F. M. L. Yates]. 1843. *Letters Written During a Journey to Switzerland in the Autumn of 1841*. Vol. 1. London: Duncan and Malcolm.

Secondary Sources

Acton, Harold. 1979. 'Introduction' to *Lady Blessington at Naples*, edited by Edith Clay, 3–8. London: Hamish Hamilton.
Adams, Percy G. 1962. *Travelers and Travel Liars, 1660–1800*. Berkeley and Los Angeles: University of California Press.
———. 1983. *Travel Literature and the Evolution of the Novel*. Lexington: The University of Kentucky Press.
Adburgham, Alison. 2012. *Silver Fork Society: Fashionable Life and Literature from 1814 to 1840*. London: Faber & Faber.
Adelman, Richard. 2011. *Idleness, Contemplation and the Aesthetic, 1750–1830*. Cambridge: Cambridge University Press.
Balshaw, Maria, and Liam Kennedy. 2000. 'Introduction' to *Urban Space and Representation*, edited by Maria Balshaw and Liam Kennedy, 1–21. London and Sterling: Pluto Press.
Barrell, John. 1972. *The Idea of Landscape and the Sense of Place, 1730–1840: An Approach to the Poetry of John Clare*. Cambridge: Cambridge University Press.
Bassnett, Susan. 2002. 'Travel Writing and Gender'. In *The Cambridge Companion to Travel Writing*, edited by Peter Hulme and Tim Youngs, 225–41. Cambridge: Cambridge University Press.
Batten, Charles. 1978. *Pleasurable Instruction: Form and Convention in the Eighteenth-Century Travel Literature*. Berkeley, Los Angeles, London: University of California Press.
Bermingham, Ann. 2010. 'The Picturesque and Ready-to-Wear Femininity'. In *The Politics of the Picturesque*, edited by Stephen Copley and Peter Garside, 81–119. Cambridge: Cambridge University Press.
Black, Jeremy. 2010. *The British and the Grand Tour*. London: Routledge.
Bohls, Elizabeth A. 1995. *Women Travel Writers and the Language of Aesthetics, 1716–1818*. Cambridge: Cambridge University Press.
Borm, Jan. 2004. 'Defining Travel: On the Travel Book, Travel Writing and Terminology'. In *Perspectives on Travel Writing*, edited by Glenn Hooper and Tim Youngs, 13–26. Aldershot: Ashgate.
Bourke, Angela. 2002. *The Field Day Anthology of Irish Writing*. Vol. 5. *Irish Women's Writing and Traditions*. New York: New York University Press.
Brand, C. P. 1957. *Italy and the English Romantics: The Italianate Fashion in Early Nineteenth-Century England*. Cambridge: Cambridge University Press.
Broderick, Marian. 2012. *Wild Irish Women: Extraordinary Lives from History*. Dublin: The O'Brien Press.
Bruno, Giuliana. 2002. *Atlas of Emotion: Journeys in Art, Architecture, and Film*. London: Verso.
Buzard, James. 1993. *The Beaten Track: European Tourism, Literature, and the Ways to Culture, 1800–1918*. Oxford: Clarendon Press.
———. 2002. 'The Grand Tour and After (1660–1840)'. In *The Cambridge Companion to Travel Writing*, edited by Peter Hulme and Tim Youngs, 37–52. Cambridge: Cambridge University Press.
Cardinal, Roger. 2002. 'Romantic Travel'. In *Rewriting the Self: Histories from the Middle Ages to the Present*, edited by Roy Porter, 135–55. London: Routledge.
Chard, Chloe. 1983. 'Horror on the Grand Tour'. *Oxford Art Journal* 6, no. 2: 3–16.
———. 1999. *Pleasure and Guilt on the Grand Tour. Travel Writing and Imaginative Geography, 1600–1830*. Manchester: Manchester University Press.
Clay, Edith. 1979a. 'Preface' to *Lady Blessington at Naples*, edited by Edith Clay, 9–19. London: Hamish Hamilton.

———. 1979b. 'Summary of the Life of Lady Blessington'. In *Lady Blessington at Naples*, edited by Edith Clay, 151–59. London: Hamish Hamilton.
Colbert, Benjamin. 2005. *Shelley's Eye: Travel Writing and Aesthetic Vision*. Aldershot: Ashgate.
Copeland, Edward. 2012. *The Silver Fork Novel: Fashionable Fiction in the Age of Reform*. Cambridge: Cambridge University Press.
Cronin, Richard. 2002. *Romantic Victorians: English Literature, 1824–1840*. Houndmills: Palgrave Macmillan.
Culley, Amy. 2014. *British Women's Life Writing, 1760–1840: Friendship, Community and Collaboration*. Houndmills: Palgrave Macmillan.
Czermińska, Małgorzata. 2005. *Gotyk i pisarze: Topika opisu katedry* [Writers and the Gothic: Topics of Cathedral Description]. Gdańsk: słowo/obraz terytoria.
Eckroth, Stephanie. 2012. 'Celebrity and Anonymity in the Monthly Review's Notices of Nineteenth-Century Novels'. In *Women Writers and the Artifacts of Celebrity in the Long Nineteenth Century*, edited by Ann R. Hawkins and Maura Ives, 13–31. Farnham: Ashgate.
Eco, Umberto (ed.). 2004. *On Beauty: A History of a Western Idea*, translated by Alastair McEwen. London: Secker & Warburg.
Elfenbein, Andrew. 1995. *Byron and the Victorians*. Cambridge: Cambridge University Press.
Erickson, Lee. 1996. *The Economy of Literary Form: English Literature and the Industrialization of Publishing, 1800–1850*. Baltimore and London: The Johns Hopkins University Press.
Feldman, Paula R. (ed.). 2000. *British Women Poets of the Romantic Era: An Anthology*. Baltimore and London: The Johns Hopkins University Press.
Ferguson, Priscilla Parkhurst. 1994. *Paris as Revolution: Writing the Nineteenth-Century City*. Berkeley, Los Angeles, London: University of California Press.
Fisher, Devon. 2012. *Roman Catholic Saints and Early Victorian Literature: Conservatism, Liberalism, and the Emergence of Secular Culture*. Farnham: Ashgate.
Flaxman, Rhoda L. 1998. *Victorian Word Painting and Narrative: Toward the Blending of Genres*. Ann Arbor: UMI Research Press.
Fludernik, Monika, and Miriam Nandi (eds). 2014. *Idleness, Indolence and Leisure in English Literature*. Houndmills: Palgrave Macmillan.
Fortunati, Vita, Rita Monticelli, and Maurizio Ascari (eds). 2001. *Travel Writing and the Female Imaginary*. Bologna: Patron.
Foster, Shirley and Sara Mills (eds). 2002. *An Anthology of Women's Travel Writing*. Manchester: Manchester University Press.
Frawley, Maria, H. 1994. *A Wider Range: Travel Writing by Women in Victorian England*. Cranbury, NJ: Associated University Presses.
Genette, Gerard. 1997. *Paratexts: Thresholds of Interpretation*, translated by Jane E. Lewin. Cambridge: Cambridge University Press.
Gettman, Royal A. 2010. *A Victorian Publisher: A Study of the Bentley Papers*. Cambridge: Cambridge University Press.
Greenblatt, Stephen. 1980. *Renaissance Self-Fashioning: From More to Shakespeare*. Chicago and London: The University of Chicago Press.
Hagglund, Betty. 2010. *Tourists and Travellers: Women's Non-Fictional Writing about Scotland, 1770–1830*. Bristol: Channel View Publications.
Hannay, Prudence. 1980. 'Lady Blessington: A Literary Club for Editors'. In *Affairs of the Mind: The Salon in Europe and America from the 18th to the 20th Century*, edited by Peter Quennell, 23–33. Washington: New Republic.
Hawkins, Ann R. 2003a. '"Formed with Curious Skill": Blessington's Negotiation of the "Poetess" in *Flowers of Loveliness*'. *Romanticism on the Net*, no. 29–30. http://www.erudit.org/revue/ron/2003/v/n29-30/007721ar.html.

———. 2003b. 'Marguerite, Countess of Blessington, and L. E. L. (Letitia Elizabeth Landon): Evidence of a Friendship'. *ANQ: A Quarterly Journal of Short Articles, Notes, and Reviews* 16, no. 2: 27–32.

———. 2005. 'Marketing Gender and Nationalism: Blessington's *Gems of Beauty*/*L'Écrin* and the Mid-Century Book Trade'. *Women's Writing* 12, no. 2: 225–37.

———. 2012. 'The Portrait, the Beauty, and the Book: Celebrity and the Countess of Blessington'. In *Women Writers and the Artifacts of Celebrity in the Long Nineteenth Century*, edited by Ann R. Hawkins and Maura Ives, 49–78. Farnham: Ashgate.

Hawkins, Ann R., and Jeraldine Kraver. 2005. 'Introduction' to *The Victims of Society* by Marguerite Blessington, edited by Ann R. Hawkins and Jeraldine R. Kraver, vii–xxvi. In *Silver Fork Novels, 1826–1841*, general editor Harriet Devine Jump. Vol. 4. London: Pickering & Chatto.

Haynes, Clare. 2006. *Pictures and Popery: Art and Religion in England, 1660–1760*. Burlington: Ashgate Publishing.

———. 2010. '"A Trial for the Patience of Reason"? Grand Tourists and Anti-Catholicism after 1745'. *Journal for Eighteenth-Century Studies* 33, no. 2: 195–208.

Hoagwood, Terence Allan, and Kathryn Ledbetter. 2005. *"Colour'd Shadows": Contexts in Publishing, Printing, and Reading Nineteenth-Century British Women Writers*. New York: Palgrave Macmillan.

Hollington, Michael, and Francesca Orestano. 2009. 'Introduction' to *Dickens and Italy: Little Dorrit and Pictures from Italy*, edited by Michael Hollington and Francesca Orestano, xiv–xxvi. Newcastle upon Tyne: Cambridge Scholars Publishing.

Hooper, Glenn. 2002. 'The Isles/Ireland: The Wilder Shore'. In *The Cambridge Companion to Travel Writing*, edited by Peter Hulme and Tim Youngs, 174–90. Cambridge: Cambridge University Press.

Hooper, Glenn, and Tim Youngs (eds). 2004. *Perspectives on Travel Writing*. Aldershot: Ashgate.

Ives, Maura. 2012. 'Introduction' to *Women Writers and the Artifacts of Celebrity in the Long Nineteenth Century*, edited by Ann R. Hawkins and Maura Ives, 1–12. Farnham: Ashgate.

Jackman, J. S. 2005. *Hibernia's Muses: The Daughters of Thalia and Melpomene. Portrait Sketches of Irish Women Writers*. Cambridge: Lutterworth Press.

Jones, Angela D. 1997. 'Romantic Women Travel Writers and the Representation of Everyday Experience'. *Women's Studies* 26, no. 5: 497–521.

Jordan, Sarah. 2014. 'Idleness, Class and Gender in the Long Eighteenth Century'. In *Idleness, Indolence and Leisure in English Literature*, edited by Monika Fludernik and Miriam Nandi, 107–28. Houndmills: Palgrave Macmillan.

Kendra, April Nixon. 2003. '*Catherine Gore and the Fashionable Novel: A Reevaluation*'. Ph.D. diss., The University of Georgia. https://getd.libs.uga.edu/pdfs/kendra_april_g_200312_phd.pdf

Kinsley, Zoë. 2008. *Women Writing the Home Tour, 1682–1812*. Aldershot: Ashgate.

Koppenfels, Werner von. 1999. 'Sunset City – City of the Dead: Venice and the 19th Century Apocalyptic Imagination'. In *Venetian Views, Venetian Blinds: English Fantasies of Venice*, edited by Manfred Pfister and Barbara Schaff, 99–113. Amsterdam and Atlanta: Rodopi.

Korte, Barbara. 2000. *English Travel Writing: From Pilgrimages to Postcolonial Explorations*, translated by Catherine Matthias. London: Macmillan.

Królikiewicz, Grażyna. 1993. *Terytorium ruin: ruina jako obraz i temat romantyczny* [The Territory of Ruins: The Ruin as a Romantic Theme and Image]. Kraków: Universitas.

Labbe, Jacqueline M. 2010. *The History of British Women's Writing, 1750–1830*. Houndmills: Palgrave Macmillan.

Lane, Leeann, and William Murphy (eds). 2016. *Leisure and the Irish in the Nineteenth Century*. Liverpool: Liverpool University Press.
Leed, Eric J. 1991. *The Mind of the Traveler: From Gilgamesh to Global Tourism*. New York: Basic Books.
Lejeune, Phillipe. 1989. *On Autobiography*, translated by Katherine Leary. Minneapolis: University of Minnesota Press.
Lipska, Aneta. 2012. 'Pictures from Southern Italy: *Lady Blessington's Neapolitan Journals, 1823–1826*'. In *From Queen Anne to Queen Victoria: Readings in 18th and 19th Century British Literature and Culture*, edited by Grażyna Bystydzieńska and Emma Harris, 299–307. Warsaw: Uniwersytet Warszawski, Ośrodek Studiów Brytyjskich.
———. 2014. 'Between Attraction and Aversion: Roman Catholicism in Marguerite Blessington's Travel Accounts'. *The New Review: An International Journal of British Studies*, Issue 4, pp. 45–59.
———. Forthcoming. '"Solemn associations": Rome, Venice and Romantic textuality in Marguerite Blessington's *Idler in Italy*'. *Studia Anglica Posnaniensia*.
Lovell, Ernest J., Jr. 1969. 'Introduction' to *Lady Blessington's Conversations of Lord Byron*, edited by Ernest J. Lovell, Jr., *3–114*. Princeton: Princeton University Press.
Matoff, Susan. 2016. *Marguerite, Countess of Blessington: The Turbulent Life of a Salonnière and Author*. Newark: Delaware University Press.
McAllister, Marie E. 1988. 'Woman on the Journey: Eighteenth-Century British Women's Travel in Fact and Fiction'. Ph.D. diss., Princeton University.
McCue, Maureen. 2014. *British Romanticism and the Reception of Italian Old Master Art, 1793–1840*. Farnham: Ashgate.
Mellor, Anne K. 1993. *Romanticism and Gender*. London and New York: Routledge.
Melnyk, Veronica. 2002. '"Half Fashion and Half Passion": The Life of Publisher Henry Colburn'. Ph.D. diss., University of Birmingham. http://etheses.bham.ac.uk/163/1/Melnyk02PhD.pdf
Mills, Sara. 2003. *Discourses of Difference: An Analysis of Women's Travel Writing and Colonialism*. London: Routledge.
Moroz, Grzegorz. 2013. *Travellers, Novelists and Gentlemen: Constructing Male Narrative Personae in British Travel Books, from the Beginnings to the Second World War*. Frankfurt am Main: Peter Lang.
Nord, Deborah Epstein. 1995. *Walking the Victorian Streets: Women, Representation, and the City*. Ithaca: Cornell University Press.
North, Julian. 2002. 'Self-possession and Gender in Romantic Literary Biography'. In *Romantic Biography*, edited by Arthur Bradley and Alan Rawes, 109–38. Aldershot: Ashgate.
O'Cinneide, Muireann. 2008. *Aristocratic Women and the Literary Nation, 1832–1867*. Houndmills: Palgrave Macmillan.
O'Dwyer, Riana. 2008. 'Travels of a Lady of Fashion: The Literary Career of Lady Blessington (1789–1849)'. In *New Contexts: Re-Framing Nineteenth-Century Irish Women's Prose*, edited by Heidi Hansson, 35–54. Cork: Cork University Press.
Orr, Clarissa Campbell. 1998. 'Mary Shelley's *Rambles in Germany and Italy*, the Celebrity Author, and the Undiscovered Country of the Human Heart'. *Romanticism on the Net*, no. 11. https://www.erudit.org/revue/ron/1998/v/n11/005813ar.html.
Ouditt, Sharon. 2014. *Impressions of Southern Italy: British Travel Writing from Henry Swinburne to Norman Douglas*. New York: Routledge.
Ożarska, Magdalena. 2013a. *Lacework or Mirror? Diary Poetics of Frances Burney, Dorothy Wordsworth and Mary Shelley*. Newcastle upon Tyne: Cambridge Scholars Publishing.

——— . 2013b. *Two Women Writers and Their Italian Tours: Mary Shelley's Rambles in Germany and Italy and Łucja Rautenstrauchowa's In and Beyond the Alps*. Lewiston, Queenston, Lampeter: The Edwin Mellen Press.

Paroissien, David. 1973. 'Introduction' to *Pictures from Italy* by Charles Dickens, 9–34. London: Andre Deutsch.

Pauk, Barbara. 2008. 'Crossing the Channel: Socio-Cultural Exchanges in English and French Women's Writings – 1830–1900'. PhD diss., University of Western Australia. http://research-repository.uwa.edu.au/en/publications/crossing-the-channel-sociocultural-exchanges-in-english-and-french-womens-writings--18301900(e43a4070-fe8f-42ba-a731-9f0156ad7415).html

——— . 2011. '"The Parisian Beau Monde": Frances Trollope's Representations of France'. *Women's Writing* 18, issue 2: 256–72.

Pemble, John. 1988. *The Mediterranean Passion: Victorians and Edwardians in the South*. Oxford and New York: Oxford University Press.

Pfister, Manfred (ed.). 1996. *The Fatal Gift of Beauty: The Italies of British Travellers. An Annotated Anthology*. Amsterdam and Atlanta: Rodopi.

Pfister, Manfred, and Barbara Schaff 1999. 'Introduction' to *Venetian Views, Venetian Blinds: English Fantasies of Venice*, edited by Manfred Pfister and Barbara Schaff, 1–13. Amsterdam, Atlanta: Rodopi.

Poovey, Mary. 1984. *The Proper Lady and the Woman Writer: Ideology as Style in the Works of Mary Wollstonecraft, Mary Shelley, and Jane Austen*. Chicago and London: University of Chicago Press.

Robinson, Jane. 1990. *Wayward Women: A Guide to Women Travellers*. Oxford and New York: Oxford University Press.

Robinson, Jane (ed.). 2001. *Unsuitable for Ladies: An Anthology of Women Travellers*. Oxford: Oxford University Press.

Rojek, Chris. 2004. *Celebrity*. London: Reaktion Books.

Rosa, Matthew Whiting. 1964. *The Silver-Fork School: Novels of Fashion Preceding* Vanity Fair. Port Washington: Kennikat Press.

Ross, Alexander M. 1986. *The Imprint of the Picturesque on Nineteenth-Century British Fiction*. Waterloo: Wilfrid Laurier University Press.

Sadleir, Michael. 1933. *Blessington–D'Orsay: A Masquerade*. London: Constable.

——— . 1947. *The Strange Life of Lady Blessington*. New York: Farrar, Straus.

Sadoff, Dianne F. 2012. 'The Silver Fork Novel'. In *The Nineteenth-Century Novel 1820–1880*, edited by John Kucich and Jenny Bourne Taylor, 106–21. *The Oxford History of the Novel in English. Vol. 3*. Oxford: Oxford University Press.

Saunders, Clare Broome. 2014. *Women, Travel Writing and Truth*. New York: Routledge.

——— . 2015. *Louisa Stuart Costello: A Nineteenth-Century Writing Life*. New York: Palgrave Macmillan.

Schaff, Barbara. 1999. 'Venetian Views and Voices in Radcliffe's *The Mysteries of Udolpho* and Braddon's *The Venetians*'. In *Venetian Views, Venetian Blinds: English Fantasies of Venice*, edited by Manfred Pfister and Barbara Schaff, 89–97. Amsterdam and Atlanta: Rodopi.

Schlaeger, Jürgen. 1999. 'Elective Affinities: Lady Mary Wortley Montague in Venice'. In *Venetian Views, Venetian Blinds: English Fantasies of Venice*, edited by Manfred Pfister and Barbara Schaff, 63–71. Amsterdam and Atlanta: Rodopi.

Schmid, Susanne. 2002. 'Byron and Wilde: The Dandy and the Public Sphere'. In *The Importance of Reinventing Oscar: Versions of Wilde During the Last 100 Years*, edited by Uwe Böker, Richard Corballis, Julie Hibbard, 81–89. Amsterdam and New York: Rodopi.

———. 2008. 'The Countess of Blessington: Reading as Intimacy, Reading as Sociability'. *The Wordsworth Circle* 39, no. 3: 88–93.

———. 2013. *British Literary Salons of the Late Eighteenth and Early Nineteenth Centuries*. New York: Palgrave Macmillan.

Smith, Sidonie, and Julia Watson. 2010. *Reading Autobiography: A Guide for Interpreting Life Narratives*. Minneapolis and London: University of Minnesota Press.

Soderholm, James. 1996. *Fantasy, Forgery, and the Byron Legend*. Lexington: The University of Kentucky Press.

Spector, Robert D. 1997. *Samuel Johnson and the Essay*. Westport: Greenwood Press.

Stabler, Jane. 2002. 'Taking Liberties: The Italian Picturesque in Woman's Travel Writig'. *European Romantic Review* 13, no. 1: 11–22.

———. 2013. *The Artistry of Exile: Romantic and Victorian Writers in Italy*. Oxford: Oxford University Press.

Sutherland, John, 2014. *The Longman Companion to Victorian Fiction*. Abingdon: Routledge.

Sweet, Rosemary. 2012. *Cities and the Grand Tour: The British in Italy, c. 1690–1820*. Cambridge: Cambridge University Press.

Walchester, Kathryn. 2007. *'Our Own Fair Italy': Nineteenth Century Women's Travel Writing and Italy 1800–1844*. Bern: Peter Lang.

Ward, Gerald. 2008. *The Grove Encyclopedia of Materials and Techniques in Art*. Oxford: Oxford University Press.

Webb, Ruth. 2009. *Ekphrasis, Imagination and Persuasion in Ancient Rhetorical Theory and Practice*. Farnham: Ashgate.

Wilson, Sheryl A. 2012. *Fashioning the Silver Fork Novel*. London: Pickering & Chatto.

Woodcox, D.C. 1996. 'Marguerite, Countess of Blessington (Marguerite Power Farmer Gardiner)'. In *British Travel Writers, 1837–1875: Victorian Period*, edited by Barbara Brothers and Julia Gergits, 50–54. Dictionary of Literary Biography. Vol. 166. Detroit: Thomson Gale.

INDEX

Addison, Joseph
  Pleasures of the Imagination 56
  Remarks on the Several Parts of Italy 35
architecture 67–76
  castles 74–76
  churches and cathedrals 69–70, 71–72, 73–74, 78
  Gothic 69, 71, 73, 74–76
  Renaissance 72–73
  ruins 67–68, 70–71, 110–11

Baedeker guides 3
Blessington, Marguerite
  Catholicism 77, 81
  childhood 6
  death 19
  first marriage 6–7
  French travels 10, 11–12, 15–16
  Isle of Wight travels 8–9
  Italian travels 12–15
  literary career 17–19, 43
  Low Countries travels 9
  Paris 10, 11, 16–17, 19
  salonnière 17–18, 102–5
  second marriage 7–8
Bracciano castle 75–76
Bulwer Lytton, Edward xvii, 17, 18, 48
Burke, Edmund
  Philosophical Enquiry into the Origin of Our Ideas of the Sublime and Beautiful 60, 62, 63, 64, 72, 73, 74, 76, 80
Burney, Frances xvi
Burns, Robert 3
Byron, Lord, George Gordon 3, 12, 14, 15, 17, 31, 32, 38, 48–51, 67, 91–97, 113
  Childe Harold 3, 71, 109–11, 112, 114, 115

Don Juan 94

Carey, Frances Jane 1
Catholic Emancipation bill 16, 40, 44
Chorley, Henry xvi
Claude Lorrain 56, 57–59, 64, 67
Colburn, Henry 5, 30, 32, 43
Conversations of Lord Byron 17, 30, 92, 94, 95
  advertising 32
  paratext 27
Cook, Thomas xiii
Costello, Louisa Stuart 1, 2

D'Orsay, Count Alfred xvii, 10, 12, 13, 14, 16, 19, 92, 102
Dickens, Charles 18, 113, 114, 115
Disraeli, Benjamin xvii, 17, 18
Drummond, Sir William 104
Duomo (Milan) 70, 73

Eastlake, Elizabeth 3–4, 5
Eaton, Charlotte Anne 1, 3, 5, 30
epistolary form 4

Forster, John 18

Gell, Sir William 68, 76, 104, 105
Gilpin, William 37, 57, 59, 64, 65, 67, 68
Gothic literature 2, 42, 46, 76, 87, 115
Graham, Maria 5
Grand Tour xiv, 1, 9
Guiccioli, Teresa 18, 49, 93, 94, 95, 96
Guido Reni 79

Haydon, Benjamin 18, 117
Horace 85

idleness 28–30, 31, 63, 82, 106
  leisure travel 1, 2, 29
Idler in France. Passim. See esp. Ch. 10
  paratext 27–30, 32, 38
  reviews 31–32, 121
Idler in Italy. Passim. See esp. Chs. 6–9
  advertising 32
  Bathurst incident 45
  Byron 48–51
  Hunt murders 45–46
  paratext 27–30, 32, 38
  reviews 30–31

Jameson, Anna 1, 2, 91, 111, 112, 113, 114
  Diary of an Ennuyée 4, 5
  literary tourist 3
  Winter Studies and Summer Rambles in Canada 2
Januarius, Saint 85–86
Johnson, Samuel
  Idler 28, 29
journal form 4, 27, 35–39
Journal of a Tour through the Netherlands to Paris 8, 36, 74–75, 77, 117, 120
  paratext 24, 25–28, 38
Julio Romano 79
July Revolution 17, 45, 117, 121–25

Knight, Payne 56

Landor, Walter 14, 17, 18
landscape 55–65
  Alpine routes 91
  artistic frames of reference 56
  Claude glass 58–59
  human elements 64–65
  picturesque principles 57–59
  sublime 59–63
Lawrence, Sir Thomas xiv, 8, 24
Leslie, Doris xvii
Lewis, Matthew Gregory 87
literary tourism 2–3

Madden, Richard Robert xvi
Magic Lantern 8, 24, 47
mass tourism xiv, 3, 5
Mathews, Charles 102–3
Matoff, Susan xvii

Molloy, J. Fitzgerald xvi
Montagu, Mary Wortley xvi, 113
Moore, Thomas 11, 17, 18, 32
Morrison, Alfred xvi
Murray guides 3, 4

Naples 99–107
  Blessington's salon 102–5
  Palazzo Belvedere 13, 100–103, 104
Napoleon I 3, 9, 10, 11, 36, 45
Napoleonic Wars xiv
national identity
  English 39–40, 86, 88, 124–25, 131–32
  Irish 40
Neapolitan Journals 99
Nostra Signora del Monte (Vicenza) 81

Owenson, Sydney, Lady Morgan 1, 5, 30, 60

Palladio 72–73
Paris 117–25. *See also* July Revolution
  fashion 118–19
  Louvre 120
  Notre Dame 78
  salons 117–18
  theatre 119–20
Parr, Samuel xiv
Patmore, Peter George 104
Piozzi, Hester xvi, 26, 112, 114
Poussin, Gaspard 56, 64, 67
Power, Margaret xvi
'Proper Lady' 99, 101, 102, 105

Radcliffe, Ann 75, 87, 112, 113, 115
Raphael 79, 111
Repealers 44
Robinson, Henry Crabb 18
Rogers, Samuel 18
Romanticism xiv, 1, 2, 60, 62, 64, 70, 71, 74, 88, 114, 125, 132
Rome 109–12
  Byron 109–11
  Coliseum 110–11
  Pantheon 111
  St Peter's 72, 109
Rosa, Salvator 56, 59–61
Ruskin, John 65, 71

sacred art and ritual
   aesthetic distance 77–88
   Catholic mass 81–82
   fêtes 83–85
   funerary 86–87
   Gothic qualities 87
   idolatry 80–81
   miracles 85–86
Sadleir, Michael xvi–xvii
Shakespeare, William 113
Shelley, Mary 1, 2, 40, 91, 114, 115
   'English in Italy' 3
   Frankenstein 5
   Rambles in Germany and Italy 2, 4, 5
Shelley, Percy Bysshe 5, 32, 115, 116
silver fork novels xvii–xviii, 30, 43–52
Sketches and Fragments 8, 24
Sketches of Scenes in the Metropolis 8
social status 29–30, 40–42, 67, 88, 123.
     See also idleness
St Etienne church (Genoa) 78–79
St Omer cathedral 78
Starke, Mariana 1, 4
Sterne, Laurence 1, 135n. 19

Strathern 48
Strutt, Elizabeth 4, 5

Thackeray, William 17, 18
Tour in the Isle of Wight 8, 35–37, 61–62, 68, 75, 77
   landscape 55–56
   paratext 23–25, 27–28
Trollope, Frances 1, 4, 5
Two Friends 43, 48, 75

Venice 112–16
   Romantic decay 114–15
   San Servolo 115–16
   St Mark's cathedral 73–74, 114
Vitruvius 72

Waterloo 3, 9
Willis, Nathaniel Parker 18
Wollstonecraft, Mary 2
Wordsworth, Dorothy 2, 3

Yates, Mrs Ashton 4

www.ingramcontent.com/pod-product-compliance
Lightning Source LLC
Chambersburg PA
CBHW021830300426
44114CB00009BA/399